Consuming Reality

Consuming Reality

The Commercialization of Factual Entertainment

June Deery

CONSUMING REALITY
Copyright © June Deery 2012.

First published in 2012 by
PALGRAVE MACMILLAN®
in the United States—a division of St. Martin's Press LLC,
175 Fifth Avenue, New York, NY 10010.

Where this book is distributed in the UK, Europe and the rest of the World,
this is by Palgrave Macmillan, a division of Macmillan Publishers Limited,
registered in England, company number 785998, of Houndmills,
Basingstoke, Hampshire RG21 6XS.

Palgrave Macmillan is the global academic imprint of the above
companies and has companies and representatives throughout the world.

Palgrave® and Macmillan® are registered trademarks in the United
States, the United Kingdom, Europe and other countries.

ISBN: 978–0–230–37996–1

Library of Congress Cataloging-in-Publication Data

Deery, June.
    Consuming reality : the commercialization of factual entertainment / June
    Deery.
        p.   cm.
    Includes bibliographical references and index.
    ISBN 978–0–230–37996–1 (hardback)
    1. Television advertising.   2. Reality television programs.   I. Title.
    HF6146.T42D44 2012
    384.55′32—dc23   2011047899

A catalogue record of the book is available from the British Library.

Design by Integra Software Services

First edition: May 2012

10 9 8 7 6 5 4 3 2 1

Printed in the United States of America.

In loving memory of
John P. Deery (1924–2010)
and
Ellen B. Deery (1933–2011)

Contents

Acknowledgments

I am very grateful to colleagues who, since this book's inception, have offered me encouragement and advice. I am especially indebted to those who generously read portions of this manuscript: for this I would like to thank Laurie Ouellette, Mark Andrejevic, Ellen Esrock, Katja Haskins, and Alan Nadel. Thanks also to my former graduate student Paul Booth for his help with this manuscript and for his stimulating conversations about the nature of fiction, reality, and possible alternatives to both. I am grateful to Josh Comer for his help with the Index and to Jim Zappen and Cheryl Geisler for their warm encouragement as department chairs. I am indebted to Greg Pitts and the National Association of Television Program Executives (NATPE) for a Faculty Fellowship, to Rensselaer for a sabbatical to work on this book, and to the Paley Center for Media (formerly the Museum of Television and Radio) in New York City for granting me access to their television archives. I am most grateful to Brigitte Shull, Sam Hasey, and Robyn Curtis at Palgrave Macmillan for shepherding this project, also to Pat Marra and Jan Darling for their always willing and unaccountably cheerful assistance at RPI.

My greatest debt I owe to my late parents, who, unfortunately, did not see this book's publication but who encouraged me throughout. This book is dedicated to their memory. Thanks also to my brother, Gavin, for his firm transatlantic support and to the rest of my loving and extended family in Ireland. Closer to home, I want to thank my children, Alanna and John, for their understanding when I had to consume so much time and so much television. Finally, thanks go to my husband, Doug, who is probably as glad as I am to see this book off my desk.

Portions of chapters 3, 4, and 7 appeared previously in "Interior Design: Commodifying Self and Place in *Extreme Makeover, Extreme Makeover: Home Edition* and *The Swan.*" In *The Great American Makeover: Television, History, Nation*, 2006, edited by Dana Heller. New York: Palgrave Macmillan. Reproduced with permission of Palgrave Macmillan.

Introduction

Displays of reality have become a display trade and a display of trade.
(Henri Lefebvre [1968]1984, 63)

Now firmly entrenched in television schedules around the world, the factual entertainment commonly referred to as reality television has provoked powerful and diverse reactions. For some it represents a dreadful cultural degradation, for others a welcome democratization, but whatever their opinion, certainly, many people have one, even (and sometimes especially) those who have never viewed this programming. Viewed or unviewed, reality TV's formats and fallouts have ignited debate everywhere—from office cubicles to the great halls of parliament. Every day millions watch, vote on, and critique reality shows in print and online. At first dismissed as a passing fad, reality television, as we currently know it, has been around for more than a decade and for some time now has been a dominant area of media production. Hence, even if the entire phenomenon were to disappear tomorrow, it would still be important to know why this programming appeared on the scene and why it lasted as long as it did. Emerging during a large upheaval in the media industry at the end of the last century, reality TV (RTV) leapt into prominence at a time when television contracts and conventions were coming under tremendous stress, and when DVRs, multiple channels, and the Internet were beginning to threaten long-established economic models. In response, RTV producers began to redefine relations between audiences, texts, and delivery systems—even between individuals and their society. Most strikingly, their programming blurred the previously distinct categories of producer versus consumer, program versus advertising, and the scripted versus the unscripted.

A primary objective of this book is to examine the integration and even conflation of programming and advertising in order to uncover the commercial motives behind the erosion of these other categories. While other studies of contemporary television have touched upon various aspects of commercialization, mine adopts a more sustained and comprehensive approach to this topic and links commercial practices to larger themes such as the sentimental dissemination of capitalist and nationalist ideologies, the professionalization of social relationships (including conceptions of self), and the integration of hybrid discourse and public relations (PR) techniques into everyday life and conceptions of reality. Upcoming chapters will illustrate how reality programming aligns private and individual interests with larger corporate and political agendas for which it offers support or compensation. This much talked about and as often dismissed programming is, therefore, a useful entry point for thinking about the media's response to larger economic and sociopolitical trends, especially the mass media's propagation of commercial culture in an era of capitalist expansion. To understand the specific relationships between reality TV and commerce, I undertake a comprehensive examination of its advertising and promotional strategies, as well as its commodification of viewers, of participants, of ideas, ideologies, and dreams. I believe that it is still possible to generalize about all of reality television if we agree, for instance, that its most fundamental commonality is its purportedly non-scripted depiction of "ordinary people" in extraordinary circumstances, or vice versa (access to celebrities). In other words, it is about the juxtaposition of familiarity and strangeness in a nonfictional and not entirely predictable setting. Beyond this, I suggest that reality TV is best understood not so much as a genre with certain textual or aesthetic characteristics but as a *relationship* between texts, agents, and technical devices. These relationships are evolving, but they remain distinct from other television programming given a common ontological base in what I will refer to as a *staged actuality*. This hybridity, this combination of the planned and the spontaneous, provides a powerful context for promoting specific goods and services as well as broader ideological beliefs and practices. In probing its power, I aim to contribute to a larger discussion regarding mediation and consumption. In particular, I draw attention to the twin ideas of mediation being a form of consumption and consumption being a form of mediation.[1]

Trade-marked Life

Not all reality series are concerned with consumption or with promoting consumerism, but a large number are. The programs I examine tend to normalize the embedding of commercial agenda into experience. They advance the notion that culture and the commercial sphere are becoming almost coextensive, so that virtually all forms of social interplay are ultimately about selling, about sponsorship, about spin. Indeed, *one of reality TV's strongest claims to being real is when it represents the reality of an increasingly sponsored, branded, and mediated life,* an experience that this programming presents as benign as well as inevitable. Rather than detracting from their scholarly worth, the thoroughly commercial nature of reality programs is what makes them such a sensitive indicator. As Bonnie Dow (1996) points out, "commercial television's relentless profit motive is one of the elements that makes it such a useful cultural barometer" (xxii), given that it has to try to capture the zeitgeist and both reflect and shape cultural trends, all in the interests of attracting a large audience. And one of the most significant cultural trends that this commercial programming captures is the very impetus to commercialize.

To say that we (in developed nations) live in a consumer society encapsulates more about contemporary experience, I suggest, than does any other single characterization. A consumer society focuses on and encourages a high level of consumption, and this affects, among other things, power, law, ethics, identity, and status. As Martyn Lee (2000) puts it, "Consumer society . . . is not just about the satisfaction of needs, but in many ways it is about the forms through which we view the world and our position within it as well as gauge the progress of our life trajectories" (x). It is our perspective and measure. Commercialization, the process of turning something into a consumer item in order to generate a profit, is clearly the main engine of this type of society and the popular programming examined here reflects the extent to which in late capitalism the driver's seat is no longer occupied by manufacturers and engineers but by advertisers, designers, and retailers (Slater 1997, 174). Upcoming chapters consider commercialization as topic and as technique in order to demonstrate how television content both depicts and enacts consumer practices. The aim is not to provide details about TV's political economy (Magder 2009; McMurria 2009; Raphael 2009; Gillan 2011), but to identify commercial strategies within its texts that are emblematic of a wider societal commingling of commercial and noncommercial agendas. My analysis takes advertising seriously as a central cultural activity that is more than a simple mechanism for shifting goods. It underlines its centrality in media production, or in what I prefer to call *media-advertising*, to represent the close ties between these two kinds of cultural production. At once among the least scripted and the most commercially shaped of media content, reality TV makes conspicuous the fact that the commercial media are, at base, cultural devices for selling things: selling not just products but also the audience's attention, its participation, and, increasingly, the *importance of being mediated*.

Throughout this book, I will be interested in narratives that position consumerism as the essence of national and social identity. Several reality series feature buying and selling as their primary or secondary focus and recognize shopping as a central component of social experience: not, it should be said, the mundane purchases of bread or eggs, but transactions that are transformative or excessive or transgressive and therefore likely to generate drama. Even the absence of shopping can be acknowledged and thematized, as when gamedocs like *Survivor* (CBS, 2000–) or *Big Brother* (Channel 4, 2000–/CBS, 2000–) deprive participants of the opportunity to shop (while commercial breaks remind viewers that they do have this privilege). My discussion will focus on series that promote specific products and/or consumerism in general, but it will also encompass series that articulate anxieties about consumption—perhaps not coincidentally in a recessionary context. Though it is not often noted, there is a strain of moralism in much reality television. When it comes to consumption this produces a range of attitudes, most shows depicting the practice as wholly beneficial and redemptive, but some portraying it as a matter of pathology and shame.

Some reality series, I contend, offer not only moral redemption but also political compensation. For example, each home makeover's efficient and privatized resolution may be enjoyed as some compensation for government failure to reshape and renovate on the national and international stage. As entertainment programming whose political charge is defused by commercialization and whose featured crises are attributed to individual bad luck, RTV transfers larger anxieties onto a more manageable scale. However, while there are analogies between micro and macro politics, between individual narratives and larger political resonances, this is not to suggest that these series are ideologically homogenous or unified. As subsequent chapters will illustrate, many series are both symptomatic and performative: that is, they provide insight into the narratives that circulate in support of the status quo, including their inadequacies, while at the same time they propagate and perpetuate those narratives, sometimes with considerable fanfare. Whereas documentary has often had explicit political and/or ethnographic agendas, reality TV does not. Yet many programs are obliged to touch upon problems of unequal resources and opportunity, if only briefly, in order for individualized and apolitical solutions to proceed. This requirement inevitably exposes some of the strategies of the larger ideological narratives on which these programs depend in order to make sense of the realities they offer for our consumption. In the discussion that follows, and without attributing causality, I will be interested in the extent to which reality TV is aligned with specific sociopolitical trends and philosophies in a late capitalist and predominantly American context.

While still the dominant medium around the world, television today is obliged to recalibrate its role in an increasingly convergent environment, whether it be a convergence of ownership, of profit generation, or of technological devices. As already indicated, one response is to engage in yet another form of convergence, that of program and advertising content.[2] Indeed, reality TV has proven to be a wonderful vehicle for all kinds of contractual promotion and for amalgams of advertising and program content that ready television for a post-advertising era when there will be few straight-forward and segregated models such as the traditional commercial break. This increased integration, something I have elsewhere referred to as *advertainment* (Deery 2004a), means that commercialization is not just expanding but is also becoming more essential, even congenital, in a range of media products.

Another strategy in a convergent era is a form of "media consumption" in which the *medium* consumes the *audience* as well as vice versa. Upcoming chapters will illustrate how RTV's consumption has destabilized traditional notions of audience and text, both of which now have to be seen as more *process* than *product*. In order to delineate the significance of this move, I offer precise definitions of otherwise often loosely employed terms such as participation and interactivity, the aim being to chart how a mass medium like television is able to incorporate dialogic and participatory elements of new media culture while also leveraging the traditional advantages and economic clout of a mass audience.[3] Reality TV is not amateur. On the contrary, it bears witness to the power of professional media production, not least of which is its ability to summon important allies in the commercial world that buoy up television as a "legacy" medium in a micro-media era. While there is much talk of amateur or unofficial participation in contemporary media, my analysis demonstrates the need to consider also the power of *corporate* participation in the form of PR and advertising. On television, as in the political arena, ordinary participation is evident, is even showcased and capitalized upon, but is circumscribed. Commercial television manipulates ideas of participation such that consumer-based narratives replace other forms of membership. Reality TV is not about giving voice to the powerless, the ordinary, the overlooked. Instead, it largely promotes the interests of the already influential: the media, the business class, the entrepreneur.

Staged Actuality

The most important thing about reality TV is that it is not fictional: this is why it entertains and why it enters our culture in a different way than do fictional texts. But determining exactly how real it is will not be the focus of this work. To declare that reality TV is an altogether transparent reflection of a universally defined reality is obviously untenable, supposing we could come up with such a definition. But so is saying it is all a sham. My discussion will employ the conventional terms "reality" and "real life" to indicate a social understanding of a phenomenon without making any absolute claim about the concept's veracity or universality. My interest, in any case, is not in the absolute epistemological limits on what can be known, but in the activity of agents (television producers, advertisers) who have a stake in establishing what the known looks like to a certain population. Without getting too exercised about any given series' degree of realism, I categorize all of reality TV as a form of "factual entertainment," denoting programming that represents the actual but is not focused on the informational or scientifically verifiable; other examples would be the broadcasting of sporting or ceremonial events, but these are not my concern here. When it comes to reality TV it appears that many viewers desire and even expect the real, the factual, the true (Hill 2007) (these terms are often used interchangeably), and while on the philosophical level we can wonder to what extent any representation can ever meet these expectations, on the production level we can speculate about the extent to which producers shape raw material and according to what agenda. That reality TV problematizes reality and truth—even as it cashes in on their nostalgic attraction—is one reason why it attracts both a popular and an academic audience. Its mixing of the staged and the spontaneous provides a form of dramatic tension that allows audience members to speculate about the authenticity of each format, whether it be the actions of participants or producers.

Today, in much cultural production, hidden or half-hidden commercial motives are masked by other more socially respected stances. This is the realm of public relations, an activity that I believe provides a useful model for understanding the status and cultural function of much RTV, particularly its popular makeover formats.[4] Though designed to be under the radar, the effect of PR on contemporary culture is pervasive and profound. And yet its cultural ascendancy is often missed by media commentators—an omission that is greatly to the advantage of its practitioners. One could argue that the oblique approaches of PR, and their enactment on reality TV, signal the limits of capitalism, a system that relies on a partial disguise of the system; for example, if it were always socially acceptable to simply go after profit, then much of the subterfuge mounted by PR firms or by RTV producers would be unnecessary. Some reality formats exploit for dramatic purposes this encountering of limits, as when they test to what extent people are comfortable with an expansion of the market and of profit taking in more intimate areas of life. Indeed, on one level, perhaps every reality show tests what people will do for money. But reality TV *tests* and *masks* both, for one of the desires it codifies, most clearly in its makeover and romantic formats, is also for a transcendence, or at least a suspension, of the market. Producers gratify this desire when they conjure up archetypal dreams, fairy tales, and even religious motifs. And behind them stands Walt Disney as a prime progenitor of the stuff that modern dreams are made on. This entrepreneur, I suggest, is helpful in understanding the cultural function of RTV, not so much because he created dreams but because he staged them in real life, because he went beyond creating fictional narratives to branding and commercializing experience outside the cinema. His idea of a theme park that would invite ordinary people into the world of television and film is in some ways a prototype for reality TV. For years, the Walt Disney Company has claimed not just to make dreams but to make "dreams come true." The same phrase is repeatedly heard on RTV formats where the ordinary is transformed into the extraordinary in answer to consumer desires. For this reason, Walt Disney could be the grandfather, if not the patron saint, of makeover TV.[5]

Such is its cultural absorption that, for some people, reality TV has already become a way of seeing or experiencing real life—at least occasionally—as when someone says of their own experience "This is just like reality TV!"[6] There have also been fictional imitations of reality programming, as in *The Office* (BBC Two, 2001–03; NBC, 2005–), *Modern Family* (ABC, 2009–), *Parks and Recreation* (NBC, 2009–), and fictional remakes of prior reality series (HBO's *Cinema Verite*).[7] NBC's flagship sitcom *30 Rock* (2006–) seems at times obsessed with its rival programming and frequently satirizes or mimics reality shows, even going to the length of embedding fake RTV shows within its narrative. In addition, there are reality shows about reality shows (reunion shows, fan shows) and advertising campaigns that mimic reality programming.[8] The influence has even been fatal, for one of the most extreme examples of reality TV's impact on real life is the case of the Brazilian producer of *Crimewatch,* who in 2009, arranged for the murder of at least five people just to produce better ratings for his crime detection show. Police got suspicious when Wallace Souza's camera crews were always first on the scene.

Political Consumption

So far, one of the main thrusts of scholarly critiques has been establishing reality TV's relationship to Foucauldian governmentality (self-governing) and to the neoliberal self as entrepreneur (Palmer 2003; Andrejevic 2004; Sender 2006; Bratich 2007; Hearn 2008; Ouellette and Hay 2008; Weber 2009). A decentered, self-regulating, and neoliberal governmentality is regarded as most evident in the way RTV manages, monitors, and enjoins its viewers to behave in certain ways in order to advance and empower themselves. Scholars refer with increasing frequency to neoliberal notions of privatization, deregulation, globalization, and the withdrawal of public or social services—though what is sometimes lost is that "governmentality" and "neoliberalism" are related but not interchangeable terms. It may be that some studies have overestimated the extent of neoliberal ideology and government contraction, especially if this is taken to be a global phenomenon (as is pointed out by Kraidy and Sender 2011, 5), but this perspective has yielded important insights into the potential impact of RTV on ordinary citizens and is something I build upon here. In line with those who suggest that television doesn't just reflect but intervenes in and governs real life, I maintain that one of its main interventions is the transformation of real life according to media-advertising standards: for instance, into beautiful, updated, and well-equipped bodies, or beautiful, updated, and well-equipped homes. More broadly, my work traces how reality TV works to *normalize* the commercialization of everyday life by other agents. The focus is not television's training of citizens as a form of government-at-a-distance or reality TV's contribution to theories of liberalism, worthwhile though these discussions are: as, for instance, in the extended studies of governance offered by Gareth Palmer (2003), Mark Andrejevic (2004), and Laurie Ouellette and James Hay (2008). My concern, rather, is how this programming markets particular versions of reality that align with commercial interests and perform ideological work largely through compensation and distraction.

As distinct from other studies of reality television, I draw most often on the cultural theorist Jean Baudrillard, because he was among the first to recognize that the analysis of both consumer behavior and the media is key to understanding contemporary life. However, I reference only certain elements of his work; most often the early commentary on consumer society that I believe is still helpful in delineating how consumption is managed by the media and how both media and consumption affect perceptions of reality. Baudrillard has not been fully embraced by media studies and is often misunderstood as celebrating the nihilism he describes (for a passionate corrective, see Merrin 2005). Clearly he is in sympathy with Marxist and Situationist arguments that consumerism breeds alienation and loss of freedom (e.g., Debord, Lefebvre, Marcuse), but his vision is not necessarily as apocalyptic or defeatist as is often thought. Baudrillard was one of the first major theorists to understand the novelty and significance of reality television, drawing attention to the 1970s PBS series *An American Family* (1983, [1987]1988) and later the French series *Loft Story*. However, there are limits to his perspective, for semiotic approaches such as his tend to pay scant attention to social practices and conceive of an overly generalized, homogenous, and passive viewer or consumer. Hence, Baudrillard's observations about traditional mass media are not always applicable to new media practices and to more active RTV audiences.

Someone who early on influenced this commentator—though this is not usually acknowledged, except by Baudrillard—is the American historian Daniel Boorstin. In the mid-twentieth century, Boorstin came up with the idea of the "pseudo-event" to describe events that are specifically designed to be mediated and so are what I describe as both actual and staged (Chapter 2).

This remains an underutilized but compelling idea that has the capacity to explain many contemporary media practices. More specifically, the pseudo-event is an excellent way to understand the peculiar status of reality TV. Though more apt than Baudrillard's full-blown "simulation," both terms draw on the latter's observation that real life is increasingly conceived and staged according to its "reproducibility" ([1976] 1993, 56). When describing reality programming and its commercialization, what I find appropriate is not so much simulation as *dissimulation* (Chapters 1 and 2).

My analysis of reality TV begins with specific commercial techniques. The first two chapters examine and catalogue advertising and PR practices, including brand extension and commodification of viewer input across different media platforms. This produces a more in-depth account of techniques such as product placement and donorship than is found in other studies of reality television, or elsewhere. The scope then widens to examine a larger promotion of capitalist and nationalist ideologies that underpin this commercial activity. Some reality TV is identified as compensatory and as drawing on elements of fantasy and religion in ostensibly apolitical narratives that complement public discourses surrounding wars and other crisis events (Chapters 3 and 4). A key consumerist invocation with often hidden political efficacy is the American Dream, a misunderstood trope whose origins I trace in order to understand its contemporary use in RTV programming and, through this example, its usefulness elsewhere (Chapter 4). Subsequent chapters concentrate on popular series that present commerce as a topic and that insist on the importance of buying and selling for identity formation and socioeconomic success (Chapters 5 and 6). These programs promote consumption as a form of mediation through which social relations are reproduced and they make acceptable commercial, as opposed to governmental, control. The expert class featured here also indicates the current extent of the professionalization of social relationships and the expansion of the market into deeper and deeper privacies (Chapter 5). Other series suggest that consumption is strongly gendered and they celebrate the theatrical and ritualistic aspects of shopping or caution against its abuse (Chapter 6). In either case, consumer-based moral imperatives are seen to turn shopping into a crucial test of individual worth. The shopping expert's call to improve the self through consumption, a theme heard throughout makeover programming, culminates in the commodification of the body through cosmetic surgery, the subject of the final chapter. Here even the physical condition of being human becomes the product of consumer activity.

As I discuss these matters, I will at times generalize about all of reality television and at other times highlight different features of specific formats. Examples will be drawn from makeovers of the home or the body, but also from docusoaps and from what we might term "trade shows" that focus on buying and selling. Some of these programs have already received scholarly attention, while several others have not been examined before or have not received as much attention as they merit, given their prominence. I focus often on makeover programming because its producers have been particularly enterprising in finding ways to commodify both content and viewers within a new media economy and because their efforts highlight some distinctive aspects of RTV's relationship to reality and its current sociopolitical formations. Emerging first as a segment on talk shows, the makeover is now a widely circulating meme with a particularly strong resonance in American culture: for though the desire to "make over" or "start over" is certainly heard in other nations, it is never more emphatically voiced than in the United States, where there is an extensive array of makeover programming.

Most television makeovers are of homes or bodies for reasons this book will explore, but one possible motivation worth noting right away is that this focus entails powerful, visible (hence televisual) transformations of entities that are close to most people's identity. Not coincidentally, concentrating on homes and bodies is also a boon to advertisers, most of whose clients are selling something to improve or benefit these two spaces, with the result that makeover shows provide one of the most striking examples of television making a real socioeconomic impact on popular culture (i.e., sales). On a more theoretical note, makeover series bolster arguments from psychology, sociology, and cultural studies about performance, fluidity, and "technologies" (Foucault) or "techniques" (Rose) of the self [9] and so they provide concrete examples of postmodern theories regarding identity formation and disciplinary control. Many offer a particularly clear example of what I suggest is the basic formula for all of reality television which is *the privatization of private lives for public consumption and commercial profit*. Reality TV's contribution to a public imaginary around homes and bodies is to position both spaces within market capitalism as projects, as commodities, and as forms of property.

In general, I don't assume that any content has a uniform or predictable impact on each or all of its audience members. I have looked at viewer responses that are posted online but not systematically or exhaustively, and I will draw on these only occasionally. My approach is also to disregard whether an effect was intentional or unintentional on a producer's or participant's part, supposing this intention could even be determined. I choose to work on the level of the series—what Ellen Seiter (1992) regards as "television's definitive form" (45)—in order to identify general patterns and broad trends. My discussion centers on American series from 2000–2011, and although my analysis occasionally takes a longer view, this is not a historical study.

Finally, regarding distribution, the material I examine was produced primarily for television screens, though I consider also associated material on computers or other mobile devices. Prognostication is not my aim, but to my mind the future of television lies in the past, for I believe what television will most resemble in the near future is the first mass medium, the book. What we currently recognize as TV programming will increasingly be accessed on portable devices (like books) that will allow the viewer to decide when, where, and what to watch (as with books). These devices might be computer screens, smart phones, or any number of venues, public and private: more significant than the device will be the availability and management of content, and hence the relationship between text and user. Like book readers, viewers will be able to select the latest title many others are currently enjoying, check out last year's most critically acclaimed works, or delve into last century's classics, all at their own time and pace. The extent to which program content will change is another matter, but in dramaturgical terms the adaptations may be fairly insignificant and will likely still entail 30–60 minute videos with various forms of integrated advertising, techniques that the next two chapters will explore.

CHAPTER 1

Commercial Participation: Post-advertising

Commercial Participants

Advertising needs to be taken more seriously. It deserves more respect and more scrutiny not because it is a significant part of many economies employing thousands of people, but because it is a major part of media production and has become nothing less than "a touchstone of our changing concept of knowledge and of reality" (Boorstin [1961] 1992, 211).[1] Looked at separately, advertising messages try to persuade us to buy specific items using simple techniques that make this communication easy to trivialize. Looked at as a whole, advertising has a profound impact on society:

> Its creations appropriate and transform a vast range of symbols and ideas; its unsurpassed communicative powers recycle cultural models and references back through the network of social interactions. This venture is unified by the discourse through and about objects, which bonds together images of persons, products, and well-being.
>
> (Leiss, Kline, and Jhally 1997, 5)

Advertising, in other words, is greater than the sum of its parts (Wernick 1991, 92), and while its first function is selling stuff, it does much more. One of its primary achievements is persuading us that promoting something is a normal form of discourse. Not surprising when today, as Baudrillard observes (with some hyperbole), "what we are experiencing is the absorption of all virtual modes of expression into that of advertising," not necessarily actual advertising copy itself but the *form* of advertising, which is "a simplified operational mode, vaguely seductive, vaguely consensual" ([1981] 1994, 87). It is this soft coercion that I will be examining throughout this book, where I go beyond a model of advertising as interloper, or interruption, to a more integrative model in which advertising becomes vital and necessary, in which advertising enables and validates experience both on and off screen, and where techniques go beyond what we are used to identifying as advertising. It is generally assumed that viewers are rarely looking for ads but are instead trying to avoid them, or at best simply put up with them as the price they pay for receiving other content (push rather than pull). If advertising is what Iain MacRury (2009) refers to as "the ever-expected but uninvited guest" (10), then upcoming chapters will examine various scenarios in which reality television (RTV) has proven to be a most welcoming host.

As previously indicated, reality programming is interesting for its experiments in not only *audience* but also *corporate* participation.

> *Survivor* is as much a marketing vehicle as it is a television show. My shows create an interest, and people will look at them, but the endgame here is selling products in stores—a car, deodorant, running shoes. It's the future of television.
>
> (Mike Sager, *Esquire*, July, 2001)

This proclamation and prognostication comes from Mark Burnett, one of the most successful of reality producers and one who is more frank than others about underlying commercial motives. Shows like Burnett's represent a privatized culture where we come to expect that all kinds of life experiences need to be sponsored and that these sponsors will, understandably, have their own agenda, though we may never be privy to what this is. Today we might find ourselves asking: Does this TV/radio host really like this product or is he/she just being paid to say so? Do these politicians or experts really think this policy is a good idea or are they just being paid to say so? Is this scientific study comprehensive and objective or does it merely serve the interests of those who funded it? Never before has the sponsored nature of all kinds of discourse been so pervasive and never before has it been quite so difficult to disentangle commercial from noncommercial motives or to detect what used to be straightforwardly known as an advertising message. The result, I suggest, is a form of post-advertising dissimulation that is not about spreading lies or false information but about disguising intentions, power, and capabilities. It is not simply a matter of falsifying but of dissembling and involves not lying but deception.

This chapter will focus on TV series that do the heavy lifting for commercial sources, where the branding of entertainment is strong and the general ethos of consumption is unmistakable. Not all reality TV is equally commercially freighted. Some programming, in fact, centers on saving money and spending as little as possible (Rosenberg 2008)—though this kind of programming does still involve some expenditure and relies on free advice and labor from professionals who would otherwise expect payment (e.g., house décor shows like *Design on a Dime*, HGTV, 2003–06). My focus will be on programming that is designed to stimulate consumption and does so by employing techniques that work best when they don't appear to be advertising, techniques that RTV producers have either pioneered or revived, such as sponsorship, donorship, and product placement, in addition to brand extension and merchandising online. The remainder of the chapter will analyze how this kind of reality programming capitalizes on ordinary people as viewers or participants and will chart the commercial benefits of RTV's peculiar status as nonfictional programming.

Product Placement

Product placement, the practice of arranging for brands or products to be embedded in media content, is sometimes achieved through virtual imposition (e.g., digitally superimposing brands on sports fields), but more typically the product actually appears in front of the camera. This appearance is generally arranged for a fee, or there may be some form of barter or other quid pro quo. Some placements are the result of a producer wishing to defray costs by receiving free props or services and others appear because an agent approached a television producer and asked for a client's product to be placed for a fee. Different degrees of attention are negotiated, from a 2-second mute glimpse to the product becoming a series-long thematic element. In most instances, advertisers hope that their client's product will both fit in and stand out, that it will be "organic" but also noticed. Sometimes the financial model for placement can shift within the same show. For example, on the first series of *Queer Eye for the Straight Guy* (Bravo, 2003–07; hereafter *Queer Eye*), items appeared on screen mostly through ad hoc barter, meaning that producers received free goods or services providing these items were shown on TV. But in subsequent seasons producers required actual payment from those anxious to place products in a now highly rated show. From then on, if anything appeared on screen there was generally a direct economic explanation for its presence—a reminder that anything that appears as media content has the potential to double as a commercial opportunity.

Presumably most viewers are aware of some of this commercial activity, but the business arrangement is not disclosed in the text: presenters do not recommend a product and then say they have been paid to do so. This practice therefore entails an omission, if not some degree of deception, on the producer's part. Compare this with the spot announcement during a commercial break: it may omit some facts, it may exaggerate, but because it appears during a break viewers know it is an ad. A placed product works by not appearing to be an ad. It can appear as a prize in gamedocs, a reward in talent competitions, a romantic gift on dating/mating shows, or an aid in makeovers.[2] It can be the thematic material of a competition, as in the products and services contestants are charged to promote on *The Apprentice* or on *Top Chef* (Bravo, 2006-). But what it does not want to appear to be is an ad. One of the earliest and most controversial examples of product placement occurred in 1886 when the prominent British artist Millais was paid to put a bar of Pears soap in one of his best-loved paintings (entitled "Bubbles"). Many commentators were horrified at what they regarded as a cheapening of fine art. With its lower cultural status, television has not been so solicitously guarded. Some examples of product placement can be found as early as the 1940s, but it was not a significant practice until the end of the 1990s and then more than doubled at the beginning of the twenty-first century, when reality TV came on the scene (Thussu 2007, 55). In recent years, placement has ballooned thanks in large measure to reality programming, and it is not only appearing in an increasing number of programs but is also increasingly employed within these programs (Magder 2009).[3]

The current prominence of product placement can be attributed to a number of converging factors affecting media production. In the first place, it responds to pressures brought on by a new media ecology: again, the DVR, the Internet, multichannel satellite or cable. Television audiences have become increasingly migratory and hard for advertisers to catch and, while they hope individual ads may generate some pleasure, media producers have always assumed that the audience's attitude to advertising is one of for-bearance or evasion.[4] With product placement, evasive actions like channel hopping during breaks or watching recordings won't work. Then there is the increased clutter within traditional commercial breaks thanks to deregulation and increased competition. With product placement the commercial signal remains, whatever platform it is viewed on, and industry research shows that the practice produces a better recall rate than do regular television commercials (Jacobson and Mazur 1995, 69); hence, its presence is now tracked by Nielsen and by companies such as iTVX that attempt to measure the effectiveness of brand integration (iTVX.com). Many advertisers fear that the old arrangement of buying time for commercials during program breaks is endangered if not doomed; witness the appearance of business advice books with titles like *Life After the 30-Second Spot* (Jaffe 2005) and half-joking references among broadcasters to TiVo being "the Antichrist."[5] Product placement is therefore looked at as a useful strategy in a post-advertising era.

The density of product placement on reality TV may be due to a variety of factors. For one thing, the relative lack of scripting means that products can be inserted with little need for motivation and fairly late on in the production process. As mentioned, products are often welcomed by participants as prizes or as aid rather than being merely tolerated or ignored. Even fairly heavy-handed plugs can work on reality programming as a matter of realism, since brands are increasingly present in the real life they portray; MTV's practice of blurring the labels of those who don't pony up on *The Real World* (MTV, 1992–) may therefore reduce its realism. As Burnett's quote indicated, reality producers are probably less inclined to wring their hands over art versus commerce than, say, serious film directors.[6] Since syndication is not always in the cards, they are also under tremendous pressure to maximize revenues from each episode aired.

The life affirming and (literally) constructive contexts of makeover programming, in particular, offer advertisers an integral and positive role. These formats provide a dramatization of the binaristic rhetoric that, thanks to repeated exposure, is a fundamental part of our cultural training: the advertiser's "Before-and-After." In many instances products integrated into makeovers rise to the status of essential thematic element, for without placed goods and services there would be no show. The commercial element is therefore no longer an irrelevant or competing discourse. Sometimes the placed product occupies a place of ritual, as in the GMC SUV that functions as a literal advertising vehicle on every episode of *Queer Eye*. Or, even when products change with each episode, they get to be privileged participants in a life-changing event. Take weddings, for example. On *My Fair Wedding with David Tutera* (WE, 2008–) the host is able to elevate a formerly modest wedding into a grand affair because of items and services provided by a variety of vendors. On the wedding day itself, he takes the bride and groom on a tour where he makes sure to mention every provider's name. Whether the happy couple can do more than feign interest in such commercial details on their big day is hardly the point. The named products borrow some of the significance of an easily identifiable and altogether positive milestone event and the commercial transaction is ennobled by a sentimental discourse of love.

Paid Programming

In many regards, makeover formats resemble infomercials, and indeed one could argue that infomercials are a prototype for reality TV. Although missing toll-free numbers or EZ payment plans, makeover shows use the same formula of problem identified, solution offered, and empirical proof of the desired transformation.[7] In both infomercials and makeover TV the results are guaranteed for real or ordinary people who testify to the featured product's worth. Infomercials typically disguise themselves by mimicking more objective programming such as news or interview formats: they are predicated, in other words, on deception, if not of product then of genre. Makeover series are similarly disguised—for example, as documentaries—but they provide a more legitimate platform than the "paid programming" whose claims are officially disowned by the broadcaster and that annoys viewers who see through its semitransparent cloaking devices. Not being legally categorized as paid programming makes RTV more powerful as a hybrid discourse and rhetorical device.

A standard feature of the infomercial is the personal testimony; that is, an appeal through the use of peer models to the ordinary person viewing at home. Whether or not the results portrayed are believable, the rhetorical thrust of infomercial programming is that it is in the factual mode. On makeovers, ordinary people can and usually do look much better after restyling or surgery. Moreover, since they were never particularly abnormal or freakish in appearance, the majority of viewers can identify with their initial problems and subsequent course of action: this is why their stories work as testimonials. The main structure of every makeover, the classic Before-and-After contrast, is repeated in internal loops throughout infomercials. On makeovers, everything builds toward this dramatic contrast but there is a little more restraint, or suspense at least. The final gratification is delayed until the program's end, with teasers along the way that show *reactions to* the final reveal but not video of the transformation itself. Like infomercial pitchmen, makeover hosts mediate theory and practice by translating abstract desires into the acquisition of particular goods or services and then demonstrating their use in an actual situation. The goal in both instances is to encourage audiences to materialize the advertising imagery and reenact the TV demonstration in their own lives. Makeovers do so in front of a prime-time audience that most infomercial producers can't afford to purchase.

On reality TV, being embedded in a dramatic narrative can change a product's status from *object* to *event,* making its integration more critical and therefore more memorable. This is what I would call *featured* product placement as opposed to a fleeting camera glimpse or brief mention of a brand. In some cases products may even become a character of sorts and play a minor role in the storyline (humorously highlighted in an ad for Diet Pepsi that had the soft drink negotiating for a starring role in a film).[8] This role-playing can occur during the regular program or in designer ads created for interstitial commercial breaks, as in the frequent use of Ford cars on *American Idol* (Fox, 2002) spots. On *The Apprentice* (NBC, 2004–)—where capitalism is itself the star in the supposedly charismatic person of Mr. Donald Trump—advertising and marketing are not simply integrated but are foregrounded in that much of the program content is advertising created not alongside but *by* the show's participants (Jenkins 2006). *America's Next Top Model* (UPN/CW, 2003–) makes advertising itself the subject matter of the show since, as fashion models, the participants are vying for a career as an advertising vehicle. The ads they perform as amateurs on the television series also function as ads for the sponsors (e.g., Cover Girl). Corporations increasingly appreciate having their products appear in a program with which viewers have a relationship, rather than in the context-less, cold turkey approach of a commercial break. Brian Shook, a senior VP at Dial Corp, reports that his company likes being on *The Apprentice* because "I think more and more consumers are TiVo-ing through the commercials" whereas viewers have a relationship with a show and so integrating a product into this environment "creates a long-term relationship with your product as well" (Lafayette 2006). The CEO of Coca-Cola describes such placement as borrowing the show's "emotional capital" in order to manage consumer relationships. Because of a convergence of "Madison and Vine" (advertising and entertainment production) he declares that companies like his "will use a diverse array of entertainment assets to break into people's hearts and minds. In that order. For this is the way to their wallets" (Donaton 2004, 30). This is what Henry Jenkins (2006) identifies as "affective economics," a new discourse in marketing that emphasizes the emotional commitments consumers make to brands as a central motivation for their purchasing decisions (Gobe 2001). An hour-long makeover episode provides enough time for the empathetic identification and vicarious emotion that shorter advertising forms cannot manage. The makeover, in other words, is an ad that has time to make us weep.

When polled, some viewers report that spotting placed products on reality TV is just part of "the game" and that they have a higher tolerance for placement here than in other TV genres (Hill 2005; Jenkins 2006, 88). Jennifer Gillan suggests that "reality TV is less often the target of complaints about [product placement] as it is already assumed to be purely economically motivated programming. Scripted programming is subject to more critique" (2011, 183). However, others find product placement of any sort objectionable and something to be guarded against. This was the opinion of the British media minister Andy Burnham, who in 2008 declared the practice a "contamination" and reason for banning its presence on all UK programming. His criticism underlines a correlation between hybrid advertisement and the erosion of authenticity and the viewer's trust. What became known as the "phone-in quiz scandals" had erupted in the previous year in Britain when it emerged that on several shows viewers were being duped into calling in to a program they thought was live but was actually prerecorded and so their chances of participating or answering a question were nil.[9] In other instances, viewers hoping to qualify for a quiz show were being misled in various ways. Referring to these incidents, the minister maintained: "There is a risk that, at the very moment when television needs to do all it can to show it can be trusted, that we elide the distinction between programs and adverts." Appealing to his own domestic brand, the minister argued that "British programming has an integrity that is revered around the world, and I don't think we should put that hard-won reputation up for sale" (Steve Clarke, *Variety*, June 11, 2008). As a result, and over strong objections from the media industry, the ban went into place. It was then lifted but with significant restrictions in 2011.[10] For example, many types of (unhealthy) products may not be placed anywhere, the placement must be editorially justified and not unduly prominent, and when paid placement does occur the broadcaster must display the letter "P" for three seconds at the start and end of the program to warn viewers that some product integration is taking place. In 2006, the European Union decided that its member states could authorize product placement but with genre restrictions: placements could not appear in news, current affairs, or children's programming (Thussu 2007, 40). None of these restrictions apply on American TV.

As American producers have discovered, home improvement shows are particularly amenable to placement because the home is something for which one can purchase goods and services almost infinitely. On television this place becomes a product, a media product, whose value is partly its being a location for placing other products. And if this space becomes full, it can be emptied out and updated. We are reminded of this during a ritual scene on *Extreme Makeover: Home Edition* (ABC, 2003–; hereafter *Home Edition*) when a huge (branded) furniture truck pulls up like some giant cornucopia from which objects pour. Cameras focus on teams of volunteers gleefully and energetically loading the house with these objects. The rapid pace highlights the sheer accumulation and the euphoria that results. The message couldn't be more simple: a home is a space for filling up with stuff. (An interesting spoof of this is a YouTube video that "makes over" a well-appointed home into something more authentically "Indian" by removing just about every piece of furniture and appliance, much to the shock and horror of the affluent Indian-American homeowner.)[11] While it would be difficult to prove a direct influence, home improvement shows and retail sales figures certainly have grown together, and companies such as Lowes and Home Depot have been happy to sponsor this kind of programming.[12] Home improvement has been a notable growth sector in American and other Western economies, and though expenditure was slowing down by 2008, it remains a big business.

On advice formats such as style makeovers, the information presented by hosts is always framed as sincere and disinterested, though the transaction behind a product's recommendation is not disclosed. This dissimulation means that viewers can be left with a great deal of uncertainty as to whether the presenter really does or does not like the product and whether the TV hosts are cultural intermediaries (Bourdieu [1979]1984; Featherstone 1991) or corporate intermediaries. As producers become more enamored of the income generated by product integration, the specter of commercial forces killing off the goose (a genuine advice show) that was designed to lay the golden egg (advertising dollars) has become a real possibility. On *Queer Eye*, clumsily motivated pauses in action mean that some program content came to resemble a 10-second spot announcement, with the presenter angling the product toward the camera whilst dutifully extolling its merits: a distortion that was humorously anticipated in Peter Weir's *The Truman Show* (1998), where subjects in a reality soap paused to highlight the merits of products in similarly staged close-ups. The incongruity of form—the filming of unscripted ongoing events versus spot advertising—was comic in the film but not intentionally so on *Queer Eye*. One of the few merits of Comedy Central's spoof *Straight Plan for the Gay Man* (2004) was that it foregrounded *Queer Eye's* commercialization by mocking its fetish for "products" and its not-so-subtle opportunities for product placement. As Jennifer Gillan notes, on fictional dramas like *The Office* and *30 Rock*, product placement is similarly parodied or overtly outed for comic effect (2011, 186–200). But in most RTV, product placement is a serious business. *Home Edition* found one way round the awkwardness of making plugs by making them mute and visual only. Yet it shares with other varieties of makeover the obligatory visit to the sponsor's retail chain, another predictable shaping of events (e.g., Sears on *Home Edition*, Whole Foods on *Top Chef*). These practices must raise the issue of credibility and realism: credibility, because viewers have to wonder how genuine the advice is, and realism, if the premise of reality television is that it films events as they occur without being scripted.

The fact is that product placement is a form of scripting and media professionals have expressed concern over its shaping of events to suit advertisers' needs both in fictional and nonfictional programming. For example, in 2005 the Writer's Guild of America (West) launched a "Product Invasion" campaign to protest the manipulation of content for the sake of product placement.[13] Of course, this is not to suggest that it would be easy to come up with a pure case of someone recommending a product unadulterated by advertising pressure: after all, most of us—hosts or viewers—encounter products through advertising. But we might expect those on a show that is not presented as an infomercial to give advice based on their knowledge of the product's merits and the subject's needs, even if both merits and needs were previously communicated through other forms of advertising. Style makeovers can therefore be seen as testing the limits of certain types of branded entertainment, not simply because viewers might find plugs clumsy and unrealistic but also because paid-for recommendations can potentially, or maybe even necessarily, weaken the whole premise of a show—and therefore its ability to attract audiences for advertising of any kind. A bigger issue than stylistic awkwardness is the larger relationship between presenters, subjects, and viewers. If this is compromised, if its authenticity is put up for sale, then clearly commercial forces may be in danger of undermining themselves.

Selling Celebrity

A more indirect form of product placement is that of celebrity—which is essentially the use of one media product (the star) to boost another (the television show), and vice versa. For example, sometimes celebrities perform as volunteers on *Home Edition*, especially once the show gained a solid reputation in its time slot. These guests frequently use their celebrity to generate donations in a benefit concert or other event, a move that provides a form of product placement in which the celebrity, in return, gets screen time and a boost to their career. The same transaction has become a key element in *American Idol*, where stars briefly "mentor" contestants and in so doing get valuable face time before a large audience. Other celebrities are home grown and come out of the popularity of the series itself. On *Home Edition* this accumulating celebritihood helps to persuade people to volunteer and to show up to cheer on site, as well as to produce good ratings at home. Beyond the show, many reality presenters are able to cash in as television hosts or guests elsewhere or as commercial spokespeople. For example, profitable cross-pollination occurs when culinary expert Ted Allen lends the celebrity he acquired on *Queer Eye* to Bravo's *Top Chef* and to Food Network's *Iron Chef America (2005–)*, *Food Detectives (2008)* and *Chopped (2009)*. *Home Edition*'s Ed Sanders did a stint as the host of the short-lived *National Bingo Night* (ABC, 2007) and *Queer Eye*'s Thom Filicia went on to host Style Networks' *Dress My Nest* (2007–) and *Tacky House* (Style, 2010–). Perhaps most interestingly, *Queer Eye*'s Carson Kressley graduated to host *How to Look Good Naked* (Channel 4, 2006–; Lifetime, 2008–), a show that persuades women who think of themselves as unattractive (usually because overweight) that they, too, are beautiful. Some reality hosts pitch products in short commercials: as "real" people, but consumer experts, their persona can travel intact from one media product to another. One of the earliest examples was when *Queer Eye*'s Thom Felicia became the official spokesman for the retailer Pier 1, nudging out the professional actress Kirstie Alley. Other active ads spokespeople are Stacy London and Clinton Kelly from *What Not to Wear* (BBC Two, 2001–03; BBC One, 2004–07; TLC, 2003–) and *Top Chef*'s Padma Lakshmi and Tom Colicchio.[14] During one *Top Chef* reunion a former contestant created a stir by criticizing Colicchio to his face for appearing in an ad for what she considered a not very healthy product (Diet Coke) and therefore for cheapening the profession—Colicchio remained unapologetic. Sometimes the interweaving of TV presenters in commercial breaks and on television shows is quite intricate. For instance, during the broadcast of an episode of *Home Edition* (aired 10/26/10) presenter Paige Hemmis appeared in a television commercial (in her *Home Edition* persona) to promote a Ford vehicle (the show's sponsor) and invited viewers to join her on Facebook for a live chat, not about the show but about the vehicle.

But by far the most active example of marketing one's celebrity and producing a commercial synergy between TV production and retail trade is provided by *Home Edition*'s host, Ty Pennington. This photogenic presenter has gone on to establish his name as a design brand in multiple media, including print, TV ads, and brick-and-mortar retail. In 2004 Pennington became a spokesperson for Sears and at the same time developed his own brand of home products to be sold in Sears' stores. In 2007 he launched the magazine *Ty Pennington At Home*, which, not surprisingly, features many full-page ads for Sears. In another interesting twist, Sears imitated the show that it sponsors in its own advertising campaign. In the 2007 Sears Christmas campaign Pennington launched the slogan: "Don't just give a gift. Grant a wish." According to cues in the commercials, this apparently means giving a major or multiple gifts from several family members to a deserving other family member: for example, not a dress but a whole new wardrobe (as in the style makeover), not a tool set but a whole new workshop (as in the home makeover). This campaign not only strengthens Sears' role as an enabler of makeovers, but also clearly improves the bottom line if it encourages viewers to think big when it comes to exchanging gifts. Pennington has also pitched for one of the world's largest pharmaceutical companies in Bayer's "Wonders of the Heart Campaign." Again echoing the television series, this campaign asks people to nominate an "everyday person" who was "worked wonders" (working wonders being a long-term slogan for Bayer's aspirin). The winner can expect a cash prize of $25,000 and a story written about them in (where else?) Pennington's magazine—a move that illustrates the wonders of synergy if nothing else. Clearly, using a feel-good TV reward formula as an advertising technique is useful for generating good public relations (PR), something Bayer AG needs to keep an eye on given its past ties to Nazism and several more recent controversies.[15] Indeed, the advertising for Bayer aspirin has for some years provided an outstanding example of dissimulation, of the effective management of fact and perception through the careful dissemination of truths and half-truths.[16] Its commercial equivocation and brand mystique perfectly illustrate the hybrid discourse of a culture that can always find work for someone who appears affable, genuine, and sincere.

Merchandizing and Brand Extension

One way to think of a television series is as a brand that can convert *viewers* into *consumers* through the totemistic purchase of merchandise associated with the show, or "entertainment property" as the industry refers to it, and the arrival of the Internet has made this commodification of the viewer's experience much more efficient. Some broadcasters frame online selling as answering a demand from viewers to interact with and to enrich their experience of the show, so it sounds like a matter of outreach and public relations. "If there is a hallmark for NBC and Bravo's interactive efforts, it is innovation that enriches the viewer experience for our programming," remarked Stephen Andrade, NBC Vice President of Interactive Development, when launching online shopping for his company's shows.[17] If things go according to plan, it is likely that others will be enriched also. To facilitate this, in 2004 NBC Universal hired a company called Delivery Agent to manage the sale of goods seen on TV or, as they term it, to "shop-enable" a range of shows.[18]

The shift from show to *showcase* is where makeover TV has been in the vanguard and its selling of show merchandize is often framed by its broadcasters as being pedagogical or a form of mentoring. They offer items for sale as a way to share the secrets or the glamour of the mass media experience. Viewers can sign up for an online "university" (offered by Donald Trump or producers of *Top Chef*), or benefit from "shopping guides" and "tips" about how to achieve the same results seen on TV. Of course what purports to inform consumers also provides information about consumers and can function readily as market research (Andrejevic 2004; Philips 2008). *The Real Housewives of Orange County* (Bravo, 2006–) experimented briefly with pop ups on the television screen, prompting viewers to go to Bravo's website to purchase items like those currently being viewed (2008, Season 4). Though thought to be the future of television, such on-screen prompts are still comparatively rare. Less crass, perhaps, are the tie-ins to other shows like *Top Chef* whose website and occasional spot announcements promote the sale of recipe books for meals prepared on the show, enabling viewers to mimic the activity they witness on TV. The content generated by such formats is twice commodified, first as TV content and then when resold as books or DVDs. Another twist is that viewers can "win" participants, as when *Top Chef* offers its viewers the chance to win the prize of having the series' winner cook for them personally. As well as selling T-shirts or mugs, broadcasters can sell other associated media content, such as games, music downloads, or ringtones. It is also worth mentioning that the physical location of the home build can function as a commercial site for merchandise sales. Thus, *Home Edition* vendors can offer souvenirs to visitors who want to materially connect to their visit to the TV building site: when I visited one such site in 2007, there were stalls with branded T-shirts, books associated with the series, and even pink tool kits marketed by carpenter Paige Hemmis.[19]

RTV producers have also extended their brand by creating many types of associated content across different media platforms: spin-off TV shows, web shows, and radio shows. Britain's Channel 4 hosted *Big Brother's Big I*, a web show that discussed the television series on the official *Big Brother* website and on YouTube. Similarly, CBS launched a web talk show called *House Calls: the Big Brother Talk Show* (CBS.com, 2004–). This low-cost venue (which has its own commercial breaks) encourages viewers to use the telephone (at their expense) to discuss a television show on a website; it also promotes subscriptions to the CBS live feeds. Back in Britain, Channel 4 also briefly experimented with articulating radio and TV productions when it developed a radio show called *Big Brother's Big Ears* to discuss *Big Brother 9*. These activities are in addition to several television programs such as *Big Brother's Little Brother* (Channel 4 and E4, 2001–) and *Big Brother's Big Mouth* (E4, 2004–). There have also been experiments with extending the TV entertainment in real life, or at least in a version of real life. For example, when David Cook won the *American Idol* series in 2008 he declared (just like the paid Super Bowl athletes) "I'm going to Disney World!" This clip invoking one of the most sacred refrains of consumer culture was then used in Disney ads that appeared within hours of the finale. But this was just a taste of the synergy to come. Echoing ABC's early financing of Disney's original theme park while it was broadcasting the hit show *Disneyland* (Nadel 2005), when Cook spoke Disney was in the process of building an "American Idol Experience" attraction at Disney World (Florida). Here "guests" can recreate their favorite show experience, either by auditioning and performing or by voting as an audience member.[20] Every day, the winner of this Disney event enters into the world of the "real" show by being guaranteed a spot in a regional *American Idol* audition (by being issued a "Dream Ticket"). Obviously, Disney is an old hand at commodifying experience and the company provides an early example of using television to promote other associated businesses, but here we see a particularly ambitious integration of a media product into real life and then back again into the media.

Made Possible By: Sponsorship

One of the earliest models for monetizing TV programming is sponsorship, a technique television inherited from early radio, where sponsoring programs was a common practice from the 1930s to the 1950s (Barnouw 1978). It was favored by advertisers because it was perceived to be less intrusive than commercials but offered the advertiser more editorial control over program content (McAllister 1996).[21] But the practice diminished after the quiz show scandals of the 1950s when it was discovered that some sponsors and producers were rigging content to maximize ratings and profit.[22] In subsequent decades, if there was sponsorship of television content it was mostly of live events, like sports, and by companies who were otherwise legally banned or restricted from direct advertising on television, like tobacco or alcohol. In other words, sponsorship was a backdoor strategy born of necessity and lack of other options. Today, there has been something of a revival of sponsorship in certain types of reality television, not for reasons of legal regulation but because of changing technology and viewer choice. As in the past, sponsors usually pay up front and enter into a business contract to help finance a show, either during the early stages of production or later in the process. Though detailed figures are not disclosed to viewers, the financial support is overt because the named sponsor wants their brand to be recognized as a magnanimous and overarching supporter of what is taking place. Early radio or television sponsorship involved a simple "trade-name publicity," where companies were content to attach their name to an entertainment with no other marketing attempts; as in the *Goodrich Silvertown Orchestra* or the *Kodak Chorus*. At most, the sponsor hoped a "gratitude factor" or "halo effect" would, as Eric Barnouw put it, drive "the osmosis of affection and trust from program to product" (Barnouw 1978, 47). But gradually the presence of the sponsor became more evident within the programming itself.

Today's sponsorship deals usually involve a package of special announcements before or during shows ("brought to you by . . . "), regular spots in commercial breaks (some of which are designer ads that link to a particular episode), and product placement. Some companies pay for naming rights in order to become part of the mise-en-scène; for example, there is no longer just a kitchen but "the Kenmore Pro kitchen" (*Top Chef*) and *Project Runway* models invariably traipse off to the "L'Oréal Paris Makeup Room" and "TRESemmé hair salon" (Bravo, 2004–08; Lifetime 2009–). Because reality TV has ritual and distinct segments, it can also attract partial sponsorships. For example, contestants use the sponsor's product (e.g., Bertolli oil on *Top Chef*) during a particular challenge and then win an associated prize furnished by this sponsor (a trip to Italy). *Top Chef* producers have also adopted the model of nominating "official brands," as though during an event like the Olympics. On its third season (2007), there was an official ice cream (Cold Stone Creamery), bottled water (Evian), olive oil (Bertolli), and spirit (Bombay Sapphire gin). By the time the spin-off *Top Chef: Just Desserts* (Bravo, 2010–) arrived Breyer ice cream was elevated to the rank of an official "partner" of the series. Today's multiplatform use also means broadcasters can sell packages of advertising across diverse media in what Michael Curtin terms a "matrix-media" strategy (Turner and Tay 2009, 15), and so sponsorship can be extended onto an associated website or part thereof. To take *Top Chef* again, Glad and Bertolli sponsor the TV series but, in addition, Glad sponsors webisodes and a sweepstakes on the show's website, while Bertolli sponsors the website's biography area (Bravotv.com).

Sponsors may come on board at the Spring upfronts (where traditionally advertisers pay up front for spots attached to Fall series that they get to preview) or they may be involved at all stages of production. Occasionally, sponsors function as coproducers, meaning that they are approached when the series is just a gleam in some producer's eye and when they sign on they have a direct say in shaping content. This kind of deep sponsorship, reminiscent of early radio, is evident in *Home Edition* (Sears, Ford) and *American Idol* (Coke, Ford). It was even more striking in the reality series *No Boundaries* (WB, 2002), which was jointly produced by a manufacturer and a media company as a vehicle for a product—in this case another type of vehicle, the Ford Explorer. Before any filming began, the production company (Lions Gate Entertainment) approached the manufacturer's advertising agency (J. Walter Thompson) who agreed on mutually beneficial terms that allowed the sponsor to be involved in the early stages of production. Ford had input into casting, named the show after its own advertising campaign, and helped choose settings that would best display its product. Similarly, Toyota advertised its 4 Runner SUV on the RTV series bearing the unwieldy title of *Global Extremes: Mt. Everest—4Runners of Adventure* (OLN, 2003). The series functioned as an extension of a marketing campaign that likewise featured the vehicle at Mt. Everest. Even the advertising copy for the SUV reflected the target demographics and ethos of the television show. The 4Runner, we are informed, is: "aspirational, youthful, sporty and most of all, genuine."[23] Exactly how an SUV can be "genuine" is not explained, but it does match the reality programming's own selling point of authenticity. In another instance, three big sponsors for the series *The Restaurant* (NBC, 2003–04) covered all production expenses. This would explain why products and services provided by American Express, Mitsubishi, and Coors were featured in a rather stilted fashion again and again.

Naturally enough, sponsors intend their association with a show to strengthen their own brand. Sears' long-term sponsorship of *Home Edition* makes sense given that the company has for generations been selling people the means to build and furnish homes, even offering quickly mounted (prefabricated) homes in its famous catalog. Sears was also instrumental in encouraging an interest in do-it-yourself home projects. As early as 1901, its catalog began to market tool kits and advice for amateur home repairs and in subsequent years increased these offerings to make the job of home improvement more accessible and more affordable (Goldstein 1998, 18). *Home Edition's* other main sponsor, Ford, also strengthens its brand by regularly giving away one of its newly launched vehicles and reinforcing the automobile's association with the American Dream. The featured vehicle is often framed as literally providing mobility out of a stagnant situation as well as a way of keeping a family together.

A more problematic example of sponsorship is Olive Garden's occasional participation in the same series. As any American TV viewer will know, this restaurant chain's slogo is: "When you're here you're Family" (the word "Family" being capitalized, perhaps because here it is such an abstract concept), an ironic claim given that this chain is putting the Mom-and-Pop model out of business (There is a similar irony in rival chain Applebee's slogan "There's no place like the neighborhood" as each neighborhood fills up with identical franchises). Or perhaps it *is* appropriate for Olive Garden to sponsor a show that likewise capitalizes on the cherished entity of the family. As with all franchises, Olive Garden obliterates locality since its standardized features of menu and architecture mean each restaurant could be located anywhere. In this case, perhaps it makes sense that one episode Olive Garden sponsored (the Hassall family, aired 7/22/06) is all about substitutes: the wife is a substitute teacher and substitute mother for two special needs children and their newly built substitute house is sponsored by a firm that substitutes a franchised "family" atmosphere for the real thing. At one point during this build, a presenter flies off to something entitled "The Olive Garden Culinary School" in Tuscany. Filming at this venue obviously tries to accomplish two things for the sponsor. It suggests, first, that the Olive Garden brand is authentically Italian and, second, that the organization has culinary heft. Whereas what chain restaurants are really about is applying the efficiencies of scale of mass production to the "assembly" of food and buildings, a process that requires little local knowledge or skills. An Olive Garden commercial during the broadcast further claims that there is homemade warmth in their dishes, another example of a commercial elision that associates one thing (mass produced items) with another thing (homemade items) that it is not, but which carries a strong sentimental currency (home, family). Associating the Olive Garden chain with building a home for a real family is a logical effort to reify an ersatz domesticity. As with *Home Edition* itself, "home" has become part of a market strategy: a simulation of home that is.[24]

Donor TV

One way the makeover format has made a distinct contribution to monetizing television is its elevation of sponsorship to donorship, a practice that can enhance not only donors but also the status of commercial support for programming in general (more in Chapter 2). The difference between a donor and a sponsor is not entirely straightforward and there is some considerable overlap, but on RTV while sponsors offset production costs, donors offer aid to individuals depicted on screen (donors may or may not be sponsors also). In other words, the sponsor supports the production and helps get the show made, whereas donors benefit individual participants. Of course, donations are made with the expectation that this gift will be duly noted during programming, so the donor's role lies somewhere between overt advertising and the freely offered aid of those who have no personal financial gain in mind. The donor's gesture amalgamates gift and market economies and can accomplish two things at once: produce appropriately targeted and organically embedded product placement (items people really need) and generate good publicity for the donor. Both of these will likely lower audience resistance to the advertising involved. This is not the behind-the-scenes "donation" of earlier barter arrangements where companies would provide goods or services to the production staff in return for some representation of these items in the film or program. Here the donation is staged and foregrounded: it is not merely a production transaction but the main thematic content. Since donations are supposed to answer the subject's rather than the producer's immediate needs, the donated products are kept by the recipients rather than functioning as background props.

While not unprecedented (e.g., *Queen for a Day* NBC, 1956–60; ABC, 1960–64), donating products to charitable causes has not been a common model for popular TV programming and is still comparatively rare. One prominent example is *Home Edition*, where for years donors have been framed as helpers, rescuers, or friends whose involvement is personal and heartfelt rather than detached and interchangeable. Hence the host will refer to "our friends at [Tyson/Sears/CVS]." To sustain the emotional capital, no one on camera completes the statement "CVS would like to help you out" with "and the company hopes this publicity will measurably enhance its profitability." There is a persistent fantasy in all makeover television that one can step outside or above the market—though only with the help of those who squarely inhabit it. This programming creates a transcendental world where the normal rules of commerce appear to be suspended and where companies simply want to help those in need. Apart from anything else, this backyard utopianism demonstrates the power of television when for just one second of the camera's attention companies are lining up to donate valuable items.

In short-term and complex contracts typical of late-modern capitalism, the producers of *Home Edition* subcontract most arrangements out to a local building firm that voluntarily coordinates donations from other businesses in their area, usually people they've worked with before. By relying on preestablished networks but asking business colleagues for donations, these firms are functioning aberrantly within a middle realm of ambiguous discourse that is hard to identify as either strictly commercial or noncommercial. What we are witnessing is not quite astroturfing (creating a fake grass roots movement) but is more like buying real but instant sod, sold by the yard—like the material they roll out on neighbors' lawns to compensate for damage done to local properties during filming. Nothing is as simple as fake. The "community" formation may be instant, but real people and real feelings are involved: this in addition to real profits.

The *Home Edition* narrative does not include the new homeowners subsequently cashing in on the donations by putting their house on the market, unlike numerous other home series that focus on resale. We know that owners of renovated rooms on *Trading Spaces* (TLC Discovery Home, 2000–08) are not even allowed to sell furniture or items by associating them with the show (e.g., "as seen on *Trading Spaces*") (Shufeldt and Gale 2007, 278). But while it is no doubt to the contractor's advantage to build a large and impressive home to showcase their work, and while it certainly helps the TV production to have a dramatic "After" shot, it may not be in the long-term interest of the new owners if maintaining the new house is beyond their means. One resident who could no longer afford his home's upkeep felt obliged to defend his decision to put it on the market. "I'm not doing it [selling] to make a profit. I'm doing it not to lose money," Eric Herbert insisted. "I just hope people understand the reality of it" (Marlisa Keyes, *Bonner County Daily Bee*, May 19, 2008). When another *Home Edition* recipient decided that he, too, would have to sell his home, his listing attracted a lot of media attention and he angrily withdrew it after only one day. A *Philadelphia Inquirer* article reports that Victor Marrero had soured on the *Home Edition* experience. When overwhelmed by bills, he tried to contact ABC but "When I got into trouble, they wouldn't take my calls," he said. "They didn't care. They made their 100 million and moved on." In summary, "I appreciate everything— this house and everyone who helped me," Marrero said. "But it's too much house" (Sam Wood, *Philadelphia Inquirer*, May 7, 2008).

While filming the transformation generates a profit for the broadcaster, the "paid talent" (design team), and the producers, no one else is supposed to make money in the process. A show like *Home Edition* depends on numerous unpaid on-site volunteers, as many as half a million so far by one account.[25] And in a sense, viewers, too, are voluntarily giving their attention, which, since this attention is ultimately why the show is produced and the family is helped, is part of the economic circuit. But when it comes to tradesmen who donate time and labor, participation might be more accurately described as volunteerism-for-profit since they can expect some financial gain from their own and others' efforts. So while donation is usually considered a form of charity, and St. Paul was famously of the opinion that "charity vaunteth not itself" (1 Corinthians 13:4), on TV discrete vaunting is rather the point. The subjects who are being helped trade their privacy for goods and services. Donors trade goods and services for the opposite, for publicity. Either way, the currency is media exposure.

The donor's participatory role affords the opportunity to personalize their brand, a strategy that is of great importance in modern commerce: for example, in its spot announcements donors thank producers for being "included" in the programming and donorship becomes an intimate transaction that makes it legitimate to say "This fridge was given to you by Sears" or "CVS wants to give you a year's supply of medicines," a scripting that articulates a personal relationship between corporate donor, recipient, and, by extension, viewer. This valuable connectivity continues the effort to humanize the "faceless" or "soulless" corporation that has been a major task of advertising and public relations since the late nineteenth century (Marchand 1998). Lest we forget to whom they owe thanks, a family returning to their new home picks up a "Welcome home" card from Sears as they enter their new building, to which the mother replies "We love you Sears!" (*Home Edition*, aired 8/10/08). Companies are mentioned by name because they appear to have come out— or rather their brands have come out—to give individuals something as would a friend, neighbor or volunteer.

It is now obligatory for every *Home Edition* kitchen to be equipped with Kenmore appliances donated by Sears and awkward scripting insists that the presenter not only point this out but also briefly extol their virtues. After a few iterations, viewers might well assume that the equipment will come from this retailer, yet in every episode the host is obliged to explicitly point it out again—not, obviously, to inform the regular audience of something vital or new but to make us give our (paid for) attention where it is due. By being framed as part of a larger donor relationship, this attention may appear more legitimate than a regular plug and almost a matter of politeness for us to give the donor due recognition. Donated goods are also often substantial: for example, subjects receive a whole room's worth of furnishings instead of a single beauty product. Hence the scale of donation is worth our attention.

Donorship and personalization, as well as high production values, elevate the makeover show above the level of its cousin, the infomercial, as can be seen by comparing *Home Edition* to a series like *Designing Spaces* (WE) that is in fact produced by a marketing firm (O2 Media Inc.). While the latter series also performs home improvements with the help of commercial sponsors, it is far less adept at hiding its promotional base. With forced enthusiasm hosts thank "guest" companies who have no doubt paid to "appear" on the "show" and engage in awkward prompts like "how can our viewers find out more about this product?" which cue a website address. This series' own website reveals (presumably to attract more advertisers/ sponsors) that the television show is a form of "Branded Entertainment" designed to "give brands a human face" and to produce "a sincere and persuasive message that easily relates to the consumer."[26] This is not a bad description of *Home Edition,* but there is much more effort to keep the commercial script more diaphanous in the prime-time show. It takes the migration to another platform to bring this out: on the show's website the featured video clips are of the moment when Ford, Sears, or whoever is donating an item to a grateful participant and this footage come across more clearly as a commercial when extracted in this other medium.

TV makeover recipients are not so gauche as to express excitement over how much donations cost. No dollar amounts are ever mentioned, since we are supposedly functioning within an economy of gifts. Of course, as Marcel Mauss ([1950] 1990) underlined, in such economies the recipient is obligated to reciprocate; not, in this instance, with another gift but by allowing producers to generate profit from publicizing the exchange. Gift giving is also about establishing status and building relationships, which is what donors and broadcasters aim to do. We get a glimpse of this agenda on the *Real Housewives* series when the women periodically organize charity events, occasions that have for some time been a way for individuals or businesses to establish social status under the rationale of donating to a "good cause." On this series, we get an inside view of individuals fighting quite viciously in order to promote their own business interests. We see that at such events different types of sponsorship are precisely priced and commercially valued and that sponsorship plays a role in many echelons of society, on or off screen. Makeover TV therefore represents not so much a transcendence of commerce as a recirculation through less direct channels that ends up benefiting several constituencies. There is a moratorium on payment but not on profit.

Ordinary Participation: Texts to Texting

Having examined how corporate participation shapes program content, the remainder of this chapter will consider the role of ordinary people as they participate or interact with reality TV programming. What becomes clear is that evolving relations between audience and text offer yet more opportunities for commercialization due in large part to the appearance of the Internet and to multiplatformicity as an economic strategy in the last half decade, a topic that is beginning to receive some critical attention but mostly as it affects fictional programming.[27] RTV provides an early and strong example of an "overflow" (Brooker 2001) from the television text onto other platforms such as the computer and other mobile devices. Indeed, one could say that RTV was born in an attempt to maximize multiplatform viewing.

Clearly, the coactive[28] or asynchronous use of multiple devices diversifies and complicates concepts like "audience" and "text."[29] I want to clarify the current situation by identifying specific articulations, especially as they expand commercial opportunities. What I want to underline is the bidirectionality whereby viewers consume texts and *texts consume viewers*. Reality TV is more energetic in both directions than is most programming, especially in its consumption of viewers as program participants and as generators of supplementary material. I describe this as the media *consuming* the audience because, like consumption, it refers to a process whereby one entity absorbs another in order to nourish and benefit itself, generally to the advantage of the consumer. My analysis will concentrate on what makes the viewer-text circuits around RTV so distinctive and will draw on examples from *The Real Housewives* series, where, like other docusoaps, people are not supposed to be competing or putting on masks in order to win a game but are just playing themselves.[30] However before undertaking this examination, it will be helpful to distinguish a few key terms and concepts.

New media like the computer are recontextualizing television: that is, they are "changing what it is that television can do, for whom it can do it, and under what conditions" (Turner and Tay 2009, 3).[31] I talk about television *and* new media because I believe the two terms remain distinct.[32] If the designation "new media" requires a full-fledged multidirectional or dialogic activity, if it involves consumers becoming producers, then current reality TV broadcasts push the televisual medium closer to new media in ways this book will explore but they still remain within the ranks of mainstream mass media. As a stand-alone medium, television does not have the Internet's many-to-many "multipersonalization" (Castells 2000, 385) nor, alternatively, its intimate one-to-one engagement. A good way to understand

TV's relation to other media platforms would be to adapt Stuart Hall's (1980) term "articulation" to refer to elements that are linked together and yet retain their distinctive identities, as in Hall's analogy of the different segments of an articulated lorry (or tractor-trailer). Increasingly, media devices are being used in conjunction with other media devices, but the likelihood is that there will always be a variety of platforms and content types to meet the desires of different consumers in different contexts; for example, sometimes screen size will be more important than mobility, or long-form narratives will be more desirable than one minute formats.

Over the last century, views about audience behavior and actual audience behavior have been shifting (this distinction is important but sometimes overlooked). Initial models of the mass media grew out of Marxist writings in the mid nineteenth century regarding the ideological role of cultural texts. In simple terms, Marx and Engels promulgated a model of the passive mass audience subject to ideological pressures from the capitalist class. Ordinary people were conceived of as largely mute subjects constrained by their roles as workers and as consumers of media. The same is largely true of the Frankfurt School in the 1940s, when Max Horkheimer and Theodor Adorno (1944) portrayed the masses as subject to a systematic culture "industry" that turned out homogenized and hegemonic fare—although, in contrast and somewhat ahead of his time, Walter Benjamin ([1936] 2006)) did articulate a shift from passive audiences to early forms of user-generated content.[33] In real practice, audiences did have little input into media production. In the 1960s, a more active model for audiences emerged in post-Frankfurt commentary coming out of Birmingham (CCCS) and elsewhere. Writers such as Raymond Williams (1980), Stuart Hall (1980), and John Fiske (1987) saw more instances of hegemony and negotiation than linear ideological control.[34] This was the start of a widespread shift from seeing audience members as having low agency to seeing them as more actively engaged, albeit at the level of interpreting already coded texts. The audience was still pictured as reacting to a media product that was produced without their help; unless one considers audience interpretation as a secondary form of "production," a claim made by various forms of Reception Theory that energized literary criticism in the pre-digital 1970s and 1980s.

Today, the appearance of new technologies, most especially the computer, has allowed audiences to push through what I elsewhere call the broadcast threshold (Deery 2003) and to transition from read-only to read-and-write cultural production. Scholars therefore need to consider more than the former passive-to-active spectrum and think beyond the viewer's reception of content on a single medium. Today's interactive user who accesses and contributes to multiple platforms moves us from the notion of the text to *texting*, not in the sense of text messaging but when referring to the open and open-ended process of producing multi-authored, user-generated material, as in an unfolding series of viewer posts on a broadcaster's website. While this activity may "overflow" the television text, it does not wipe out its boundaries: an overflow, after all, is distinct from a confluence. The television text remains and is archivable, but there is potential (not a necessity) for more. Online activity doesn't change the status of the television text as a one-to-many—or more accurately few-to-many—mass medium and for the foreseeable future the model of producing a fixed text for a large audience will be as important a part of the television experience as is the newer associated interaction. I agree with Su Holmes that it is important to "retain the notion of the TV text as an analytic category, while at the same time acknowledging the changing parameters within which this is now formed" (2004, 217). At this point, the TV broadcast remains the primary, self-sufficient, and originating text: for example, only in very rare instances do producers try out a show first online (Gillan 2011, 38; Ross 2008, 110).

Participation versus Interactivity

When it comes to a viewer's relationship with media content, the terms "interactivity" and "participation" are often used interchangeably so that by now their scope threatens to reduce their usefulness. I will therefore distinguish two types of activity in order to clarify different forms of textual engagement and their potential for commercialization. "Participation" will refer to involvement that *directly affects the primary media text*. It can mean being present in a bodily sense (TV cast members) or technologically mediated (viewer votes or comments). In contrast, "interactivity" will describe any actions that engage with but *do not directly affect the primary media text*. In other words, subjects participate *in* or interact *with*.[35] The key distinction is that even the most energetic audience or fan interactivity is, as Henry Jenkins (2006) noted (after de Certeau), a form of "poaching."[36] It feeds off but takes place independently of the production of the official text and does not alter its original form.[37] These boundaries need to be clarified because viewer interactivity does not impact production as much as appears to be the case when the term is also used to describe activities that do affect program content. For example, TV sports fans notoriously confuse interactivity and participation when they imagine that their role as viewers affects the game and some viewers (and critics) of other television content do the same. On reality programming, audience engagement—whether participatory or interactive—is often officially sanctioned and even vital, but thus far it has not entailed any radical shift of power or agency. Interactivity and participation are often presented as empowering, as techniques of self-expression or as the means for customizing goods and services to better serve the viewer's needs. However, as Mark Andrejevic (2004) has convincingly argued, online technologies also allow others to extract commodifiable information about TV viewers and conduct economic surveillance. My aim is to extend this discussion by looking at other ways in which television capitalizes on its audience.[38]

The basic premise of all commercial television is that, however passive, viewers constitute a labor force that can be commodified in the form of ratings (Smythe 1981; Jhally 1990). Reality TV producers have explored ways to increase their income, first by simply expanding platforms and viewing time. Jon de Mol purposely launched *Big Brother* in order to articulate TV and Internet activity and thereby turn online video streams into additional revenue streams. The idea of offering viewers live online feeds was built into the design of the show, the aim being to broadcast to a large mass audience but also engage a smaller but demographically significant group of younger viewers who were beginning to migrate to narrowcasting online.[39] At first rolled out for free, these online videos were subsequently only available for a fee.[40] For many viewers in America and in Europe, this was their first experience of watching videos online and so it introduced them to dual media use, although not many producers followed this particular lead.

Participation

The invitation to step into the screen, to transform from viewer to participant, is of course a selling point of reality TV and is meant to contribute to its real-ness. It is also a vital part of its economic strategy. It hardly needs saying that this use of unpaid or lowly paid non-unionized labor is cost-effective, but it is interesting that profits are made precisely because viewers enjoy the spontaneous and ordinary effect that occurs when less is spent on production than in most other programming. Investigations are just beginning into the labor status of RTV participants and the extent to which they might be subject to the same rights, protections, and compensation as other workers. As Francois Jost (2011) and Mark Andrejevic (2011) note, a court ruling in France determined that participants in some reality formats are indeed subject to existing labor laws (e.g., the French version of *Temptation Island*). One of the legal arguments is that, like most jobs, RTV involves subordination to an employer and the execution of tasks under this authority, so that while activities might be entertainment for viewers they are not necessarily so for participants (Jost 2011, 36). Among other things, producers demand the full availability of the participants and the signing of contracts. Yet while one contestant on the gamedoc *Wedding Wars* (VH1, 2011) wore a T-shirt with the lettering "For Rent: By the Hour" it is unlikely that his stint on the show was lucrative.

While ordinary people may participate in the broadcast content, they do not participate in the production process and this remains a crucial distinction. To participate means to "take part," but it *is* only a part and like other (theatrical) parts is often an assigned role, whatever the format. RTV participation is usually strictly circumscribed so that even when a participant's presence appears central, his or her role can be quite passive. Yet what is not often observed is how participants can make their appearance profit themselves despite restrictive contracts. Being a participant on a RTV series produces the added value of accruing some degree of fame and therefore brand potential. Hence some ordinary participants mimic corporate participation by plugging their own businesses or wares in a form of unofficial product placement. In fact, some cast members reveal (usually off camera or on behind-the-scenes reunion shows) that this commercial opportunity is the main reason they joined a series, whether it be to promote an already existing business or to launch a new one. This is a tactic similar to *la perruque* where one produces one's own work while on the job and disguises this private work as work for one's employer (de Certeau [1980]1984, 25), the difference being that *la perruque* is not usually designed for profit. A particularly stark example of unofficial plugs is the *Real Housewives* franchise, where if the participants didn't have something to publicize when the series started, most do by the time they have accumulated some TV capital and a modicum of celebrity. This is one advantage of being on a series rather than appearing in only one episode (like makeovers). Almost every one of the housewives eventually produces a book (usually ghost written), a song (electronically enhanced), or something else that they get to publicize while on the show (wigs, skin care products, bags, dresses, wine, jewelry). They create their own pseudo-events that, thanks to being filmed in the series, are guaranteed a national audience: so launch parties replace lunch parties and other cast members become focus groups. Many also use their television fame to extend their promotion of products on other platforms.[41] In fact, the turning of the self into a brand became the main theme of a spin-off series *Bethenny Ever After* (Bravo 2010) in which former *Apprentice* and *Real Housewives* participant Bethenny Frankel revealed her quite successful attempts to parley her RTV fame into a sustainable commercial brand. This kind of determined self-promotion certainly stretches the premise that the *Real Housewives* series is just about the social life of a group of friends. At least one cast member thinks it is overdone: Kelly Killoren Bensimon of *The Real Housewives of New York* complains, "This is something that really annoys me about being on the show. I cannot stand how these women promote products so blatantly."[42] On other reality formats, too, hosts and clients can simultaneously promote their business interests since the real life that is being displayed exists also on the business plane. Another use of RTV is to create what we might think of as media zombies in the form of past celebrities who stumble around in a half-dead, half-alive state hoping the television exposure will fully revive their careers. Many seem disfigured and unsettling because they no longer resemble the image we had of them in their prime; for example, any number of participants on show like *Celebrity Apprentice* (NBC, 2008–) or *I'm a Celebrity . . . Get Me Out of Here!* (ITV, 2002; NBC, 2009–). Others up-and-coming may try to cash in on their more recent fame by having people pay for them to simply show up in real life in some off-screen venue such as a nightclub or store.

A distinctive feature of reality television is that, since participants don't have a prior script, they don't know in advance how they will be portrayed after final editing. So as episodes air they also become first-time viewers of an edited version of their lives (most receive DVDs only a few days ahead of the broadcast). Again, *The Real Housewives* producers capitalize on this by requiring the women to blog as *participant-viewers* (they don't use this term) and so open up new veins of drama and conflict due to a collision of different levels of insight and viewing access (the women now know what others said behind their back both on television and in blogs). During filming, participants seem, perversely, to forget that the purpose of the camera is to make a record. Future drama is generated, therefore, because of the difference between technological and human memory (because TV cameras record exactly and later produce only what editors decide to exhibit) and because there is a temporal and experiential gap between filming and broadcasting—which suggests that the ultimate topic of reality TV could be what it means to be mediated on television.

Audience voting is another feature associated with reality TV. It may be interactive or participatory, but in either case RTV producers demonstrate an important formula: a mass medium can generate income by selling back to audiences content created by audiences. When viewers are invited to vote on talent contests considerable profits go to telecom companies as well as TV broadcasters and producers, who sell the audience the information they helped create (which contestant won or lost the vote).[43] When *Pop/American Idol* came along, it greatly encouraged the use of mobile devices (phones and texting) and this articulation of media became a crucial marketing device for the telecom industries (Jenkins 2006, 59). Similarly, when wanna-be contestants apply to participate in a quiz show, their telephone charges fund the program (e.g., *Who Wants to be a Millionaire?* ITV, 1998–). When they vote, the aggregation of many individuals' input becomes a valuable commodity that has no value outside the series created by producers; in fact, producers guard as private property information on how many votes were cast and for whom. If some viewers do not contribute financially by actually voting, they may still be drawn to the show because many others are drawn to, and vote on, the show. Success breeds success.

Even when voting can be seen as a form of audience resistance or counter-organization it still creates a profitable circuit: in fact, if resistance means viewers become more active, then all the better for associated business interests. For example, some viewers inspired more by regional pride than by an objective judging of singing ability have voted against official criteria in various versions of *Idol* around the world. Enthusiastic viewers of *Indian Idol* (SET, 2004–) have in the past set up telephone voting booths, distributed prepaid mobile phone cards, hired people to vote, funded marketing campaigns, and so on (Punathambekar 2011). US viewers have also periodically organized a vote-for-the-worst campaign, their aim being to subvert *American Idol* so its producers can no longer claim they are discovering real talent or cynically use audiences as focus groups for future sales. This counters the PR work for the music "industry" that the open competition is supposed to provide. However, while such efforts have made producers anxious at times none have ultimately scuttled the production (the most popular "worst" candidate, Sanjaya Malakar, did not win) and all have enriched broadcasters, producers, and telecom companies. A more serious financial tug-of-war occurred in Britain in December 2009 when a few viewers organized a boycott of the single produced by the winner of *The X Factor* (ITV, 2004–) because they were frustrated by the predictable nature in which the winner would go on to secure the Christmas number one single slot and guarantee profits for the producers of the show (as it had for four years running). They encouraged people to buy instead a 1992 song by a left-wing, anticorporate rock group Rage Against the Machine. This did outsell the *X-Factor* winner, but only by a small margin.

In other instances, limited viewer input is officially incorporated into the television program in the form of emails, texts, or tweets, though this generally occurs on reunion and associated talk shows rather than on the regular series.[44] These viewer comments, individually or combined, can have a greater impact on the TV text than someone just physically appearing somewhere on the series, so the form and degree of activity (participation or interaction) are separate from agency and the power to impact. What these contributing viewers are doing is supplying, free of charge, material that others sell for profit—as is spelled out in the fine print regarding such submissions.[45] Legally the viewer's input becomes the property of producers and broadcasters who may exploit it as they see fit.[46] Another trend that is only beginning to take off is using viewers as focus groups: we've seen this in *American Idol* and another version is when Current.TV viewers can vote for which viewer-generated pieces they would like to see on air (Ross 2008, 115). None of this activity is salaried and even when it comes to professionals (of fictional or nonfictional programming) a labor dispute is mounting about how much, or if, they should get paid extra for going beyond writing a television script and creating, say, a website or blog. There is a problem of classification in some instances, for these paratextual activities might be categorized as advertising or promotion rather than regular editorial material.

Some RTV voting is interactive only, but this, too, can be profitable. For example, when viewers are asked how they feel about something on a show by voting in online polls or text messaging, this information can double as market research. Occasionally viewers think they are participating and having an impact on program content but in actual fact they are not, as in the British TV phone-in scandals where viewers thought they were participating in a live show which was actually recorded and its outcome already determined.[47] Voices were raised, even in parliament, about the low odds of anyone winning when calling in to quiz shows and the subsequently huge profits generated by alliances between broadcasters, producers, and phone companies. One parliamentary committee in London considered reclassifying vote-in reality shows a form of gambling that should come under government control.[48] Actually, since RTV voting began, commentators have been interested in its relation to real-life political elections and what these latest destabilizations might suggest to a cynical observer is that if participation in reality TV is curtailed and managed in both visible and hidden ways, then far from distancing it from real-life voting, far from making it appear trivial, these examples might make television voting all the more analogous to the citizen's participation in the larger political sphere.

Interactivity

The most common form of interactivity among television viewers is when they communicate with each other on the broadcaster's official website or other site. We saw the potential for web advertising and merchandising, but online activity can also play an important role in sustaining viewer interest, so important in an age of channel surfing and time shifting. Online forums can build brand loyalty for a television series and encourage people to watch the program so they can be part of the conversation. New technologies even encourage appointment viewing since some viewers will want to watch the very latest episode at the same time as others so they can discuss it together either during or immediately after the initial broadcast, an anticipatory effect that may impact their viewing. Internet use, in other words, can fortify traditional features of the mass medium, including the notion that the television show is a synchronous event for large numbers of viewers. It returns us, in some ways, to the early days when television watching occurred in family groups—with one significant difference: today's remote, interpersonal conversations take place in public forums that, because they are public, are also commodifiable, whereas family conversations were not. They are commodifiable because online space can be sold to advertisers and because each hit constitutes an advertisement for the show. Viewers, too, can build their own associated sites and even commoditize them by putting them up for sale.[49] Many websites promote the idea that the television audience can become a community, a particularly useful epiphenomenon when it comes to attracting and retaining the desired Facebook generation—though determining whether any given website does, in fact, constitute a "community" is complex and beyond the scope of this study.[50] In any case, any increased attention to a media product generally adds value to it—even negative criticism, since some viewers who dislike a TV show will nevertheless watch it in order to criticize it online (as in sites like Television Without Pity or Survivor Sucks). In the past, such disgruntled viewers might have stopped watching but now, whether fans or anti-fans, all are included in the ratings.[51] Online fan activity today can be enormous, some of it directed by the broadcasters and some entirely viewer-generated; for example, interactivity surrounding the fictional series *Lost* (2004–10) has given rise to a constellation of websites (real and fictional), a wiki *(Lostpedia),* and an ARG (alternate reality game) (Booth 2010).

Persistence of Vision

Because reality TV involves real people, sometimes viewer interactivity can affect participants in a delayed and asynchronous manner, as when they modify their behavior in future episodes not because a writer alters a script but because of the affective relations between participants and viewers as mediated by the Internet. We know this because participants acknowledge this viewer influence on reunion shows or other venues. Viewers can try to influence writers to change fictional characters, too, but the effect is not as immediate or as often countenanced. Unlike fictional characters, RTV participants persist beyond the broadcast, and the real social slights and humiliation they experience when reading viewer comments can deepen the drama and affect future episodes. How they are perceived by viewers is also monitored by producers and may affect who is offered a contract renewal. This can be empowering for viewers who become engaged with the show because they know their remarks can impact the people they watch on-screen. It gives rise to a new form of real, albeit highly mediated, intimacy that at least in some regards constitutes a mutual relationship. A similarly indirect effect can be felt in gamedocs, but in this case the interaction is a cat-and-mouse game between producers and viewers. As Henry Jenkins (2006) and others have noted, viewers of competitions like *Survivor* spend some considerable time interacting online in order to guess the outcome of the series. In order to preserve their primary selling point (the winner's identity), producers react by editing material both on television and online in order to throw viewers off the scent. Though apparently amicable, this interaction is at base antagonistic and constitutes a move to protect profitability, whereas the more affective relation between viewers and participants of docusoaps like *The Real Housewives* is meant to impact them as real-life people beyond their role on television. Of course, this activity also creates or solidifies interest in the media product.

TV participants can go online, too, and, in fact, some are contractually obliged to do so. Typically they produce a regular blog in which they comment on the show they appear in or other shows in the broadcaster's repertoire. Many use this space to present an orthodox interpretation of their TV roles in a form of damage control, apparently sometimes with the help of professional PR agents. This opportunity is especially important if they desire their persona to become a profitable brand. Indeed, some TV participants use their blog to plug their own businesses, or pretend to be ordinary viewers who respond to this blog in order to mount a stealth promotion or defense. The *Real Housewives of New York* cast member Jill Zarin is suspected of doing both. She has been accused of adopting multiple personae to defend herself in online viewer exchanges and apparently has been caught using fake reviews to boost sales of her book on Amazon.com. Needless to say, this deception, or trespassing, attracts a great deal of viewer disgust and ire, not least because it threatens to undermine the authenticity and integrity of the entire program-viewer interaction. More officially sanctioned is another experiment mounted by RTV producers in which participants directly interact with regular viewers. Within Bravo's *Real Housewives* "Talk Bubble," participants watch shows alongside regular viewers and chat with them live by communicating on Twitter, Facebook, or mobile devices. Given that these "virtual viewing parties" (Bravo's description) have won a *marketing* award it looks like others in the industry think Bravo may be on to something.[52]

On the *Real Housewives* website, some viewers characterize their criticism of TV participants as a right and the women's blogs as an expected engagement on their part. This could be considered part of what Tincknell and Raghuram (2002) identify as the audience's feeling of "ownership" when it comes to reality programming (211). Viewers complain if, as sometimes happens, the participants stop blogging (perhaps out of hurt feelings or anger).

They assert that as viewers they are an important part of the economic circuit and point out that the participants' celebrity and income depends on them. When cast members complain about having their feelings hurt, discussions arise about the etiquette and parameters of online viewer discussion. Some viewer posts insist on a civility that would be expected in an offline, face-to-face encounter, while others reject this as anachronistic and inappropriate for the new kind of interaction the Internet allows. These also maintain that expectations about privacy and personal honor have to shift when someone signs on for a reality show. Clearly, as the media continue to converge and texts give rise to texting, the power and entitlements of viewers and participants are still being negotiated. Some new media features alter the television viewing experience. Others return to earlier models of viewership. All are open to commercialization.

CHAPTER 2

Public Relations

Truth? What is truth?
I don't know anyone in this business who talks about "truth."

(PR executive to a colleague)[1]

Sponsored Reality

We have all received at some point a memo from a commercial company, bank, or administrator announcing that a new policy is going to be much better for us, the consumer/employee. Except that as we read the effusive language about how much better it will be, we realize with a sinking heart that probably the opposite is the case. This is the increasingly common experience of being at the receiving end of doublespeak, of deliberately ambiguous communication that spins and obfuscates. It is just a minor example of a huge and largely unexamined area of cultural production that goes by the professional name of public relations (PR). My argument in this chapter is that if we are interested in the media and its impact on society, then we have to look at the huge role public relations plays in mediating our reality. For if, as is often said, ours is an information age then much of this information is PR of one sort or another and there is little in the public realm today that isn't the result of diligent preparation on the part of some agent who wishes to disseminate a paid-for version of reality. Yet despite being drenched in this anonymous and powerful discourse, surprisingly few commentators have noted its extent. Evidence of this extent, I argue, can be seen in popular factual entertainment and, in particular, in reality television's propagation of a PR-based reality.

To the extent that reality TV exploits its status as a pseudo-event and shapes actuality in order to promote commercial interests we have to consider it as part of the now pervasive activity that goes beyond straightforward advertising to consuming reality in the form of commercializing and commodifying everyday life. This process does more than create publicity. It creates reality—or at least our perceptions of reality. We can call this activity publicizing or promotion or marketing, but I will employ the established term that covers all kinds of persuasion, which is public relations. The discussion that follows will expand the examination of commercialization to look at how reality TV embraces and normalizes PR techniques. At a time when the mass media are in a critical transition, reality programming doesn't just advertise: some of its producers are intent on creating good relations with TV's own public and with others who wish to impress this public and will provide financial support to do so. Makeover formats, in particular, perform well as PR vehicles due to the previously discussed transaction of free goods or services for screen exposure. But, more profoundly, these programs' "reality" status offers an attractive environment for performing PR: like public relations, reality TV derives its power—which boils down to the power to attract attention—from its use of the actual and the real. Understanding that the staged actuality of reality shows makes them amenable to PR helps us understand further how they work, why they work, and how they relate to the wider culture.

On the most basic level, some shows build a good image for commercial entities in order to receive their financial support, a transaction that capitalizes on the power of the camera to create market value through media exposure. But PR has philosophical and ethical implications that are more complex than regular advertising and reality TV's deeper affinities with this practice brings to light important features of this programming's ontological status and cultural impact. Like reality TV, and as distinct from advertising, PR tends to destabilize and distort categories such as fact, truth, authenticity, and privacy, sometimes by simply conflating them with their supposed opposite (true/ false, fact/fiction, private/public, etc.). Any fictional work could portray a business or profession in such a way as to enhance its public image. But PR is most effective, because most credible and convincing, when it has a presence in the realm of fact. Hence the embedding of PR material within the news cycle. Hence also the interest in being part of the popular factuality of reality TV. The televised makeover is particularly advantageous because it is both empirically real and a good act. When contractors or retailers participate viewers may well work out that they do so for the publicity they garner for themselves, but unlike print advertorials that must publicly declare themselves an "advertising section," no one on a television makeover is going to point to the commercial transaction underneath, neither the host nor the participants and certainly not the commercial donors who are hoping for good PR—though the latter would no doubt be indignant, if not litigious, if their name or logo did not get mentioned on air. Instead, all is sublimated into narratives of volunteerism and good works, a sentimental currency that is meant to increase the *authenticity* of the virtuous act and distance it from advertising.

Reality TV evidences what I term the PR effect, when so many of our statements and beliefs are the product of commercially sponsored and commercially advantageous discourse, whether we are aware of it or not. If it is successful, we are not. My claim is not that these series are directly produced by PR professionals (though these agents are sometimes involved), but rather that this programming often functions as PR and, more importantly, is emblematic of a larger PR culture that, in both public and private life, produces a hybrid discourse blurring fact and deception. Upcoming chapters will demonstrate how makeover programming fulfills the traditional tasks of public relations in the realms of commerce and politics, given that its formats offer broad ideological support for capitalism, for imperialism, and for specific business sectors (retail, real estate) and professions (builders, designers, cosmetic surgeons). The appearance of representatives from these sectors is not arbitrary, nor is the programs' wholly positive image of their services. Some participants appear to be interested in establishing a new type of profession (personal advice services) and others to improve an already established but poor image (cosmetic surgery). In either case, their using a broadcast program to present one smooth, controlled, and monologic picture is no doubt invaluable. While much PR is as much as possible hidden, the quid pro quo on reality TV is often less subtle. I suggest that many programs offer a kind of hegemonic assurance that it is *only to be expected that there is a commercial motive for the presence of something on our screens and in our lives*. We can assume in real life, too, that work is often being done on behalf of a known or unknown client, though precisely what motives are in play in any particular instance is not necessarily clear. This is the kind of disorientation where PR becomes most powerful and where reality TV can become instructive, because on such programming this PR is often both unacknowledged and unmistakable.

A comprehensive history of public relations is beyond the scope of this book, but it is clear that there have been two main, and ultimately related, thrusts.[2] One has been to boost corporate images, business opportunities, and capitalism. The other has been to manage public perception in the realm of politics, including creating support for war. Reality TV contributes to both. The next chapter will highlight programming that promotes nationalism in a time of war and the chapter after that the promotion of consumer capitalism. But first I will sketch the historical and contemporary significance of public relations as a profession in order to appreciate the contribution made by reality TV, followed by examples of makeover TV's promotion of specific trades and professions.

The first fact that should give anyone pause is that in the United States there are now more people working in public relations than in journalism and more and more media content is being generated by PR firms. Estimates from within and outside the industry suggest that from 50 percent to 90 percent of news stories in newspapers or on television originate entirely or in part from a PR agency (Baran 2008, 346). So if journalists shape and filter the news (a common topic of media analysis), there is another level of news management that happens before they get to it (not as often discussed).[3] Many nonprofit organizations invest in PR, but that is not where most of the dollars and therefore jobs are: conservative estimates are that about 70 percent of PR practitioners currently work in the private sector (Cutlip, Center, and Broom 2006, 31). One growing sector is PR activity in government and the military, as is seen in the tens of thousands of registered lobbyists on Capitol Hill and thousands more in the Pentagon (Herman and Chomsky 1988). Not to mention the politicians' use of countless Public Information Officers (PIOs) at all levels of government.[4] In its simplest terms, PR is performed for a client who pays someone to create or maintain good "relations" between this client and another constituency. This means making the former look good, crafting a positive image, performing damage control, conveying a favorable self-image, and so on. Whereas an advertiser generally pitches a product during corralled "commercial breaks" or advertising "sections," the PR agent aims to embed material within the program or news story without viewers or readers realizing where that information originated: as they say in the industry, the best PR is invisible PR. In other words, the task is successful when something doesn't just appear *in* factual media content but appears *as* factual media content. A classic textbook uses the following definition: "Public Relations is the management function that establishes and maintains mutually beneficial relationships between an organization and the publics on whom its success or failure depends" (Cutlip, Center, and Broom 2006, 1). Whether these relations are, in fact, "mutually beneficial" is up for debate, but this is the kind of positive interpretation (PR?) that appears in contemporary manuals. In common practice, PR generally entails some spin, some selecting of the most advantageous pieces of information and omission of the less flattering.

A PR campaign may include the use of advertising as well as other activities such as marketing, fund raising, or lobbying. Whereas advertising is a controlled method of placing messages in which you pay up front or "above the line" for guaranteed media time, PR is usually broader and less direct. Instead of persuading an audience to buy a specific product or service, PR often aims to enhance the image of a whole company, industry, or political agenda. Its consultants frequently draw on a media or journalistic background in order to accommodate the needs and parameters of media production and thereby increase the chances of their agenda being incorporated into its content. A good PR executive will transform events into narratives that are both media-worthy and media-ready and will find ways to match what works for the client with the goals of the media producer and the target audience. This leads to what is perhaps the most important insight into public relations, which is that one of its tasks is to *sell private interests as a public good*: "private" meaning privately owned and commercially motivated. Understanding this relationship between private and public, and between expediency and altruism, will become important when we look at the ways in which reality TV doesn't just advertise but tries to enhance its public relations.

The fact that the oblique and powerful production of PR has been little recognized outside the industry is perhaps a testament to its success. There are surprisingly few overviews of PR's role in institutional politics, in business, or in popular culture. Most titles on the subject offer practical advice on how to succeed at it rather than critical analysis of its cultural impact.[5] Among the handful of critical scholars who have focused on PR in the United States are Andrew Wernick (1991), Stuart Ewen (1996), Roland Marchand (1998), and Daniel Boorstin ([1961] 1992).[6] A few scholars have taken a look at PR in the British political scene, for example, Aeron Davis (2002), and David Miller and William Dinan (2008).[7] The significance of PR as a form of propaganda is a thread within the writings of public intellectuals like Noam Chomsky (Herman and Chomsky 1988; Chomsky 2002) and Jurgen Habermas ([1962] 1991), but there is no detailed investigation of specific political or cultural consequences.[8] Critical accounts of political communication either by political scientists or media sociologists sometimes include discussions of PR as one theme among many (Franklin 1994; Negrine 1996; Lilleker 2006; McNair 2011). When scholars do consider PR's relationship with the media, the focus is overwhelmingly on news production or specific political campaigns; otherwise, awareness of the PR industry is scattered widely among journalistic accounts and practitioner anecdotes, most either boosting the profession or worrying over some immediate political repercussions.

Recent television has occasionally glanced at the PR industry, again from a largely uncritical stance; for example, American TV produced Lizzie Grubman's *PoweR Girls* (MTV, 2005) and more recently *Kell On Earth* (Bravo, 2010) and *The Spin Crowd* (E! 2010). The above mentioned Lizzie Grubman is perhaps the most famous, or infamous, American PR agent/celebrity publicist. In 2001, showing her disdain for the public she seeks to manipulate, Grubman ploughed through a crowd of people outside a nightclub in her Mercedes SUV, injuring 26 while allegedly shouting "Fuck you, white trash." She reappeared on reality TV when one of the *Real Housewives* daughters (Ashley) went to work for her as an unpaid intern, but there is no hint of this notorious event. Focusing on the clash of egos in boutique firms, PR docusoaps do not give any impression of the huge and largely invisible presence of PR beyond those creating publicity for minor concerns. Since being on television automatically creates the publicity these firms are trying to generate, these reality series *are* PR rather than analyze PR. More satiric analyses of the industry have occasionally emerged in fictional content, as in the British comedy series *Absolute Power* (BBC Radio 4, 2000–04; BBC Two, 2003–05), the US version of *Free Agents* (NBC, 2011), and in a small number of films, most memorably *Wag the Dog* (1997). But, for the most part, popular culture gives little evidence of the major impact of PR on contemporary society.

Advertising has been around for as long as commerce has existed, but public relations became a profession only in the twentieth century. PR agencies exist today in most developed nations, but it is a particularly American phenomenon, with more firms and employees practicing PR in the United States than anywhere else, though there is intense activity in the United Kingdom also. One could argue that, as a nation, the United States owes its success to public relations since one of the earliest forms of PR was the marketing of America to a European audience. In the seventeenth and eighteenth centuries, there were explicit ads for land and economic opportunity, but traveler's accounts and pamphlets were also used more indirectly to entice Europeans to venture over the Atlantic (Sivulka 1998, 7–9; Cutlip, Center, and Broom 2006, 88; Baran 2008, 345). Despite actual hardship, many representations painted a picture of a utopian society of free land, free sex, or free political or religious expression, depending on the target audience (Lefler 1967).Once settled, the need for more concerted PR grew with the rise of mass industrialism and pronounced socioeconomic hierarchies. According to Edward Bernays (the skillful self-promoter who claimed to be the grandfather of modern public relations), by the early twentieth century PR had become so crucial a power as to constitute an "invisible government." He maintained (with some pride in his own profession) that "We are governed, our minds molded, our tastes formed, our ideas suggested, largely by men we have never heard of," these being executives working in public relations ([1928] 2005, 37). In the early twentieth century, some PR techniques were used to fight the rise of organized labor and do damage control for the reputations of the robber barons (e.g., Ivy Lee's work for John D. Rockefeller), but public relations really grew as a profession during more concerted efforts to fend off the threats of socialism and consumer activism that spooked Big Business in the 1930s. What spurred American business to look in earnest for professional media advice—or "propaganda" as Bernays still termed it—was the need to convince the population after the Wall Street Crash that capitalism had not failed, that capitalism still provided everyone with their best shot at success and that it was inherently part of a democratic system. And in recent years, PR has been key in the push toward late-capitalist neoliberalism and privatization (Miller and Dinan 2008), which, as indicated earlier, are an identifiable ethos in makeover programming.

Sponsored Discourse

The exponential growth of professional public relations in recent decades can be attributed to a number of commercial factors.[9] The push to increase privatization and reduce government oversight has meant more opportunities for private bodies to step in and offer assistance when public services are lacking; in other words, privatization is why PR opportunities occur and privatization is often what is being promoted. Then there is the more commonly observed pressure on the Fourth Estate to transform news-making into a profitable enterprise, which has meant a reduction in the number of journalists, in investigative reports, in foreign bureaus, and in "hard news" segments. At the same time, in a 24/7 news environment the demand for content is huge. Hence journalists have become increasingly dependent on the "information subsidies" of press releases and video news releases (VNRs) generated by PR agents. Hence more graduates of journalism schools can find employment as PR specialists than as journalists and many experienced journalists end up "crossing the street" to join PR firms.

It is one thing to declare, as a postmodern relativist might, that there is no authentic grand narrative and no absolutes or objectivity. It is another to persuade people by knowingly employing half truths and masking one's true intentions. This is the difference between philosophical skepticism and the manipulation of facts, between recognizing epistemological limits to arriving at truth and intentionally hiding or distorting what is known. PR, because it does strategically manage facts, makes a huge contribution to what Daniel Boorstin identified as a "new Gresham's law of American public life," whereby "counterfeit happenings tend to drive spontaneous happenings out of circulation" ([1961]1992, 40). The PR consultant's goal is to create a particular version of reality that exists within a liminal zone of the dissimulated, the specious, and the spun. In the opinion of the sociologist Robert Jackall, in the public relations firm "creating the impression of truth displaces the search for truth" (Jackall 1995, 365). By spinning endless interpretations, its practitioners create "the ambiguity that allows the momentum of exigency to triumph" (Jackall and Hirota 2000, 112). This is the zone of viral marketing and brand pushing,[10] of astroturfing and greenwashing, of advertorials and complementary copy, of airbrushing, digital alteration, and numerous other forms of advertising disguised as something else. This is also the realm of reality TV, another paid-for version of reality.

Pseudo-event

The question of how authentic or accurate is reality TV's representation of real life (however defined) is at once too complex and too naive to satisfactorily answer here.[11] As indicated earlier, a more useful approach would be to recognize that reality series are closer to a pseudo-event than to fly-on-the-wall documentary; though, as the grand old man of British documentary himself pointed out, even documentary involves "the creative treatment of actuality" (John Grierson, circa 1926).[12] A pseudo-event is something that is actual *but is designed in order to be mediated,* designed typically by those working in PR who seek some favorable news coverage for a client. Daniel Boorstin defines the pseudo-event as a happening that is not spontaneous but planned and planted "primarily for the immediate purpose of being reported or reproduced" ([1961] 1992, 11). Its success is therefore measured by how widely it is reported in the media. Reality series have all the main features of pseudo-events as defined by Boorstin: they are paid for, planned, dramatic, easily understood, conveniently distributed, and advertised in advance (Boorstin [1961] 1992, 39–40). As a pseudo-event, reality TV offers referential realism. It is an experience, a happening, a 3-dimensional phenomenon whose reason for being is, always, its mediation.

With some formats, the process of creating the pseudo-event also creates opportunities for immediate and real-time PR. Local journalists report from every *Home Edition* site because these places not only have a real impact on their local community but also possess the aura of a national television production site. In other words, they attract journalistic attention both because they are real (part of everyday physical reality) and because they are to be mediated. And producers need to publicize the event so they can attract volunteers and local advertising. Hence professional PR firms are hired to manage local media coverage and ensure good publicity for local companies involved in the build even before the show goes to air.[13] While the event is always already mediated, it is also already an economic reality before its full profitability is achieved.

Reality TV's usefulness in this regard is validated by one popular business account. In their description of today's "experience economy," management consultants Joseph Pine and James Gilmore (1999) describe a "progression of economic value," all stages of which still coexist but each of which unfolds from the previous development. Their contention is that if you customize goods this turns them into a service and if you customize services this turns them into an experience. Reality TV is a prime example of this stage of capitalism in that it customizes and stages experiences for individual consumers, an experience that is then packaged and sold to millions of viewers, so that packages of these viewers' experiences may be sold to advertisers at a certain rate per thousand (CPM—cost per thousand).[14] However, Pine and Gilmore go on to suggest that nowadays businesses need to offer not just experiences but also personal "transformations" (46), something that will "guide customers to change some dimension of self" (47). Clearly makeover TV fulfills this economic stage. But the parallels between reality TV and the commercial world go further for, in a follow-up book to *The Experience Economy* (1999), Pine and Gilmore identify a consumer desire for the real and the authentic as the next business trend. *Authenticity: What Consumers Really Want* (2007) identifies also the difficulty of meeting this desire through commercial means because, the authors assert, commercialization inevitably destroys authenticity. They cite communications scholar Corey Anton who notes that authenticity cannot be bought because money "works as a system of exchange and substitution. And substitution . . . is counter to particularity and originality, hallmark characteristics of authenticity" (88). So their best advice for businesses is to "render" authenticity, a term that is never fully explained but which seems to entail businesses being *perceived as* authentic (phenomenologically) even if everything they offer is fake (ontologically) given that it is a commercially motivated social construction. Somewhat paradoxically, the aim is therefore to create the *appearance* of authenticity. The authors mention in passing that reality TV succeeds in doing just this and so might be a model for businesses to follow (2007, 89).

It is not often that TV entertainment is presented as a model for business practices, but perhaps this is not a bad way to view what reality TV is doing: attempting to "render" the real and the authentic, even while its claims to authenticity are being undermined by its commercialization. Or are they? One could argue that by including commercial design reality TV is an authentic, as in accurate, representation of real life, since being commercially sponsored is, today, as real as it gets. The programming is in this sense authentic *because* commercialized, not despite it. Another intriguing possibility opens up when the commercial impact becomes painfully obvious, when there are awkward close-ups of placed products or forced and dutiful mentions of program sponsors. This may have an effect similar to that of Disneyland as Baudrillard famously saw it (1983, 25), which is to say that it could make the rest of our life seem less commercially inflected and in that sense more authentic: a perception that would be quite useful for those who are busy trying to commercialize our experience and fear we will stop tolerating their efforts. Hence, to the extent that reality TV illustrates commercial pressures, it is an accurate reflection of our everyday lives. To the extent that this effect is more obvious and clumsy than we normally experience it, reality TV may constitute a distraction that, instead of defamiliarizing what is really going on in our lives, offers a comparison that renders everyday commercialization less noticeable.

Face Lift

When it comes to examining reality TV's promotion of specific trades and professions a good example is cosmetic surgery, a field that often suffers from bad PR. This is an appropriate place to begin since, as PR pioneer Ivy Lee quipped, all of PR can be seen as a metaphoric cosmetic surgery (Ewen 1996, 76). Indeed, Baudrillard later took this metaphor further in the essay entitled "Operational Whitewash" ([1990]1993), where he identifies the desire to make over everything into something ideal as a widespread social compulsion. He observes that "We are under the sway of a surgical compulsion that seeks to excise negative characteristics and remodel things synthetically into ideal forms" (45), these things being history, nature, events, public opinion. "To this end a gigantic campaign of plastic surgery has been undertaken" (45). Baudrillard was probably inspired by Boorstin, who earlier remarked that when corporations want to change their image (rather than policy), this "face-lifting operation can usually be done for hire, by the new professions of plastic surgeons and cosmetic experts," that is, PR agents ([1961] 1992, 189). On several makeover TV formats, the metaphor is translated into a literal surgery that is regarded as a rational and empowering act by both presenters and patients; for example, on *Extreme Makeover* (ABC, 2002–07), *The Swan* (Fox, 2004–05), *10 Years Younger* (Channel 4, 2004; TLC, 2004–),[15] and *Bridalplasty* (E! Channel, 2010).[16] Whether or not any individual viewer is impressed, producers frame these makeovers as a positive experience and present surgery and surgeons in a positive light.

It may be that the demonstrations provided by makeover programming are one of the most striking examples of television making a real socioeconomic as well as a physical impact on popular culture. At least this is what both patients and doctors claim. Currently, cosmetic surgery is one of the fastest growing areas of medicine in the United States. From 1997 to 2007 there was a 457 percent increase in the total number of cosmetic procedures. In 2009, in the midst of a recession, there were over 10 million cosmetic procedures and almost 10.5 billion dollars spent in the United States.[17] The exact extent to which makeover programming has contributed to this boom is hard to determine, but just as *Queer Eye* is reported to have helped expand the market for "male products" and a metrosexual attention to appearance (Cava 2004; Florian 2004), it seems other reality shows have helped sell plastic surgery to a wide audience. Surgeons featured on these programs have seen a tremendous increase in their business and patients report seeking procedures after viewing reality TV makeovers. One of the most widely circulated studies was published in *Plastic and Reconstructive Surgery* (the official journal of the American Society of Plastic Surgeons) in 2007. It found that four out of five first-time patients said reality TV shows had influenced them to pursue cosmetic surgery, with nearly one-third feeling "very much" or "moderately" influenced. The influence was particularly strongly felt among "high intensity" viewers, meaning those who regularly watched reality surgery series. These shows were found to influence both their expectations and choices of potential cosmetic surgery (Crockett, Pruzinsky, and Persing, 323). However, although these statistics were widely broadcast, it is worth noting that the sample size was a very modest 42 people.[18] Larger numbers have been sampled by other scholars working in psychology and media effects. Their studies, too, find correlations between viewing makeover television and having a positive attitude toward cosmetic surgery (Delinsky 2005; Nabi 2009; Sperry et al. 2009). Charlotte Markey and Patrick Markey (2010) surveyed 189 college students and found that after watching one episode of *Extreme Makeover* respondents were more likely to indicate a desire to have cosmetic surgery than those who did not watch the show. Other surveys show more people today report that they approve of undergoing cosmetic procedures even if they aren't planning on going under the knife themselves.[19] Perhaps as Meredith Jones (2008a) suggests, TV makeovers work as a kind of "cultural anesthetic" that makes the step to real-life surgery a little bit easier (520). Certainly more and more people are putting their resources into cosmetic surgery not only in North America but also in other parts of the world. While there isn't firm data about global activity, in South America, in Europe, and in parts of Asia both domestic patients and "tourist" patients appear to be on the increase.

From its inception, cosmetic surgery has developed alongside and has been bolstered by mass media, but rarely has the relation between material design and image generation been more conspicuous than on TV makeovers. While one of the most revered titles in many societies is doctor of medicine, cosmetic surgery is one of the most thoroughly commercialized and, perhaps as a corollary, one of the least reputable areas of medical practice. What distinguishes cosmetic surgery from other medical services is that it is often performed on perfectly healthy bodies yet may entail considerable risk. Highlighting its perversity, Meredith Jones notes that cosmetic surgery "involves the killing of a living human part (skin, muscle), and the replacement of the live with the dead (an implant)" (2008b). Cosmetic surgery is generally "private," meaning insurance companies don't cover costs because they do not consider it justified on medical grounds. The work is also without the respectability granted by referring physicians. Hence, cosmetic surgeons have had to advertise to attract clients from whom they have to extract payment: indeed it is the one area of medicine where doctors use the term "clients." TV makeovers take the whole process out of the market by presenting another narrative we have seen before, that of donation. Here the clients are charitable cases whose motives for undergoing surgery involve deeply rooted (though largely unexplored) psychological needs and whose doctors are not conducting business but are performing a virtuous act. This feel-good programming bolsters their professional standing, a commodity that cosmetic surgeons can ill afford to ignore. In order to appreciate why surgeons are anxious to promote their profession, we need to look back at the early formation of this specialty and some of its practitioners' previous attempts to acquire a better reputation.[20]

Although there are precedents in ancient civilizations, the practice of cosmetic surgery is largely a Western and twentieth-century phenomenon. Most accounts mention that some primitive forms of cosmetic surgery were performed in India as early as 600 B.C. (Haiken 1997, 4), but since early operations had to be performed without anesthetics or antiseptic conditions they were sufficiently dangerous to be rarely attempted. Modern cosmetic surgery began under the larger umbrella of "plastic surgery," which was at first mostly what we would today refer to as reconstructive work.[21] This practice took off during the horrible injuries inflicted by trench warfare in World War I. Prior to this were some attempts to improve the appearance of those who were simply visually unattractive, but aesthetic work remained a minor field. Whereas reconstructive and more medically sanctioned surgery is not generally advertised, practitioners of aesthetic or cosmetic surgery have for a long time tried to attract media attention. Early on, they produced books, interviews, and even entertainment events. Some lectured in department stores or performed surgeries before crowds. For example, in 1931, J.Howard Crum performed a face lift (using a local anesthetic) on a woman in a hotel ballroom. A similar event featured accompanying piano music (Sullivan 2001, 52). Medical colleagues shunned such obvious showmanship and its practitioners were frequently exposed in the media as quacks and charlatans who were taking advantage of a lack of regulation. Still, many people did seem intrigued by the possibility of radically improving their appearance on other than medical grounds. While men (soldiers) were the majority of early subjects, the attention later switched to women's bodies.

It was the emergence of visual mass media that played a crucial role in consolidating the public's interest, not isolated publicity stunts like Crum's. In the 1920s, millions went regularly to see their Hollywood idols and large numbers of people began to emulate these movie stars and to scrutinize their own appearance with portable devices such as compact mirrors (Brumberg 1998, 70). What worked on camera became influential on and off screen, so that photogenicity began to alter aesthetics (Lakoff and Scherr 1984, 74; Blum 2003, 210–11). Beauty was becoming defined as media worthiness and for those who felt they measured up, the Miss America pageant was established in 1922 to offer amateurs a chance to establish national fame and fortune. These trends suggest that at the beginning of the twentieth century both the degree of public scrutiny and the prevalence of media imagery were intensifying. But while some clients looked to surgery to match screen ideals, it was years before cosmetic surgery was accepted as a legitimate medical practice. Those in reconstructive plastic surgery who performed cosmetic procedures often did so in secrecy or as a low-key but lucrative sideline. Gradually, however, cosmetic surgery gained a better reputation and in 1950 the American Society of Plastic and Reconstructive Surgeons hired a full-time director of public relations (Haiken 1997, 137). In the 1970s, the stigma surrounding cosmetic surgery eroded to the point where it became a field in which students could train, as a subset of plastic surgery. Henceforth, the practice really took off, both in terms of patients and professional standing. New procedures such as breast augmentation and liposuction became popular in the 1970s and 1980s and these led to a noticeable growth in patient numbers.

For some time, medicine had established its high status by its very separation from advertising, this after an earlier period of patent medicine advertising whose wildly false claims threatened to jeopardize not only the medical profession but even advertising. Perhaps concerned that direct advertising would reduce their profession to a trade, professional societies initially banned the advertising of medical services. But in the mid 1970s the Federal Trade Commission forced the American Medical Association to lift this ban and cosmetic surgeons were among the first to embrace this way of attracting business, a move that, while it may not have helped their image among their colleagues, was vital to a specialty that still largely depended on attracting private clients. Later on, cosmetic surgeons again led the way in marketing through websites and other media before other medical colleagues followed suit.

While they are not shy about direct advertising, cosmetic surgeons have also recognized the merits of more indirect PR. Since the 1980s, professional organizations such as the American Society for Plastic and Reconstructive Surgery (ASPRS) and the American Society for Plastic Surgery (ASPS) have spent considerable time and money issuing information brochures and conducting "public education" programs, this in addition to marketing campaigns undertaken by individual cosmetic surgeons. The need for PR work became particularly urgent with the breast implant crisis in the early 1990s when, in light of some evidence that silicone breast implants were dangerous, the Food and Drug Administration imposed a moratorium on all such procedures. As a result, cosmetic surgeons mounted an aggressive but not terribly successful PR campaign to counter this bad press. TV makeovers emerged in the wake of this crisis and have taken their place within a fairly extensive PR push in the last few decades to place favorable accounts of cosmetic surgery in the media. More specifically, reality TV's charitable makeovers can be seen as part of the PR campaigns that since the mid 1990s have stressed voluntary work undertaken by plastic surgeons, usually helping Third World patients with cleft palates and other disfigurements. Recognizing the influence that the media have in recruiting patients, publicity agents have been steadily supplying the media with stats, kits, and VNRs (Sullivan 2001, 90ff) and Meredith Jones notes how, today, surgeons' websites often publicize their charitable work and pro-rata surgeries for the underprivileged (2008b). Perhaps, therefore, it was only a matter of time before there emerged full television programs to extend these efforts.

Compared with the widespread marketing of beauty products, ads for cosmetic surgeons have appeared only in limited niche markets, in specific magazines, yellow pages, occasional local television ads, or billboards in certain urban locations: none of these particularly wide-reaching or sophisticated techniques. Giving center stage to actual procedures on popular national television therefore has tremendous commercial value. That cosmetic surgeons would use television to showcase their services also makes perfect sense since the visual medium provides a demonstration of the results they are selling. And while earlier attempts to drum up business by creating entertaining spectacles only added to the image of charlatanism, a television series such as *Extreme Makeover* appears to be above reproach. Instead of disreputable showmanship, we witness sober and charitable operations conducted by fully credentialed experts who are again attaching themselves to an entertainment format but with quite different results from hotel room facelifts. By making surgical procedures public, these programs accomplish a couple of things. They shine the light of publicity not in a "gotcha" narrative to shame a celebrity who was hoping to keep her nose job a secret but to suggest that more viewers should consider cosmetic work themselves. Each episode reinforces the notion that cosmetic services are not indulgent or vain but life-enhancing and often profoundly necessary. Clients show off their new bodies to great applause, and they are presented not as spoiled and narcissistic but as likeable and unassuming. TV makeovers gesture toward cosmetic work being more of a right than a privilege, something that should be entered into by all, with their (soon to be enhanced) heads held high. TV surgeons are introduced as kindly avuncular figures who have agreed to take part in an egalitarian effort to serve low-income clients. Their being thanked not with cash but with hugs and smiles helps to modify stereotypes of profit-oriented doctors pandering to self-indulgent clients. Only on some series are costs ever mentioned: for example, the UK version of *Extreme Makeover, Brand New You* (Channel 5, 2004–05), and the more documentary style *Plastic Surgery: Before and After* (Discovery Health Channel, 2002–07). There is no reference to the fact that the patients are not being charged in this instance because they are cooperating in making a profitable television show. Nor is there any hint that these professionals are interested in drumming up business.

Ordinarily, stories about cosmetic surgery enter the media only when there is some brand new procedure or when a celebrity is unable to hide botched results. Occasionally there are serious reports about the risks attached to undergoing multiple procedures or becoming addicted to surgery. There are also occasional programs of the Plastic-Surgery-Gone-Bad variety, usually focusing on celebrities.[22] On TV makeovers, however, there are no addictions, mistakes, or disappointments. Some of the pain of recovery does appear on screen, but viewers are assured by patients that any discomfort is well worth it. In US productions, warnings about the potential risks of surgery, which are presumably issued to every patient prior to their operation, tend to appear in the final cut only if some minor infection or setback later occurs, but this is rare. *Extreme Makeover UK* does display a warning at the end of each episode to "always consult your doctor," which could be interpreted not only as a legal disclaimer but also as an advertisement. In any case, every ending is happy and every reveal demonstrates the surgeon's skill. The term "reveal" goes back to Allen Funt's *Candid Camera* (1948–2004) but it has quickly gained currency as a trademarked segment of reality makeover shows, especially of the surgical variety. To reveal means both to uncover and to display; on surgical makeovers, the new body is uncovered (which could be done privately) and simultaneously displayed to a dual audience of family and television viewers. This generates maximum suspense and a heightened emotional climax, all of which impresses upon us the wonders wrought by the surgeons involved. Clients are always pleased with the predictably good results—and in this field pleasing the client, not curing an illness, is how success is measured.

We often hear that cosmetic surgery is an artistic endeavor, but much of the authority and hard-won credibility of the field comes from its scientific status. TV makeovers offer solid PR for the white-coated medical class by reinforcing the power and authority that comes with their status as scientists. Their labor supports the centuries-old scientific proposition that one can and should alter natural processes for the greater glory of humankind (or mankind). In the case of cosmetic surgery, there is also something powerful about manufacturing and guaranteeing, through a premeditated act, a quality as elusive as beauty. Hence, *The Swan* ironically counters Hans Christian Andersen's original tale of the "Ugly Duckling," which admonished that nature will take its course and does not need our intervention. What makeover programs demonstrate is that nature lets us down and that human devices such as money and technology can and should correct it. The doctors' highly technological environment mirrors the act of mediation that is taking place around them, for visual devices have become an important part of medicine (MRIs, laparoscopes, cameras). There are, however, some interesting omissions. For example, we know that cosmetic surgeons can project simulations of their postsurgical patients on a computer screen before operating and that many do so as a form of marketing. Yet television makeovers do not broadcast this image, perhaps because not doing so creates more suspense and avoids disappointment if the surgeon fails to match the projection.

On TV makeovers, the provider's formal education and credentials are emphasized, thus reinforcing their professionalism. Although some claims seem a bit far-fetched, as in the description of a cosmetic dentist in London as a specialist in "implantology and smile design" (*Extreme Makeover UK*, aired 7/21/08). Cosmetic dentistry is another elective field not usually paid for by insurance companies and so inclined to advertise. A regular on the *Extreme Makeover* series, Dr. Bill Dorfman is a particularly enterprising individual who believes dentists need better PR because of past representations. He notes:

> Before *Extreme Makeover*, dentists got a pretty bad rap in the media and were not represented very well in pop culture. Remember the Nazi dentist in the film *Marathon Man* or Steve Martin's sadistic turn as a dentist in *Little Shop of Horrors*? This is what we were up against! *Extreme Makeover* made dentistry the hero week after week on prime time television.
>
> (2006, xv)

Dorfman owns a company that manufactures dental products promoted on the show. He also works on the professional smiles of Hollywood's celebrity class and has found time to compose a bestselling book whose proceeds, we are told, are going to charity but which also promotes cosmetic dentistry in general and his own business in particular. As the title suggests, Dorfman's *Billion Dollar Smile* (2006) links the aesthetic directly to the financial and to the television show that made the author into a celebrity brand.[23] Other surgeons run clips of their television appearances on their professional websites, as though being televised confirms worth and prestige. Some reality TV surgeons leverage their media exposure into the sale of other branded products (DVDs, books) or they resurface on other TV formats to promote spin-off brands: for instance, Garth Fisher, a surgeon who frequently appeared on *Extreme Makeover*, has sold skin care products on shopping channel QVC (2010). Cosmetic surgery therefore owes much to the media for creating demand and for enabling the satisfaction of that demand (on screen and in real clinics advertised online) in order to amplify the demand further.

Damage Control: Builders

Another sector that could often do with better public relations is the construction business. In Gallup's annual "Honesty and Ethics" poll, building contractors generally rate as middle to low, as do the associated professions of realtors and insurance brokers.[24] In addition, whether or not it is valid, there is a linkage in many Americans' minds between the construction industry and organized crime. Some Mafia bosses have been tried and imprisoned for illegal practices in construction, though the full extent of this involvement would be difficult to determine.[25] Nevertheless, there is a common perception that the American Mafia have some real hold on large construction companies (at least in the cement end of the business) and though this may not affect small-scale home building much it is still clearly a public relations liability for the whole trade.[26] Smaller businesses also have their own image problems. Stories of home builders failing to do a good or timely job are a big part of suburban lore: in fact, so frequently do people get stressed or even divorced over these matters that at least one US psychologist has begun to specialize in "Renovation Psychology."[27] Much of this sector is unregulated and unlicensed and hence open to those who may not be particularly skilled or competent: what in Britain are popularly referred to as "cowboy builders." British TV, which has a strong tradition of programming aimed at protecting consumers from fraud, has offered several reality shows that provide cautionary tales of what can go wrong, such as *Tradesmen from Hell* (LifeStyle Channel, 2004) and *Rogue Traders* (BBC1, 2001–). *Construction Intervention* (Discovery, 2010–), *Cowboy Builders* (Channel 5, 2009), *Cowboy Trap* (BBC1, 2009–), and some episodes of *Home Edition* also offer a chance to repair this image. For example, on one *Home Edition* episode the Ali family is helped after suffering at the hands of a previous contractor who walked off after taking their money, leaving their house roofless and uninhabitable (aired 10/31/04). Now the "good" contractors come in to rescue these victims and undo the damage of property and of business reputation. Sal Ferro, the *Home Edition* contractor, makes this explicit:

> The biggest outrage for me is that someone in my business took advantage of this hard-working family, stole their money, and left them homeless. When *Extreme Makeover* asked us to step in and undo the damage this contractor did, we threw ourselves into the job, body and soul.[28]

The "damage" here is clearly both to physical structures and to business reputation. Another series that is built around the concept of good contractor versus bad contractor is the Canadian *Holmes on Homes* (HGTV Canada, 2001–08; also shown on the US HGTV), where a trusted and skilled builder goes in to repair the damage caused by either less skilled or less scrupulous others.

Home Edition does damage control by stressing, more than professional skills, the contractors' ethics. As the seasons have progressed, there has been an increased showcasing of contractors who are now ritualistically invited to speak at climactic moments in the narrative. Their tears, hugs, and heartfelt wishes indicate that these firms are comprised of good and caring people. This is not the sexy, exciting, but ultimately selfish capitalism of, say, *The Apprentice*. Here the hero is a small business whose members mediate between faceless conglomerates and individual people. Featured contractors underline that they, too, are families who are building not just an edifice but also relationships. In an era of accelerating conglomeration, it is significant that many home construction firms are family operated and have historically been a way for immigrants and for the relatively poor and uneducated to quickly establish themselves. Appearing on television can be used by a local firm not so much to expand business nationally—few are equipped to do so—but to boost their profile in their own district and amplify their one-episode appearance in subsequent local advertising. *Home Edition* contractors are encouraged to extend the promotion both of the television show and of their own businesses by writing an account of their participation in the home build on a "Community blog" at the show's official website. So they at the same time personalize and commercialize their participation. As for motives, does a building contractor show up on site to help people or to help his business? The television show frames the motive as the former, but the real motive could be the latter, or both: even those involved in the transaction may not be able to distinguish their own motives. However, and this is the larger point, as far as the recipients are concerned—and presumably, by extension, the viewing audience—it isn't worth asking and it doesn't much matter. This is when PR is most potent, when we can't be sure of the commercial or private agenda and we don't care to ask, whether this be in business or politics.

Home makeovers present something that is not often seen on television screens, which is a positive image of manual labor. On many home and garden shows there is little input from ordinary workers who grunt their way under the direction of designers and managers. In American programming, these are typically silent Latinos or other minorities who can be glimpsed performing manual tasks while (usually white) experts discourse in the foreground. On *Queer Eye*, home transformations occur in the background, as though by magic. But on charitable makeovers like *Home Edition*, *School Pride* (NBC, 2010) or *Construction Intervention* labor is foregrounded and even romanticized. Workers (mostly white) are noble volunteers, not paid help. Their skills are lauded and their physical input greatly appreciated as they perform their labor of love. Contestants on competition shows like *Project Runway* or *Top Chef* also work hard at creative tasks, but all their effort is to further their own careers. On *Home Edition* there is a strong fantasy that the market is not just about competition and that business is not just about profit: or at least we can enjoy the feeling of a temporary truce. The only competition is about who can be the most generous donor of time and physical exertion.[29] Many can identify with the idea that we have to work to deadline, that we never have quite enough time, that our efforts will be monitored and judged, but on home makeovers regimentation and surveillance are made enjoyable. *Home Edition*'s Ty Pennington is the caricature of a boss going around yelling at workers through a loudspeaker, but it is all framed as good fun. Lead designers find time to perform comic antics, compose songs, or go on trips even in the midst of a work crisis; one local news report suggests they have time to visit a tanning salon (Mark McGuire and Jennifer Gish, *Albany Times Union*, March 25, 2007). Suffice it to say that this general ethos of labor as entertainment (for laborer and viewer) picks up a significant socioeconomic trend in 24/7, mobile cultures where there is an erosion of the industrial distinction between work and leisure/ non-work.

At the same time, in a post-manufacturing, information economy there is something reassuringly material about home makeover shows. Since we still think of the material as the real (*res*), the bricks and mortar of a home makeover compensate for our dizzying transition into all kinds of nonmaterial and virtual non-places. The shows tap into a nostalgia for a level of craft and customization that in industrialized countries is increasingly a matter of privilege. But it goes further than affordability. As advanced economies switch from largely manufacturing to largely information operations, there has been an evaporation of the material into symbolic form. Instead of producing tangible stuff, information and financial services produce numbers and symbols. These can turn out to be too removed from real conditions, with serious real-world and material consequences (as in the US home mortgage crisis). Hence the relief of observing honest people toiling within the material realm—though of course for television viewers this putting form on matter is also vicarious and mediated.

The physicality of the site offers distinct commercial advantages. Once built, the house becomes a "model home" for showcasing goods and services. Cameras enter at the pristine point of first occupancy when there is no ugly mess due to anyone actually living in the space. Décor, not evidence of daily life, dominates the scene, just as in magazine photos of rooms that are perfectly arranged to look as though they represent a lived-in space but are attractive precisely because they do not. One delighted recipient in the poor Watts neighborhood of Los Angeles declared after viewing her *Home Edition* makeover: "now I got what everybody in the magazines and TV have" (aired 3/28/04). Another subject sums up her impression of her new bathroom as: "It was like a magazine" (aired 8/10/08). In a more explicit formula, TV Guide Channel produced the series *Ready, Set, Change!* (2005–06) that made over viewers' rooms to resemble the sets of specific television shows, a more literal attempt to make something media-worthy.

On *Home Edition,* the houses also showcase the TV show. A big feature of every episode is the presence of multiple television monitors reflexively displaying the logo of the show. This is a branding of an event that at the same time provides a model for the everyday integration of the television medium into the family home. When televisions were first introduced, TV programs showed people proudly watching their sets, but when the novelty wore off watching TV was largely given a lower-class status (e.g., *Rosanne,* ABC [1988–97]; *The Simpsons,* Fox [1989–]; *Married with Children,* Fox [1987–97]). For years, high-end fashion dictated that television sets should be hidden away in armoires or entertainment centers. However, with flat screens, TVs have once again become desirable aesthetic objects (sometimes framed like a work of art) that can now be displayed on TV itself, as in the flat screens of *Home Edition.* But beyond the device, the final promotion we witness on makeovers is of television as a profit-making enterprise that does social good.[30] Since the Reagan era, many American broadcasters have attempted to translate "public interest" into market forces: that is, they have defined public interest not as what might be in the best interests *of* citizens but as what viewers are interested *in,* as demonstrated by ratings. To those who support a broader view of the public interest—as is still the case in European public broadcasting though it is under considerable stress—this implosion into the mere calibration of ratings appears to be a cynical attempt to increase corporate power by reducing civic obligations. Hence the significance of makeover series that popularize the notion that television can make a profit while at the same time perform easily demonstrated units of social good—but not because it is obliged to do so. What happens when television shows attempt to build good PR on a much larger scale is the subject of the next chapter.

CHAPTER 3

Nation Building

Homeland Security

In building homes, reality makeovers also participate in the building of nations. At least it is my contention that the series *Home Edition* can be read as styling not only personal but also national identity as it reaches to bring the powerful currents of nationalism into the commercial sphere.[1] Collectively, makeover narratives provide physical and psychological security by mapping fears about the "homeland" onto the home in highly patriotic as well as commercially charged settings. In this way, national identity is privatized and national pride made commercially productive.[2] Premiering nine months after the invasion of Iraq, *Home Edition* may be enjoyed as a substitute for government failure to deliver on promised makeovers across the larger geopolitical scene, as in the attempt at nation building in Iraq or Afghanistan or even the delayed memorial for the twin towers attack in New York—all projects that are bogged down, behind schedule, or falling apart.

Politics is to an increasing extent about image and even a light entertainment series such as *Home Edition*—in many ways because it is a light entertainment series—can play a role in this image making. Part of this series' entertainment value is that it works to improve the nation's public relations (PR) and to reassert nationhood as a public good. In so doing, it demonstrates how, despite global capitalism and global media, mass media programming is still being used to express national identities and to demonstrate the resilience of nationalism as a concept. One could argue that as much as reality television (RTV) is about globalism and the diffusion of formats internationally, it is also about a glocalized diffraction of broad narratives into local indigenized versions, with economic and political motives and consequences. Few series are as overtly nationalistic as *Home Edition,* a series in which viewers are taught nothing about how to use power tools but much about how to support one's country. In James Carey's ([1975] 1992) terms, the series is more ritualistic than informational, more about the sharing of an experience and the communication of values (sacrifice, loyalty, patriotism) than about the passing on of practical techniques. This is not to suggest any conscious political agenda on the producers' part but merely their tapping into a common zeitgeist in order to engage with viewers who, along with producers, occupy a particular political landscape. As is usually the case in commercial television, its creators shun overt political critique and controversy, but significant political crises have been the context for the making and the viewing of this series and it can't help exposing weaknesses and tensions on the political scale, even if only implicitly. The show's main work is not critical but compensatory, offering solace for disaster, for war, for terrorist attack, and, less traumatically, for stresses on the middle-class family.

One contemporary problem is America's image at home and abroad. By 2004 (following the invasion of Iraq), a majority of Americans reported that they believed their nation was losing both respect and popularity around the world. Furthermore, they believed this loss of image was a major problem.[3] This widespread concern about a loss of standing is unprecedented. But those looking for reassurance that the United States is a good as well as a great nation whose inhabitants are decent, caring, and fair-minded need look no further than ABC's *Home Edition*. Its mediated transformations not only create local and television communities but also invoke the larger imagined community of the nation, a nation that is, it seems, in need of some restoration. But despite failures abroad and gaps at home, *Home Edition* viewers are reassured that in America the good are rewarded for being good and for holding on to traditional values. America's corporations, too, enter as domestic heroes, instead of one reason why the country is enmeshed in war. All work in unison to restore the nation "one family at a time." And lest we miss this larger promise, the 2007–08 season selected one house from every State, presumably as an attempt to unify the nation as well as remind people of its great extent.

There is something deeply nostalgic about this series' focus on the family. Indeed, it may be one of the last robust examples of "family viewing" on a national TV network: in this case, a viewing of families by families. In an era of globalization, *Home Edition* producers have looked resolutely inward to recreate the wholesome image of small-town, rural America. Each episode's barn raising capitalizes on a perceived societal need for a greater sense of community by underscoring that American culture is one of good-hearted neighborliness—even, as we shall see, in its international entanglements.[4] The irony is that the consumption so celebrated on this series is in some measure responsible for the loss of local community for which it seeks to compensate. For it is the organization of shopping itself, into big box malls, strip malls, or the Internet, that has shaped and channeled social interchange with a resulting disappearance of Main Street and the family store.

While its producers avoid overt political discourse, *Home Edition* has been used for electioneering and politicking by those who recognize the power of its wholesome portraits. More than one prominent political representative has understood that its "authoritarian populism" (Hall 1988), its strong appeal to common sense and commonly held interests, could be useful for building their own image. First Lady Michelle Obama, then First Lady Laura Bush, and former Secretary of State Colin Powell have appeared on *Home Edition,* as have several governors (to date, of California, Maryland, New Jersey, Minnesota, and Kentucky). For example, on one episode, the governor of New Jersey put in a rather stilted performance as a gardener (as in "the Garden State") and Idaho governor Butch Otter went so far as to proclaim July 18, 2007 "The Stockdale Family Recognition Day" in honor of the family being helped by the *Home Edition* team. Also in 2007, George Amedore, Jr., parleyed his appearance as a contractor on *Home Edition* into a seat in the New York State Assembly. He was not shy about playing up his connection to the reality show and during his campaign stated that his aim was to perform an "economic makeover" of the State.[5] Candidate Barack Obama's 2008 campaign site linked to the ABC Better Community site associated with *Home Edition* and to the theme of "making over": at the Obama site, visitors were invited to sign up to help change not a house but a country.[6] These public figures have little to lose, it seems, by sharing this popular platform and associating with something patriotic and positive. What could be more down-to-earth or universally heartwarming than helping a family build a new home? What could be more worthy or patriotic than honoring a wounded vet? A cynical response might be: not much that also yields such easy political capital or healthy media profits.

"Nation building" of course applies internally and externally, especially when a country is at war. Its contribution to a "national imaginary," to a set of common images and narratives that people share when they think of their nation and of themselves as citizens of that nation, has been one of television's most significant functions since its introduction (Nadel 2005, 6).[7] A nation is not a natural unit, a simple land mass say, but rather a social construct, a sense people have of being a people. If a nation is "an imagined political community" (Andersen [1983] 2006), then for its entire run *Home Edition* has contributed to defining and improving America's image of itself as a community. It has done so as a popular, socially cohesive, and mass-mediated event that joins, or even conflates, images of nation and family. The nation as family or motherland/fatherland is a trope that has historically served to build unity and gloss over socioeconomic disparities, "because, regardless of the actual inequality and exploitation that may prevail in each, the nation is always conceived as a deep, horizontal comradeship" (Andersen 2006, 7). In addition, the idea of a nation has a certain moral grandeur that encourages sacrifice and thinking beyond one's own concerns, an important stimulus for the volunteerism on which *Home Edition* relies, as do larger national agendas. Regarding America's role abroad, some episodes directly link to the combat in Iraq and Afghanistan by honoring and rewarding those who have served in these campaigns. Support for the war is expressed in the effort to compensate those who have suffered because of it and in terms of a general and combined pride in the military and the nation. This support comes as a matter of principle, without debate about the particular rights or wrongs of government policy or execution.

The United States is a particularly self-conscious nation. From its inception, it was conceived of as a "second creation" (D. Nye 2003), as a deliberate design that threw off prior models to produce its own novel constitution. Even before they reached its shore, John Winthrop famously admonished the pilgrims: "For we must consider that we shall be as a City upon a hill. The eyes of all people are upon us" (1630), thus anticipating (perhaps presumptuously) that the new country would for a long time be aware of itself as an experiment against which others would measure themselves. Centuries later, President Bill Clinton still affirmed that "America is far more than a place. It is an idea" (Jillson 2004, 1), an idea housed in the collective imagination of generations of immigrants for whom the new territory was a second chance, a new start, a rehabilitation. Early commercial notices appealed to the entrepreneurial spirit in potential colonists, but centuries later the official narrative was revised so that the brutal capitalism of Jamestown was overshadowed by accounts of the goodly people of Plymouth when stoic piety and sacred justice became a more acceptable public face for the nation. A declared desire for justice also drove perhaps the most famous PR event in early American history: the Boston Tea Party of 1773. This event, still remembered as a successful use of a pseudo-event to capture media attention (Boorstin [1961] 1992), was more recently invoked in the right-wing Tea Party movement, a seemingly grassroots political association that is largely bankrolled by the wealthy. To this day, self-conscious and competing narratives of what is authentically American and what best guards or enacts its constitution are a huge element in American politics.

The Gulf

Whatever their political persuasion, few inheritors of the idea of America can ignore the missteps and failures of recent years. One painful example occurred when hurricane Katrina slammed into the Gulf coast in August of 2005. For many, this event provided a spectacular demonstration of how American citizens best not depend on public support during or after an emergency. This partly man-made disaster made visible another gulf, that between rich and poor. In particular, it made the government elite look indifferent to the governed, expressed spatially by the president's distant fly-over of the scene. The New Orleans' evacuation plan appeared to consist of warning car owners to leave town and save themselves: in other words, an individual solution using private means for those who could afford them. Others (mostly poor Blacks) were left literally stranded.[8] In fact, it took some time for the administration to react to, never mind attempt to redress, the situation. The perception of government failure was compounded by the lack of response by both local and federal agencies. FEMA (the Federal Emergency Management Agency) became a national embarrassment when it became clear that it and other emergency agencies were underfunded, understaffed, and in the hands of political cronies such as the now notorious "Brownie" (Michael Brown), who Bush appointed to head FEMA and defensively praised for doing "a heck of a job"—all evidence to the contrary.

The media created better relations with its public during this crisis than did the government. Television reporters often got to sites of disaster before any federal agents and in raw and unembedded footage explicitly expressed their disappointment and even outrage at official ineptitude. One notorious, unguarded media incident laid bare a fundamental tension in American politics concerning the role of public versus private aid. On September 8, 2005, while live on CNN, Vice President Dick Cheney was blandly reassuring viewers that the government was making progress in the cleanup effort, when a passerby is heard off camera, shouting: "Go fuck yourself, Mr. Cheney!"[9] The latter chose to awkwardly laugh this off while on camera, though, off camera, his Secret Service attachment pursued, handcuffed, and briefly detained the offender; though no charge could be brought against him. It turns out that the passerby was ER doctor Ben Marble (who was deliberately echoing Cheney's remark to Senator Pat Leahy on the Senate floor). Marble reports that he was frustrated by the government's lack of support following Katrina as well as its waging of the war in Iraq.[10] When interrupted, Cheney had been talking about the issue of using public funds to clean up private property. This is something the VP indicated was a "problem" that needed to be resolved and hence one reason why government aid was so lacking at the time.

It is perhaps not entirely surprising, then, that First Lady Laura Bush should appear on screen to do some damage control for the Bush administration. She did so by attaching herself to *Home Edition*'s modest efforts to help out hurricane victims. Katrina occurred two years into *Home Edition*'s run and it simply could not be ignored, though producers and staff admitted that there was only so much they could do to help. While *Home Edition* was in Mississippi filming an upcoming episode, Mrs. Bush touched down for a few hours on September 27 (a month after the hurricane hit) and was filmed handing out clothing provided by *Home Edition*'s longtime sponsor, Sears. Clearly her mission was to try to control the public perception of the government's response. She was also endorsing, along with *Home Edition,* the role of private, corporate charity and religious or "faith-based" groups. Indeed, it did prove to be the case that, with little government funding in place, much of the clean up and restoration had to be performed by church volunteers and other private parties. In other words, the model that *Home Edition* employs was writ large in a national disaster relief—though not large enough. In any case, *Home Edition* served the administration's purpose and received what looked like an official blessing by attracting a major political celebrity. Everyone was happy—except perhaps those who missed the handouts or were perplexed that in a moment of extreme crisis a government representative was taking her lead from a television show.

In the episode featuring Mrs. Bush and in some subsequent episodes set along the Gulf coast, both the effectiveness and inadequacy of a television series are brought clearly into focus. In so overwhelming and long-term a crisis, *Home Edition* has only managed to make a few well-meaning visits and make over a small number of structures, extending its single family format to rebuild a few churches and community centers that were able to offer private aid.[11] More significantly, in a move that has brought the series closest to political advocacy, presenters and subjects have articulated on camera their desire to use the mass medium to draw attention to the plight of those still in need. Echoing military bravura, one plaintive voice declared when the series revisited New Orleans in May 2008: "This is America and we don't leave our people behind" (aired 5/18/08). This was not a pledge from a public or military figure but a private citizen, builder Craig Gallagher, speaking in the face of government neglect. The host articulated on camera that all a television show can do is generate some hope and some public attention by showcasing a few local "heroes" who've survived the hurricane and helped others out. As *Home Edition* cameras plainly reveal how little progress has been made, there is still no overt criticism of official authorities, only a focus on the good that some individuals can do. In the two-hour New Orleans finale of 2008 (aired 5/18/08), the series galvanized what the host repeatedly referred to as a "coalition" of different contracting firms from around the country, most of which had appeared on the show before. These distant firms were contacted because local New Orleans firms were so stretched they couldn't contribute much. But it also seemed that the show was attempting to construct an ersatz national response—albeit two years later—to a disaster situation that had largely depended on a patchwork of private volunteer groups. International anxieties were also being invoked by the appearance of these so-called coalition forces that in this instance gratified viewers by pulling off the mission and completing the job on time. Lest we miss the analogy, one of the subjects being helped in Louisiana explicitly compared his local scene to the devastation of war-torn Iraq.

9/11

There will be more to say about Iraq later, but first we need to consider the event that precipitated its invasion, at least according to the official rhetoric. This was, of course, the attack of September 11, 2001. Nothing could have been more shocking to America and its allies or have such a profound effect on the national psyche. The wreckage at Ground Zero, as it soon became known, gave the nation as a whole a searing sensitivity to how America is regarded by hostile others. While the events of 9/11 are only explicitly mentioned now and then in *Home Edition*, its narratives repeatedly address some of the deeper anxieties caused by this symbolic, as well as material, attack on Western economic and military structures. With the international scene being intractable and not well understood, it is no doubt a lot less daunting to turn inward and to undertake domestic improvements as witnessed on this popular series. So it was perhaps not altogether surprising that on September 11, 2009, President Obama chose to commemorate the terrorist attack by also participating in a charitable home build. In a well-publicized event, he and his wife painted a room on a Habitat for Humanity site.

On that infamous September morning eight years earlier, the American sense of invincibility and impermeability had been suddenly and severely damaged—this being the intent of terrorists, to bring risk down to the level of the civilian, the private, and the everyday. We see this fear of the *compromised interior* (after all, the terrorists trained in America) being addressed on *Home Edition*, where, naturally enough, the focus is on buildings with weak structures and lack of physical support.[12] But beyond this, producers frequently seek environments with some hidden and insidious threat to the family's health, such as mold or radiation or some other airborne danger. These one can see as a reflection of larger fears about threats to the nation and the need for not just watertight basements but also watertight national security. Whereas lifestyle makeovers are concerned with a person's lack of resources, taste, or simply time, *Home Edition* goes deeper than consumer dissatisfaction or ignorance into a darker realm of real physical risk (though with no mention of government or corporate culpability for industrial or domestic pollutants). The linking of a home rehab to health and survival increases the power of the drama but it is also politically cathartic to witness dangers being so objectively identified and swiftly eradicated. On *Home Edition,* there is no manufactured evidence, no loss of life, no endless delay; instead, the end result is a strong foundation, impregnable walls, and technology that quite literally filters everything noxious from the environment.

Then there is the matter of demolition. The image of the twin towers' collapse haunts all who saw it (and few did not), but the demolition on *Home Edition* only clears the way for something better. Its benign and repeated reconstruction offers a strong contrast to the utter destruction seen in the video compulsively played across the globe. Much has been said about America's need to "rebuild," but the most iconic site of all, New York's Ground Zero, for years remained a void as politicians squabbled over what to do. It therefore comes as something of a relief to reverse the tape and to witness *Home Edition* crews erect structures again and again at lightning speed.[13] One episode entitled "Friends helping friends" performed a mini-makeover of the apartment of two firefighters who lost comrades and who helped out at Ground Zero after 9/11 (aired 5/6/04). In an inadvertent display of coalition sacrifice, Englishman and *Home Edition* carpenter Ed Sanders injured his hand while creating a wood carving of the American flag for an ex-marine who helped rescue two Port Authority police officers from the rubble of the World Trade Center (aired 2/11/07). Their story was comparatively rare because one of the horrors and frustrations of the twin towers attack was that there were so few people whom anyone could rescue. On *Home Edition,* teams reliably produce people to rescue people week after week.

In 2009, ABC tried a different and more direct approach when it launched the not-so-subtly titled *Homeland Security USA,* a series that promoted a positive image of hardworking officials securing the borders of the United States, mostly from illegal immigrants and drug peddlers. Acknowledging the great PR potential for domestic authorities, producer Arnold Shapiro told *The Hollywood Reporter,* "I love investigative journalism, but that's not what we're doing. This show is heartening. It makes you feel good about these people who are doing their best to protect us" (Ed O'Keefe, *Washington Post,* March 10, 2009). Certainly, politicians have long recognized the power of popular entertainment to rally support for a war. Shortly after the 9/11 attack, President Bush twice summoned Hollywood moguls to the White House to urge them to produce content that would support the war on terror and his chief political adviser, Karl Rove, made a similar appeal to tens of media executives in a Beverly Hills hotel (Faludi 2007, 6). Years later, First Lady Michelle Obama went to Hollywood to ask the Writers' Guild (WGAW) for more stories about military families to help create more support for this part of the war effort.[14] Just a few weeks prior to this (May 2011), a series premiered called

Surprise Homecoming (TLC, 2011–), which features the highly emotional reunion of military families hosted by country singer Billy Ray Cyrus, and there may be more to follow. Less explicit than *Homeland Security USA, Home Edition* has nevertheless worked consistently over many years to raise national pride and morale. Like the former, it enacts a reassuring and non-journalistic scenario but focuses on restoring the "heartland" rather than guarding the perimeter.

Like most TV entertainment, *Home Edition* rarely looks at the 9/11 attack up close, perhaps because even implicit references to such a tragedy could make its commitment to commerce appear crass or irrelevant. This is where the model of donorship, and in this case also patriotism, is key, for linking consumption to charity and to patriotism was also the strategy favored by advertisers in the aftermath of 9/11. One of the uncanny aftereffects of this attack was the absence of advertising: not only were the skies silent, so were the advertisers. For a few days, there was little or no commercial interruption of continuous mass media news coverage, and when ads did reappear, they eased into the atmosphere of national mourning via patriotic giving. Some early retail ads suggested people donate to charities rather than buy goods, or at least companies promised to donate a percentage of their profits to named charities (Dickinson 2009). For example, Sears was quick to announce that it was donating to relief efforts for 9/11 victims and Home Depot's advertising suggested people donate to United Way's September 11th Fund in its stores because—in a strong echo of *Home Edition*—the company declared: "We can get back to building our own house soon enough. Right now it's time to help our neighbors" (Dickinson 2009, 303). Indeed, being a neighbor is an advertising trope that major American corporations have long used to soften and localize their image. For decades one American insurance company's slogan has been "Like a good neighbor, State Farm is there." Similarly, in 1915 AT&T attempted to stave off threats of public ownership with the slogan "Making a neighborhood of a nation" (Marchand 1998, 70) and, in 1923, GM used a very similar approach in its "Making the nation a neighborhood" campaign (Marchand 1998, 139).

Immediately after 9/11, consumption was linked to patriotism by political leaders, who declared that it was the citizen's duty to shop in order to support the national economy and, by extension, Western capitalism. According to Bush and Blair, going to the mall became almost a military strategy, a defiant normalization that would repudiate terrorist aims and ideology. Fifteen days after 9/11, President Bush stood beside the CEOs of the two airlines whose planes were used in the attacks and urged Americans to "Get down to Disney World in Florida. Take your families and enjoy life, the way we want it to be enjoyed" (Dickinson 2009, 307). Not for the first time was Disney being used to encapsulate American capitalist pride and Bush went on to assert that visiting Disney would demonstrate that although the terrorists think they have "struck our soul," they have not (Dickinson 2009, 307). This was indeed an apt reference, since traveling to a Disney theme park has come to be regarded as a quasi-sacred pilgrimage for Americans (and others), an apotheosis of consumption that is often donated to lucky *Home Edition* families. However, years after Bush's speech, Disney's attempt to attach itself to 9/11 became a PR fiasco when the company tried to trademark the name of the elite Navy unit that killed Osama bin Laden, the alleged mastermind behind the 9/11 attacks. Just two days after the raid in Pakistan, Disney filed an application to trademark "Seal Team 6" (an entity the Navy officially denies exists) with the US Patent Office (May 3, 2011), the plan being to make the killing of America's Most Wanted into various forms of entertainment, from TV shows to video games to snow globes and Christmas tree decorations. In a defensive maneuver, the US Navy promptly applied for a counter-trademark for the words "Navy Seal" and "Seal Team" and, as they got quickly embroiled in a public relations nightmare, Disney decided to withdraw its application.

National Renovation

In the 2000 presidential election campaign, candidate Bush had declared that he had no interest in "nation building." During a debate with Vice President Al Gore on October 11, 2000, he famously affirmed:

> I don't think our troops ought to be used for what's called nation-building. . . . I think what we need to do is convince people who live in the lands they live in to build the nations. Maybe I'm missing something here. I mean, we're going to have a kind of nation-building corps from America? Absolutely not.

Bush repeated this sentiment, to great applause, in many stump speeches during the campaign. Yet, soon after taking office, the new president set his sights on what was framed as the makeover of a nation into a new center for democracy: the first makeover occurring in Afghanistan and the second, with greater fanfare, in Iraq. The invasion of both countries was positioned rhetorically as a large-scale rehabilitation. On the eve of the invasion, President Bush declared to the Iraqi people: "We will tear down the apparatus of terror and we will help you to build a new Iraq that is prosperous and free."[15] Turning Iraq into a modern consumerist society would also make it safe for American business, of course, but as is usually the case with such ventures, the populace back home heard rhetoric about "freedom" and "democracy," not "great business opportunity." Again, we are reminded that a chief PR strategy is promoting private interests as a public good, and certainly the rehab in Iraq has profited many private companies, which have received generous US federal funds while presenting their businesses as performing a public good for both Americans and Iraqis.[16]

It is perhaps an understatement to say that neither the makeover of Iraq nor of Afghanistan has gone particularly well. The original script anticipated American soldiers being greeted as liberators and enjoying a quick and successful denouement on both fronts.[17] Apparently the CIA was so sure that American soldiers would be greeted warmly that one operative suggested "sneaking hundreds of small American flags into the country for grateful Iraqis to wave at their liberators." The plan was to "capture the spectacle on film and beam it throughout the Arab world." But this plan was dropped and the spectacle didn't materialize (Gordon and Trainor 2007, 157). Indeed, as things began to quickly unravel in Iraq, it became apparent that, among those who conceived the campaign, there was bad planning and weak execution, or just no planning at all. Secretary of Defense Donald Rumsfeld notoriously would not even entertain planning for a long-term engagement and at press conferences was defensive when pressed to reveal how much post-invasion strategizing his department had undertaken. Not so on *Home Edition,* which with smooth management and expert planning gets the job done according to schedule and leaves no mess behind. Here viewers can every week enjoy the real satisfaction of a "mission accomplished," in contrast to Bush's 2003 May Day fiasco. Here they are able to witness the repair of the nation's damaged collective psyche, including a revamped pride in the capitalist market. One contractor said of being on the show, "Doing this is half like going to camp and half like going to war" (*Official Companion Book,* 28), a notion reinforced by the now conventional charge of worker-warriors up to the target house, which producers call the "Braveheart" scene. On *Home Edition,* there are no allegations of corruption or cronyism. The mission is clear, the result is unambiguously good, and there are no enemies but time.

Nations are often most self-conscious when at war and when politicians are obliged to create a collective will to further "national interests." But building public support for these most recent wars has been difficult. During the First Gulf War, the US military control of journalists generated press conferences that, like any good product infomercial, sold the incursion as precise and clean (this so-called Nintendo war famously displayed "smart bombs" accurately hitting distant unmanned targets). Also effective was the publicity stunt created by the prominent Washington PR firm of Hill and Knowlton when a young Kuwaiti girl testified before the Congressional Human Rights Caucus (a group that had the appearance of an official congressional committee but with looser perjury standards). She tearfully affirmed that she had witnessed Iraqi soldiers throwing babies out of hospital incubators. A year later it was discovered that her narrative was a fabrication, that she was coached by Hill and Knowlton, and that her father was the Kuwaiti ambassador to the United States (Stauber and Rampton 1995). But the intended effect had already worked its way through the system and the incubator story was repeated everywhere: in Congress, at the United Nations, and repeatedly by (the first) President Bush. Rivaled only by the infamous stories of German soldiers bayoneting babies in World War I, this graphic account became a useful flashpoint for provoking the visceral anti-Iraqi sentiment needed to move a populace to fight for a not-so-democratic former British colony that few Americans had ever heard of and still couldn't find on a map.

In the run up to the next war against Iraq the PR campaign was perhaps less poignant, but fear-mongering about WMDs, supposed links to 9/11 and Al-Qaeda, and the conventional demonizing of the enemy leader, former US ally Saddam Hussein, seemed to work reasonably well. From the start, the Bush administration apparently saw its foreign policy as something to be sold to the public, not unlike a marketing campaign. In fact, White House Chief of Staff Andrew Card spoke, perhaps too frankly, to the *New York Times* on September 7, 2002, about the decision to launch a September campaign to invade Iraq: "From a marketing point of view you don't introduce new products in August," he explained (Isikoff and Corn 2006, 33). Despite the optimistic launch, things began to crack in this military/marketing campaign and a credibility gap quickly opened up. At first, both sides—the so-called coalition forces and various Arab states—were able to convince their respective audiences that all was going well. But after Hussein was ousted and the war dragged on, there was a burgeoning awareness in America and in Europe of the lies and half truths that had brought a nation or nations to war—an awareness that was in part due to the less controlled information flow on the Internet. Of course, propaganda as a form of ideological PR has always been a primary weapon of war, but the targeted populace doesn't usually witness the strategies unravel in such an unmistakable manner.[18] Painful retrospective reports on the absence of WMDs, on pseudo-events such as the orchestrated toppling of Saddam Hussein's statue, the staged flight-deck victory speech of May 2003,[19] and even the fake turkey Bush served up in Iraq—all of these exposés of PR tactics big and small—made increasing numbers of Americans and their allies feel victims of manipulation or incompetence or both (David Barstow and Robin Stein, *New York Times*, March 13, 2005). *Hubris: The Inside Story of Spin, Scandal, and the Selling of the Iraq War* (Isikoff and Corn 2006) is a popular book on the subject that captures this sense of being marketed to and manipulated.[20]

Yet the US administration continued to have such faith in the ability of public relations to create a desired reality that in his second term (2004–08) Bush spent more on government PR (or "public diplomacy") than any prior administration and sought to alleviate tensions in the Middle East, not by rethinking American policy but by establishing public relations committees to try to craft a better image of America in Muslim eyes, in part to protect American business interests.[21] One strategy, even, was to produce reality TV shows in Arabic to try to improve America's image in the Middle East (McMurria 2009, 195). Madison Avenue executive Charlotte Beers headed a group that was charged with making "American values as much a brand name as McDonald's hamburgers or Ivory soap"—or, more plainly, to "sell the war" (O'Shaughnessy 2004, 206).[22] But not much came of these branding efforts and foreign leaders complained that Beers and others in the administration simply did not listen to the reasons for hostility to American policy, such as its apparent privileging of Israel.[23] What is striking is that it seemed reasonable for a president to work on image rather than substance, on one-way PR rather than diplomatic dialogue. However, this was also understandable: after all, PR and image management are what get people into office in the first place.

This faith at the center of politics that problems can be resolved on the rhetorical level alone is evidence of the extent of the PR effect referred to earlier and it is encapsulated in television's selling of its versions of reality for its own ends and those of its sponsors. The way in which reality TV turns real life into a commodity resembles the larger political milieu of mis-information, disinformation, and doublethink, where bills are presented with Orwellian flair as The Patriot Act (reducing civil liberties), Welfare Reform (cutting public support), and The Clear Skies Initiative (allowing increased pollution). Former Vice President Al Gore was moved to write about a dis-cursive shift among contemporary leaders whereby "reality itself has become a commodity that can be created and sold with clever propaganda and pub-lic relations skills" (Gore 2007, 60). As a latter-day Habermas, the former VP bewails the loss of a public sphere for clear and open discussion and the inadequate substitution of PR strategies for delivering a client's message. And it is indeed striking how much the fundamental relations between govern-ment and citizen are today being managed according to the principles of advertising and PR (marketing, focus groups, polls).[24] This is the era of lob-byists, of pseudo-populist talk show hosts, and of Think Tanks (or "Policy Shops") with patriotic sounding names that pose as unaffiliated and unspon-sored research bodies (while the universities they mimic are under increasing pressure to commercialize).[25] In addition, many thousands of government employees work diligently every day to produce PR in the Pentagon, in the military, and in overseas and domestic broadcasting (Voice of America, Radio Sawa, domestic Video News Releases), as well as in heavyweight PR firms that are, not coincidently, based in Washington D.C.[26] The hybridity that all of this PR produces can affect who has power, who has profit, and even who lives and dies. In their selling of reality, the pseudo-events of reality TV can be seen to normalize this manipulation, though of course with much lower social costs and consequences.

One of the most famous and (at the time) successful of wartime pseudo-events, and something that would resurface on *Home Edition,* was the rescue of Private Jessica Lynch on April 1, 2003. Millions of television viewers were captivated by grainy military video of a young, blonde-haired US soldier being carried on a stretcher from an enemy hospital by US Special Forces (for some reason clutching an American flag). The vulnerable and pretty female, the virile and alert rescuers, it was as dramatic as a Hollywood script and it turned out the scene was indeed scripted to some extent. What was staged was the appearance of an immediate military threat (actually there were no Iraqi troops around), Lynch's identity as a brave soldier who fought back before being captured (she later said she didn't fire a shot), and the idea of her being rescued from mistreatment or even torture at the Iraqi hospital (Lynch was treated well by the hospital staff and a local Iraq tipped off the US forces that she was there). Lynch's doctor at the hospital had even tried to send her back to the US military two days before her "rescue" but her ambulance was fired on at the American checkpoint and had to turn back (Faludi 2007, 171). As for the flag, this was handed to her by her rescuers, presumably as a patriotic prop in an otherwise drab scene. None of this staging was identified until much later and the video, meanwhile, served as an effective morale booster.

Lynch eventually went to Congress to complain about this manipulation both of herself and of the truth (April 2007). But, before this, she appeared on a two-hour *Home Edition* finale (aired 5/22/05) in order to honor a fallen comrade, a Native American killed alongside her in Iraq.[27] Apparently Lynch had applied to be on the show in order to provide for her friend's surviving family. Like Lynch, her comrade Lori Piestewa had joined the military in what is sometimes referred to as "the economic draft" so that she could better her own poor economic conditions. On this occasion, Lynch offered no criticism of her government, its military, or needing to enlist in an army in order to get an education. As always, producers were careful to gloss over any political controversy, keeping the focus firmly on honoring veterans killed in battle or who came home alive. Hence, as well as building a home for her friend's family, designers constructed a veterans' community center for the reservation. Some attention was paid to the fact that Lynch's friend was the first Native American woman to be killed in combat while serving in the US military and the designers piously claimed to be honoring the larger tradition of Native Americans fighting on behalf of the United States, a potentially uncomfortable nod to a domestic imperialism (the United States versus Indian Nations) that this series, needless to say, does not pursue (Gillan 2006).

Most *Home Edition* episodes feature the narratives of less well-known veterans who have no potential for controversy. On more than one occasion we are informed that the sacrifice made by individual soldiers is being repaid by the "sacrifice" of workers who have volunteered to build them a home. Of course, likening some days spent on a building site to serving for years in Iraq or Afghanistan and returning dead or wounded might trivialize or even nullify these good intentions. Moreover, glossing over the fact that the volunteerism and sacrifice of the builders are part of a commercial transaction may nevertheless bring to mind the same truth about war: that those who propagandize typically downplay financial motives in favor of ideological arguments for making sacrifices that tend ultimately to protect larger economic interests. On *Home Edition* the exchange is framed as individual patriotic donors honoring other patriotic individuals. Neither the economic link to recruitment among the lower classes nor the apparent lack of veteran care afterward is up for discussion. Individual and ordinary support for the military appears when support functions are depicted on the set. For instance, one episode featured someone who was organizing a letter writing campaign for soldiers in Iraq and another showed women making up care boxes for the military serving abroad in order to send the troops "a little bit of home" (aired 5/1/11). Despite this tagline, neither of these activities are strictly part of the program's regular business (building a home) but are indicative of the series' overt support for the military, at least at the level of individuals involved in the war. The assumption that everyone can rally around individual troops allows for the common conflation of support for the military with support for the policies that dictate their actions. For some years, support for troops in Iraq and Afghanistan has been a persistent though not central element in this series, creating a stable ethos that no one on camera is ever impudent enough or "unpatriotic" enough to question.

On one episode, the headliner was none other than former Chairman of the Joint Chiefs of Staff and former US Secretary of State Colin Powell (aired 5/3/09). As secretary of state, Powell's job was to garner domestic and international support for the invasion of Iraq, this despite his own reservations. In hindsight, his career seems emblematic of the pressure that facts come under during a time of intense propaganda. On *Home Edition*, Powell meets a Gulf War veteran (Jeff Cooper) to thank him for his service and it turns out that this former serviceman is showing signs of Gulf War syndrome, a condition that was another site of contestation when government authorities initially denied its symptoms were real and therefore deserving of (costly) medical attention. But rather than touch on official misinformation or cover-up, this episode channels patriotic outbursts about freedom and sacrifice. The builder performing the makeover presents as his motive an exchange of freedoms: he says he wishes to give the wheelchair-bound vet the freedom he deserves for fighting for the freedom of others. The construction company's website encouraged people to join a military parade on the show and to "come in full attire, with banners, flags, hats, uniforms, jackets, etc" because "This parade is to honor all service men and women, and to highlight the sacrifices of Jeff Cooper."[28] Meanwhile, Ty declares "war" on their old house as cannons fire at the dwelling. Extending the military pride further, Cooper's daughter (age 16) reveals that she has enlisted in the National Guard, her brother gets a police themed room, and one of the designers visits the local disabled veterans' chapter. Another episode built a home for a National Guard sergeant whose outfit, that very week, had accomplished one of the few spectacular US successes of the war in Iraq: the capture of Saddam Hussein (aired 2/15/04). But fear of a lack of security in the homeland is evoked when a house is built for an absent father serving in Afghanistan (aired 5/1/11): his eldest son gets a surveillance camera in his room because he is now, we are told, "the man of the house." What he is looking for or guarding against is not clear.

The fear of internal lack of security was realized nationally when a US army psychiatrist and Muslim fundamentalist opened fire on fellow soldiers in Fort Hood, Texas, on November 5, 2009. One *Home Edition* episode tackled this attack head on, showing news reports of the incident and then undertaking to aid a soldier wounded at Fort Hood by building a home and, at the same time, army morale (aired 2/20/11). After host Ty Pennington and others arrive inside Bradley vehicles (tanks) to perform their "mission" of providing Staff Sgt. Patrick Zeigler both with a new home and a military wedding, they take time to commemorate those killed and wounded in the attack and to honor the servicemen who make sacrifices "for country, for family, for us." The designers then team up with a charitable organization called "Operation Finally Home" that provides land and homes for returning troops. Their first act is to formally install an American flag in front of the many helpers who are in military uniform. A strong narrative thread thereafter is the loyalty, and devotion, of the soldier's fiancée that intersects with the military and political tropes to provide masculine and feminine versions of the same core virtues. She is rewarded with a recuperative shopping spree (on the iconic Rodeo Drive) in preparation for her wedding. This turns out to be a full military affair, with traditional cavalry horses and carriage, an officiate and guests in military uniform, and the emergence of bride and groom under a line of crossed swords. In the watching crowds are seas of American flags and signs saying "support out troops." Not surprisingly, on this episode the charity prompt was "to learn how you can support our brave men and women go to a abettercommunity.com." Other episodes that thank injured war veterans for their service feature new homes for Sgt. Luis Rodriguez, who lost a leg in Iraq (aired 9/25/05); former Marine Sgt. Daniel Gilyeat, who also lost a leg in Iraq (aired 2/10/08); and veteran Patrick Tutwiler, who was shot in the neck by an Iraqi sniper (aired 1/25/ 09). All are presented as self-sacrificing heroes who bashfully reject this title. *Home Edition* has on numerous occasions also honored as domestic heroes anyone involved in fighting crime and providing security, such as local police and firefighters. These are some of the remaining public services in the United States, having grown from earlier private arrangements.[29] Here they represent the best of local-but-national authorities whose presence is a reassuring part of Americana: their flag-festooned vehicles have for generations taken pride of place in every small-town parade and this is the patriotic and celebratory image we receive of them here. Police officers and firefighters also figured prominently in coverage of 9/11 and they came to represent the best of America in their stalwart, masculine, and self-sacrificing response to that attack. After 9/11 they were elevated to heroic status, perhaps in part to fulfill some need for mythic strength and manhood after this incredible vulnerability (Faludi 2007).[30] Hence, post 9/11 ads were full not only of flags but also of images of these sacrificial figures.[31] On *Home Edition* these kinds of public services are frequently commandeered for private purposes (media profit), especially when a home is being built for someone who is or was serving in the military. In these episodes, some wing of the military and/or police invariably shows up to contribute labor and equipment. The US Department of Defense has had a formal liaison with Hollywood since the 1940s and has been willing to provide personnel and technical support for blockbuster films like *Top Gun* or *Black Hawk Down* so long as the Pentagon gets to vet content (Thussu 2007, 123–4). But here we have the conjunction of military force and a domestic setting. In one episode (aired 5/1/11) for the family of a soldier serving in Afghanistan, the old house was exploded with the help of marines and one of the interior designers flew overhead in a jet posing as a military pilot. Later, the local police appeared in a staged and slapstick arrest of another designer for supposedly picking up traffic cones and street signs. This is ironic given that while he is being lectured on not using public resources (cones) the show itself is using police time for an entertainment skit. It is not clear who for years has been paying for the uniformed police escorts, the firefighters filling a pool, the jets, the bulldozing tanks, the military guards and so on, but the benign cooperation of law enforcement agencies certainly provides great theater and heartwarming PR. This PR function was highlighted in the montage created to promote the show's having built 100 homes (aired 11/25/07), when editors went out of their way to foreground images of the military, the flag, and expressions of patriotism, capped by one subject who says with simple sincerity that he would die for his country.[32] Publicly displaying the stars and stripes was the first response of millions of Americans to the attack of 9/11; as Jennifer Scanlon notes, Wal-Mart alone sold 116,000 American flags on September 11, 2001 (Scanlon 2005, 177). For a while flags festooned every ad and, as Douglas Kellner notes, they were even computer generated to appear on top-rated TV dramas such as *The West Wing* (NBC, 1999–06) and *Law and Order* (NBC, 1990–2010) (Kellner 2002, 149). American flags still appear in almost every episode of *Home Edition* as a kind of national-corporate logo accompanied by many statements of national unity and pride. Any nation's flag summons in its citizens powerful and uncritical sentiments and unquestionably *Home Edition* producers wish to tap into this emotional seam. Repeated visual elements are reminiscent of the iconic "It's Morning Again in America" ad campaign (1984), which used pious images of family, faith, and flag to solidify the Reaganistic neoliberalism that we have observed in this and other makeover series.[33]

In a view from the other side, it is ironic, perhaps, that those devastated by America's invasion of their country resorted to the *Home Edition* format to try to heal some wounds. *Labor and Materials,* a popular Iraqi series that began in 2004, undertook a televised home reconstruction similar to that on *Home Edition.* As in America, the show sought to compensate for lack of government aid by organizing private charity—the difference being that in Iraq the building was deliberately destroyed by US military forces who made no offer to rebuild it. Less surprising perhaps is that the show's format has also been mimicked by American troops serving in Iraq, who in one spoof posted on YouTube pretend to plan a "makeover" of an insurgent's empty house—by exploding it.[34] In this military version there is no rebuild, but, given their situation, the destruction is no doubt perceived by the troops as a therapeutic and constructive act, linking them to a feel-good narrative back home as they are forced to inhabit a confusing geography of ever-present danger.

Family Structure

The coverage of the events of 9/11 was in many ways a peak for television as a mass medium, for during this period it was still playing a primary role in creating a sense of national unity. The targets of the 9/11 and other terrorist attacks were commercial and military, but the trauma of 9/11 soon got turned into a threat to families and to domestic homes and so "nesting" programs began to appear on television schedules by 2002. Observing this cultural aftermath, Susan Faludi concluded that "the cultural troika of media, entertainment, and advertising declared the post-9/11 age an era of neofifties nuclear family 'togetherness' " (2007, 3). Dana Heller also identifies a post-9/11 yearning for "familial nationalism" (2005, 7), meaning a desire for faith in the unity and continuity of the American family. By twining family and nationalism, the always wholesome *Home Edition* may also be trying to recapture the powerful but short-lived sense of national unity after 9/11. More emphatically than other home improvement series, it asserts the primacy of the nuclear family as a moral and socioeconomic structure and it takes as its particular focus the home as the embodiment of a family bond. "Home" and "family" become mutually dependent terms: a home is where a family lives and a family lives in a home.[35] This mutual dependency accords with the insights of Henri Lefebvre ([1974] 1991) and others that space and society are mutually constitutive, that space is both produced through social relations and embodies social relations. As a materialization of the social order, a family home represents many things: a nuclear or core family grouping, capitalist ownership and investment, a certain degree of technological sophistication, and the social and legal organization of various forms of expertise and labor. The home is also associated with nationhood. In many cultures, pride in home ownership is linked to pride in one's nation and owning and maintaining one's home is interpreted as supporting the nation. All of this is showcased on *Home Edition* when it asserts the importance of the conjugal family home, but at the same time RTV opens it up to public viewing in order to profit from the titillation that comes from the fact that this space is ordinarily intensely private, a privacy that grew out of the industrial separation of work (public) and family home (nonwork, private). On reality TV, the home is again a place of work, and not just for designers.

Validating people who live in this space becomes a central ideological thrust of this type of programming (Palmer 2007, 2011). A veneration of the family and of having children may be another reaction to the loss experienced after 9/11—at least this was a recuperative act commonly promoted in the popular press after the attack, as observed by, for example, Susan Faludi (2007), even if statistics did not show any great increase in births or marriages. Certainly, in all levels of society there is today an orthodoxy about declaring that being a family member or parent is one's most important role (though stepping down in order to "spend more time with one's family" is generally a euphemism for involuntary resignation). *Home Edition*'s producers go to great lengths to bring family members together, even under the constraints of a war that has taken its toll on this social unit. For example, when building a home for the family of a marine on active duty, they first arrange for location parity by having both the family (now in Disney, Florida) and the soldier (in Afghanistan) watch the demolition at the same time via a webcam. Later, all through the unveiling of the house, the soldier appears on a screen in each room and views the new space alongside his family. Designers even provide a recording of his voice saying goodnight to his youngest child, again using media technology to compensate for absence (aired 5/1/11).

Yet on *Home Edition* only certain kinds of family are sanctioned. Producers like to feature blended families, adopted children, different races living together, and so on. But homes are not being built for single people or gay couples or the divorced; rather they are to accommodate some variation on the heterosexual-parents-plus-children scenario. Children, in particular, are essential. If one parent is missing—and this is quite often the case—it is due to catastrophe and death; it is a lack and not a choice. The immediate family is isolated, with no extended family members in evidence or explanation why they are not. There is some suggestion of a broader inclusivity in the quasi family of the onscreen talent, a group that usually includes at least one gay male. However, these people appear to live on a bus, and when it comes to the association of a settled family and home there is a much stricter orthodoxy. Unlike Fox's *Renovate My Family* (2004), where both house and family were rehabbed (in a week no less) because both structures were regarded as broken, ABC's series rewards those families whose basic emotional structure appears to be strong but who need some help in functioning better as a unit. The spatial layout therefore aims to better manage the distribution of domestic and reproductive labor and to alleviate some compromises and pressures. First, designers usually recognize the importance of the centripetal experience of coming together as a family; hence, the standard ground floor "open plan." But the second principle is the desire for individuality, which designers accommodate by producing highly differentiated bedrooms for each child. These rooms were often shared by family members in the past, but only because of economic constraints. After the makeover, the newly individualized bedrooms are presented as expressions of each inhabitant's interests or even inner being, though in some instances we witness a staged placement where the room's design promotes a commercial product such as an upcoming film (e.g., Disney's *Horton Hears a Who*, aired 2/10/08, or Warner Brothers' *Speed Racer*, aired 5/4/08).

The typical house makeover also supports the modern and largely Western notion that marriage is not only a matter of household management but also of romance. The latter means that each couple receives a separate "master suite" and a large bathroom that is almost always equipped with a Jacuzzi complete with the romantic cliché of floating rose petals. Although a primary focus of the series is good parenting, designers invariably define the parents' suite as a refuge or haven from family responsibilities and, more discretely, as a way of preserving a romantic-sexual relationship within the considerable demands of family life. Being showered with luxuries and transposed from previously modest homes into much grander affairs makes for good television. But perhaps this excess is more than dramaturgical. Perhaps, as Gareth Palmer suggests, the luxurious resolution is a rather desperate attempt to disguise a more widespread breakdown of families due in no small part to the logic of American capitalism and its shrinking of public services (2007, 173).

Looking at parenting makeover shows like *Supernanny* (Channel 4, 2004–; ABC, 2005–11) and *Nanny 911* (Fox, 2004–07; CMT, 2009–), Ron Becker (2006) similarly underscores the symbolic weight RTV families carry in the context of a post-welfarist US society. He argues that by beginning and ending with individual families, these programs obscure the wider social forces and government policies that have helped put many American families into crisis. Again, we encounter distraction and compensation, perhaps overcompensation. Little thought is given to long-term consequences such as higher property taxes and utility bills or the social fallout of plopping a McMansion in a poor neighborhood. (Supersizing a home can drive up local property tax bills when these are assessed according to the average value of homes in the neighborhood.) What matters for producers is the immediate dramatic moment, so there is little attempt to follow up or to examine the situation with a wider lens.[36] Occasionally donors provide funds for future upkeep, for college education, for spaces that will generate an income (home offices). But, to borrow a well-known metaphor, generally they bestow a one-time present of a huge barrel of fish instead of instructions on how to go fishing—again, because the short-term payoff of handing over the barrel and admiring its dimensions makes for better television. Clearly there is a push to validate and support the idea of the family as with the larger family of the nation, but it looks like a dramatic compensation again distracts attention from deeper and more systemic problems.

Joining Forces

A culmination of many of the themes I have been tracing in this chapter came in the season premiere of *Home Edition* in September 2011—just after the nation's ten-year commemoration of 9/11—when the designers' bus drew up at the most famous residential address in America, 1600 Pennsylvania Avenue (i.e., the White House). This two-hour spectacle (aired 9/25/11) managed to combine all the key elements of strong support for the military, prominent political figures, much flag waving, references to the American Dream, a sanctification of the family, Sears as donor, and, once again, Disney. A full panoply of military personnel from the army, the navy, the air force, and even the coast guard appeared on screen. But even more impressive was the fact that it was America's first lady who ran out to meet the design team, as so many ordinary citizens have done before her, when Ty Pennington stood on her lawn and shouted through the loudspeaker "Good morning Obama family!"—thus tapping into a convention of American politics (left or right) where those in high office are happy to be portrayed as "just regular folk." This show clearly harnessed Michelle Obama's official sanction and celebrity, but she, in turn, harnessed the power of media attention and, given her particular political platform, it was not altogether surprising that she chose to cooperate with this series.

As volunteers helped rebuild a homeless shelter for women veterans, the president's wife was able to publicize her signature causes, most especially support for military families (an initiative entitled Joining Forces), but also growing one's own healthy food (the White House now has a vegetable garden) and obesity prevention: all a good fit for a show that had for years been lending support to military families in a domestic setting. For her opportunity to promote her (traditionally feminine) causes, the first lady returned the favor by promoting television, praising both this series and the medium in general. During filming, she talked about the great power of television and particularly of *Home Edition,* which she cited as an example of what TV does best. In associated print interviews she reinforced this point: " 'We live in a media age, and one of the things we still share is our love of television' and the stories it can tell so effectively, Obama said. 'We thought this was an extraordinary venue to highlight the struggles and challenges and triumphs of a special family' " (Lynn Elber, *Seattle Times,* September 24, 2011). Publicity surrounding this episode suggested that *Home Edition* reinforces the family structure in the White House too. " 'I love that all of us can gather around to share in these stories of triumph every week,' the first lady told *People*" (David Jackson, *USA Today,* September 21, 2011).

As this season opener unfolded, all of the old allies reappeared. This included Sears, who tied the episode to their charitable venture called "Heroes at Home," which, among other things, aims to help veterans get civilian jobs by guiding them in marketing themselves. As well as the usual display of the stars and stripes, a folded ceremonial flag became a nodal point in the narrative when it was sent by the first lady to the protagonist, who ran the veterans shelter. It was formally presented to her during a patriotic military parade at Disneyland, just as two fighter jets flew overhead. But one curious addition to this episode was a small-scale model of the White House that was built by designers and placed in the new shelter's backyard. There was little rationale offered for this extra building other than it would be fun for any children present. But, as well as simply linking the home project to the home of the star guest, this miniature replica could be interpreted as representing a political philosophy that calls for "smaller government" and for performing for oneself, in one's own backyard as it were, services that in other countries are provided by the government. Not a government *for* every home, in other words, but a government *in* every home.

New media scholar Henry Jenkins characterizes contemporary Western culture thus:

> The new knowledge culture has arisen as our ties to older forms of social community are breaking down, our rooting in physical geography is diminished, our bonds to the extended and even nuclear family are disintegrating, and our allegiances to nation-states are being redefined.
>
> (2006, 27)

Community, geography, family, nation, all are apparently losing relevance in large part due to evolving media arrangements. Both technological features (e.g., a reduction of face-to-face interaction) and media content (e.g., prioritizing individual gratification over communal goals) are typically cited as reasons for a reduction in social cohesion and civic engagement (e.g., Putnam 1995), though empirical studies have come up with mixed results.[37] What is striking, therefore, about home improvement programming is its effort to counter many of the trends Jenkins identifies and its determination to disprove claims about the demise of local social structures and the "end of geography" (Negroponte 1995).[38] One could argue that *Home Edition* remediates some of the features of new media and of digital culture in order to preserve traditional elements of the social order. Each home build is, in one sense, a triumphant mass-medium version of flash mobs and crowdsourcing[39] that at the same time underscores the importance of physical location and local community. At least this is the theory. In practice, the build disrupts the local neighborhood and draws attention to the fact that neighbors come out to help because of the catalyst of the television show. From the early morning bullhorn on, producers take for granted that their media presence constitutes such an important event that ordinary life can be suspended. Real-life neighbors are inconvenienced if not exiled: some are offered a per diem compensation if they have to move out (due to 24/7 lighting and noise) or if their lawns or gardens are destroyed. But what is not negotiable is the turning of their homes into a public media location. (When I visited one site I noticed a rather futile handwritten sign on a neighbor's lawn that read "Privacy Please!") If other local people show up to help out, we may well ask: Where were these people before the cameras rolled in? Is what we are witnessing on television a triumph of local community or a symptom of its failure?

Local, physical place clearly matters here, but it matters because it is mediated: more significant than physical change is the transforming of physical into mediated space. One would have to say then that the home makeover's validation of localism is more compensatory and nostalgic than a serious reversal of the trends Jenkins noted.

The scale of *Home Edition* enables media consumption to encompass social groups more extensive and varied than single individuals and it suggests that these structures of family or nation have not been superseded. However, the staged nature of their representations, particularly the fact that aid appears to mobilize only because of mediation, does to some extent weaken the proffered proof of their continuing strength. Regarding the health of the nation, in choosing to interpret America's foreign incursions as a sacrifice for freedom, makeover producers reflect government rhetoric and naturalize support for war. What we witness is not aggressive propagandizing but rather the constant promotion of national pride and a steady optimism that, as well as attracting solid ratings, may well enhance the morale of a people at war. The periodic and ongoing representations of those involved in the longest war(s) in American history may have the effect of domesticating warfare and the nation's perennial campaign against a nebulous enemy most commonly referred to as the abstract noun "Terror."

CHAPTER 4

Caring Capitalism

Creating Good(s)

American Express advertising urges its "members" to volunteer for good causes; Pepsi wants soda drinkers to "refresh" the world through charitable giving; the oil company Citgo declares "We share a common goal. It's called the common good"; Toyota is inviting people to use its technology "to improve the world"; and the big-box retailer Target affirms that it "is committed to social, economic and environmental well-being in every community."[1] The list, as they say, goes on. So what *is* going on here? One might conclude that these corporations were not in the business of making money but of giving it away, or at the very least that a primary function is leveraging their customer base in order to do good works. Some contemporary television reinforces this impression and to underline why it is so in tune with current economic trends, this chapter will make a broad assessment of the socioeconomic relations being reproduced on reality programming, relations that allow television to emerge as a form of "social media." We have seen *Home Edition* trying to alleviate domestic pressures accentuated by America's exporting of capitalism abroad. Now it is time to look at television's promotion of consumer capitalism at home—capitalism as a system, a philosophy, perhaps even a theology.

So far we have seen different levels of commercial input into reality programming. On the first level, we find techniques that enable the provider to pitch a product or secure brand exposure. Then there is a more active sponsorship that generates prestige for the sponsor as well as brand impression. But when financial support involves private businesses helping individuals in need, this scenario works on a higher, ethical plane that it shares with a new phase of corporate philanthropy, something we might term "caring capitalism."[2] This outreach has become a central component of modern business discourse in the United States and elsewhere, and we see it play out on reality television (RTV) when companies employ television as a mechanism for positioning themselves as a producer not only of goods but of social "good." The venture still ultimately ratifies the supremacy of the individual, of self-interest, and the economic status quo, but it is a form of public relations (PR) that attaches itself to the moral high ground. If regular advertising is a form of metonymy where one product stands for many other products, then this kind of PR is more of an allegorical dramatization of a commercial entity's worth (whether a company, a sector, or a system).

A particularly rich text for illustrating the mechanisms of caring capitalism is, again, *Home Edition*. This long-running series will be the main focus of this chapter, but much of the discussion applies to makeover TV in general. Programs that have imitated *Home Edition*'s building format include *Three Wishes* (NBC, 2005), *Town Haul* (TLC, 2005–6), and *School Pride*, while other formats that showcase caring capitalism include the clandestine *Secret Millionaire* (Channel 4, 2006–; Fox, 2008–) and *Undercover Boss* (Channel 4, 2009–; CBS, 2010). In each of these series ideological as well as physical work is taking place within a neoliberal paradigm in which capitalism is the hero, privatization is a solution to both business and personal problems, charity substitutes for social programs, and work bleeds into leisure. Viewers can only speculate as to the political intentions of those involved in this programming but it is possible to identify an interesting confluence of dramatic needs, commercial opportunity, and implicit political ideology. The need to make a profitable drama explains the focus on one family, on their pathetic circumstances, on their moral virtue, and on a happy ending, because the spectacle of benign forces raising up a lucky few just makes for better television than roundtables on social reform. The fact that private companies are helping only a handful of people is not criticized; rather the small scale comes across as heartwarming and even generous. This kind of sentimental depoliticization is a concern of, among others, Richard Sennett ([1974]1992), who laments what he regards as the widespread tyranny of intimacy that has come to replace public action with individual feeling and so weakens macro politics (339). One takes root at the expense of the other. On makeover TV, inadequacies are actually inverted, so that the paucity of support is capitalized on, via mediation, because it generates drama/ ratings.

Producers of makeover programming prefer to focus on rescue rather than root and on individual narratives of hard luck that ratify the central ideology of buying one's way to happiness. Nevertheless, not everything is smooth sailing once viewers venture even a little outside the dominant code (Hall 1980).[3] Some discrepancies are hard to miss. For instance, the basic thrust of charitable makeovers is that corporate America is great and good, but the underlying corollary is that a capitalist economy has serious flaws if people are in such need of rescue and, it is agreed, thoroughly deserve help. In fact, these programs are one of the few places viewers will see portrayals of struggling lower-middle-class (or in European terms, working-class) families on American TV.[4] However, the recipients of aid offer no criticism of the system. They feel no sense of entitlement. They display only stoic patience and deep appreciation for the aid they are given.

Such basic tensions, even contradictions, within capitalism have been managed on RTV, as elsewhere, through the central trope of the American Dream, a durable political apparatus that has long been used to smooth over socioeconomic disparities. There are implicit and explicit references to this concept throughout reality programming, though the phrase is particularly prominent in home makeovers, so closely is the concept tied to home ownership: for example, the current slogan for the National Association of Realtors is "Homeownership. The foundation of the American Dream" (2011). As a core capitalist faith and an indispensable component of American culture, the American Dream deserves more critical attention than it receives. This chapter will have room only to highlight some key aspects of the origin and current interpretation of this populist fantasy sufficient to give a sense of how this concept is being invoked on reality TV. Upcoming remarks will show how the significance of the privately owned family home as a materialization of the social order is both underlined and undermined by TV's privatizing of the American Dream of home ownership. Reality programming, I will argue, portrays the capitalist system as so potent that it appears to possess magical or even supernatural powers. Certainly, all makeover TV combines equally strong elements of the real and the fantastic. Unlike real life, there is no conflict with family members, no surgical mistakes, no problems with planning permission, not even bad plumbing. In this reality, television is the authority and can be relied upon to produce a fairy-tale ending. Some formats even appear to restage religious narratives, but it remains to be seen if they rise to the full height of spiritual transformation.

Welfare Capitalism

Makeover formats model a post-welfare circuit of privatized giving that implies that governmental aid has (for reasons unknown) been superseded. Government bureaucracy or public help of any kind are simply absent from the picture and those who offer private aid are lauded both for caring and for being so efficient about it. In their promotion of privatization, conservative governments from Bush to Cameron have emphasized charitable volunteerism. The 41st president used "a thousand points of light" (1988) to describe the beauty of having a constellation of many private contributions to the social good, and in announcing his major initiative of "the Big Society" (2010), British Prime minister David Cameron urged his nation:

> We've got to get rid of the centralised bureaucracy that wastes money and undermines morale. And in its place we've got to . . . open up public services to new providers like charities, social enterprises and private companies so we get more innovation, diversity and responsiveness to public need.[5]

In this neoliberal worldview, a reduction of public support is presented as empowering the individual and offering initiative and choice. This echoes the policies begun by Reagan and Thatcher in the 1980s and, though it is not often remarked upon, a net result of this neoliberalism is an increase in opportunities for generating PR. In this "kinder, gentler" marketplace, corporate entities can choose to transcend regular commercial parameters and through their largesse generate good PR not only for themselves but also for the economic system that supports them.

More significant even than the absence of government support is the erasure of any *expectations* of public support. What is offered instead on makeover TV is private agency made "public" only because it is mediated, not because socially mandated or tax based. In other words, the act of giving to those in need is public only to the extent that it is performed on camera. Moreover, this making public on camera is its genesis. As a pseudo-event, the transaction occurs because it will generate "publicity," a commercially valuable outcome. This, presumably, is what motivates private givers, rather than elected legislators, to offer support and to do so on an individual or personal basis (Deery 2006). That there is no shortage of people who need help is not the concern of producers or donors.

Laurie Ouellette and James Hay (2008) mount a convincing argument that television has a pragmatic and instrumental role in shifting the burden from public to private welfare in what they refer to as charity TV, a category that they suggest includes *Home Edition, Three Wishes* and *Pimp My Ride* (MTV, 2004–07). Their analysis underlines the extent to which reality TV is a "cultural technology" that aligns with, or synchronizes with, government policies regarding governing at a distance and with the need for neoliberal, self-enterprising individuals to manage themselves. TV thus becomes a sort of quasi-governmental agency offering viewer-citizens pragmatic skills and advice. These authors don't attribute agency to this strategy nor try to establish any direct link between government officials and TV producers, but they do effectively illustrate how RTV operates within a post-welfare context. My analysis attributes much of what goes on in makeover programming to the pressures of commercialization and to the promotion of businesses and commerce in general.

Whereas lifestyle programming (clothing, makeup, décor) tends to focus on individuals and a small core of change agents, *Home Edition* demonstrates television's capacity for much broader social networking. It goes beyond the basic model of attracting and selling viewers to producing a complex network of mutually reinforcing constituencies in the form of business networks, social networks, and inner audiences who, along with home viewers, all feed off each other's involvement in the programming. This mutually dependent structure proves television's reach and clout within national networks of capital. And while the on-screen construction of face-to-face social networks has the appearance of an ad hoc, tactical groundswell, it is also a successful strategy on the part of producers to make the most of the mainstream nature of their medium and its large audiences.[6] On a program like *Home Edition,* we are to admire how efficiently business organizes material and labor, how valid is the capitalist focus on the precise organization of space and time, and how immediate is the power of locally and nationally organized capital to change lives. Of course, it takes some behind-the-scenes advance planning to carry this off. Some weeks before filming producers engage with local business and political networks. A month in advance they engage a local building contractor and lumber company to prefabricate the building structure off-site. They also secure expedited building permission, ask special consideration from building inspectors, and ensure the cooperation of local police and traffic authorities. That aid comes not through government support but through corporate charity should not surprise anyone in an era when Reagan's heirs successfully redefined government aid as interference and icons such Gates, Buffet, and Bono now rival government intervention both nationally and internationally. The trend, today, is for private philanthropists to manage their donations like a business and, as economic missionaries, to import the model of market capitalism into other cultures as a force for good that can be universally applied. Their effort serves to support the axiom that capitalism begets democracy and that democracy is capitalist. Makeover programming can be seen as supporting, and as subverting, this onward march.

As alluded to above, whether or not it is ultimately self-serving, an idea building steam in advanced economies is that commercial providers can, and should, be socially responsible, philanthropic, and ethical—or at least appear to be. This stance is not new, but currently the pressure does appear to be mounting for capitalist organizations to display good citizenship and community involvement as well as profit. Corporate Social Responsibility (with an official abbreviation of CSR) is, today, a business philosophy that has spawned numerous manuals[7] and just about every corporate website has a page outlining its good citizenship mission. It seems companies now feel the need to establish not only that their product or service is good (high quality, affordable), but also that they are doing good as a company. This is where the makeover showcase becomes valuable. The involvement of private companies in such programs is presented as though someone at Ford or Sears had a good idea about how to help a particular family so this aid was freely given and not because the company wanted to launch a new vehicle or appliance. Or rather, since there are no representatives from these companies on camera, it is "Sears" or "Ford" the brands that offer timely aid and become an ethical role model for the viewer.

In an excellent account of nineteenth- and early twentieth-century corporate relations, Roland Marchand (1998) notes that as industrialized companies expanded beyond family concerns their advertising began to publicize the company's philanthropic outreach, not unlike the PR that is reemerging on reality programming. In the late nineteenth century, he notes that businesses felt the need to counter public suspicions that "soulless" corporations had become too big and too profit oriented to be trusted. There was a crisis of legitimacy as businesses and their "cathedrals of commerce"[8] began to dwarf religious and community organizations yet were unsure of their wider social role. Soon "the quest of large corporations for enhanced social and moral legitimacy went forward with an almost evangelical ardor" (Marchand 1998, 4). Fearing government regulation, late nineteenth-century industrialists could no longer simply dismiss wider sociopolitical grumblings with the infamous nonchalance of William Vanderbilt's "The public be damned!" In a defensive maneuver, they began to engage in—and, perhaps more importantly, to publicize—good works, either within their own company structures or in a wider but still local community. As paterfamilias, company heads (and often founders) boasted of their provision of worker housing and education and their involvement in the local community, in order to counter the notion that corporations were "faceless" and unaccountable. But at the same time, company publicity stressed that large is good and that, by being large, corporations were able to serve the nation. In an effort to stave off unionization and class conflict, businesses were projected as hierarchical but loving families under the benign directorship of a founding father, notable early examples being Cadbury's in Britain and NCR (National Cash Register) in the United States, where corporate care extended to stipulating that employees had salt-free and fat-free diets (Marchand 1998, 20). This "welfare capitalism" (Marchand) helped with the discipline, morale, and retention of workers, but it also served a larger strategy of protecting capitalism and private ownership when these were under scrutiny. When Roosevelt's New Deal posed a serious threat and the president promoted the four freedoms (of speech, of religion, freedom from want, freedom from fear) business leaders proposed spending money on PR to defend what they insisted was the "fifth freedom": the "US system of free enterprise" (Jackall 1995, 359; Marchand 1998, 322–3).

This combination of large-enough-to-help but localized-enough-to-care is a strong current in contemporary business PR and is well demonstrated by corporate participation in reality makeovers. In recent years there has been no shortage of bad PR due to corporate scandals, bad business practices, and the vision of a greedy capitalist class prospering at the expense of the ordinary person (Enron, AIG, Wall Street, and the banks). At the same time, in a transcendence of mere production, many of today's major companies have evolved from simple manufacture to the maintenance of a brand, to the creation of an attitude or philosophy that transcends but adds value to goods and services (Klein 2002). Since a company's image and reputation, as embodied in the brand, carry both symbolic and stock market value, it has become more imperative than ever to maintain a good, including ethical or socially constructive, image.[9] This is something economists Joseph Pine and James Gilmore (2007) recommend as the latest focus in capitalist development. Addressing some higher social cause lends a company "influential authenticity" (72), which they maintain is an invaluable asset in today's economy. Certainly more and more corporations feel obliged to authenticate grandiose "community statements" with online reports proving the extent of their philanthropic work. Take the world's largest retailer, Wal-Mart (ASDA in the United Kingdom). This company has for some time been positioning itself as "a store of the community" that gives back in local aid—at the same time as it generates bad publicity over its own labor practices that one could argue help precipitate this kind of need.[10]

A related trend is to present an individual's act of consumption as a form of charity, giving the consumer a feeling of participating in a larger social context.[11] For example, buying tampons in the First World will trigger Tampax (Proctor and Gamble) to provide tampons for girls in Africa. Or the aforementioned Pepsi campaign (endorsed by Andy Cohen, producer of several reality series), suggests that its customers can help support charitable causes and vote for their favorite cause online.[12] In another twist, ABC's parent company has used its sponsorship of independent consumer volunteerism as a way to promote its own image and services. One of Disney's 2010 advertising campaigns promised a one-day pass to its magical kingdom for anyone who volunteers for a day in some charitable task: the television ad portrays people building a home (reminiscent of *Home Edition*). Such efforts mean that the middle-class consumer is having their charitable giving managed by (and for) larger corporate entities, another efficiency like that of conglomerates eliminating middle-class and independent local proprietors, thereby deconstructing older models of "community."

By playing *its* role in philanthropic networking, TV entertainment is positioning itself as a form of "social media." Ordinarily this term simply refers to the use of widely accessible web technologies for interactive communication that may or may not produce outcomes in the offline world: anything from arranging a date to starting a revolution. As previously discussed, television is not itself a highly interactive medium but is increasingly articulating with technologies that afford interactivity and, in the case of makeover programming, this articulation does support action in the offline world by mobilizing viewers to do some social good. With very little outlay, TV broadcasters are able to utilize the Internet to link viewers to already established charitable organizations and so, however cynical we might be about underlying business motives, this move brings technical convergence into the realm of the ethical. An early example is ABC's Better Community Outreach Program, which was launched in 2005 (also discussed by Ouellette and Hay 2008). At some point during every *Home Edition* episode a member of the design team encourages viewers to go the Better Community website to learn how to become involved in other charitable projects recommended by ABC. The website for *School Pride* (NBC's answer to *Home Edition*) similarly offers visitors the opportunity to become involved in independent volunteer organizations. During the show the traditional NBC rainbow icon is tied to a "make a more colorful world" slogan, thus associating a legacy brand with new ventures in good deeds. Both networks suggest that volunteering for charitable organizations is a matter of individuality and of entertainment. ABC's Getting Involved page opens with: "Sometimes, the hardest part of volunteering can be finding an opportunity that fits your personality. Below are some great tips to help you get involved, and to make your volunteer experience a more enjoyable and rewarding one."[13] Indeed, as Ouellette and Hay (2008) also observe, on this site volunteerism is being framed as "consumer choice and lifestyle maximization" (56). They link this and other public-private partnerships to the Bush (Sr.) notion of civic entrepreneurship and the Points of Light initiative. Interestingly, the Points of Light website employs business-speak to declare the foundation's intention to "Mobilize corporations to tap the human capital of businesses to achieve impact."[14] Individual volunteerism is a resource to "tap," with no need for anything as crass as payment. This is a sentimental capital that TV makeovers also know how to tap. The fact that these series attract hundreds of volunteers reduces labor costs in many instances to zero, an ideal endpoint for capitalism: for anyone who can convince workers that their unremunerated labor is really leisure, or that their work is a moral or spiritual obligation that is its own reward, will likely profit.

Another good example of TV-web philanthropy is the role of CVS, a prominent *Home Edition* sponsor since 2008. In line with their donations to the TV show, spot ads during the television broadcast position CVS as a company made up of individuals who care deeply about their community. After a series of soft and hazy animated graphics, a voiceover asks: "Isn't it nice that there's a pharmacy that cares as much as you do?"; at which point, a URL appears on the television screen.[15] The URL is for a site that invites users to share stories about everyday individuals who care about others. The impetus is a company-sponsored competition to select the grand winner amongst these care givers. The site therefore rewards ordinary people with media attention and a few with financial prizes, but also works to the company's advantage by reinforcing the theme of its ad campaign and its contributions to the popular TV show, adding to its mutually flattering claim that the company "cares as much as you do." The more expensive TV ads gesture toward the notion of a caring community; the website attempts to fulfill the rhetoric and create one. Not to be outdone, another longtime *Home Edition* sponsor, Ford, launched an online competition where people are asked to write in to nominate a "local hero" (echoing the rhetoric of *Home Edition*) who will receive an F150 truck and some prize money, perhaps to target a more masculine demographic.[16] And yet another sponsor publicizing its community outreach as well as its connection to *Home Edition* is Sears. Recent marketing has revived the company's early association with home-building and seized on the notion of the American Dream, a phrase Sears practically tried to copyright for its own purposes when in 2002 it launched the "Sears American Dream Campaign[sm]" with "ambassador" Ty Pennington from *Home Edition*.[17] Company rhetoric connects private home ownership, nuclear family support, and, of course, acquiring a full range of appliances. Sears' website builds further synergy by itemizing how many of its products were used in each *Home Edition* episode and urges visitors to "Start building your own dream now," presumably by shopping at its stores.

But while companies seek to capitalize on the larger implications of their involvement in charitable programming, producers never propose a solution that entails collective political action. This decontextualization is typical of what Ulrich Beck (1992) refers to as a "second modernity" where a sub-political individualism ignores institutional and collective needs and means of reform. Reality producers offer only a partial and depoliticized back-story with just enough context to encourage viewers to have some emotional reaction.[18] Any deeper digging into the sociopolitical substructure is meticulously avoided by an industry that tends to fear anything that could be considered controversial lest it scare off advertisers (whether or not it scares off viewers). A certain amount of depoliticization is due also to the fact that television reaches large numbers of people but doesn't reach them collectively as a group. So by itself it is *not*, in this sense, a social medium.

Those whom *Home Edition* rescues are portrayed as unusually unfortunate. They experience extraordinary medical problems or misfortunes due to a natural disaster or war. So while the stress this puts on the system suggests something is not adequate, no one on camera complains about a social arrangement in which a medical emergency or serious injury plunges a family into dire need. Nor does anyone ask about contributing factors such as a steady decline in middle-class incomes. Refusing the social scale, the media industry and its sponsors apply a heartwarming band aid to a chosen few. The focus is on families, on mutually supporting groups who are rewarded for having tried to make it on their own without getting bitter. An appropriate subject for a home makeover is a family who is exquisitely reluctant to ask for help. Producer Tom Forman reveals: "The kinds of families we're looking for don't say, 'Gee, I need help.' They're quietly trying to solve their problems themselves and it's a neighbor or a coworker who submits an application on their behalf."[19] As Ouellette and Hay (2008) note, such candidates are rewarded for modeling neoliberal responsibility and self-empowerment even if they are having a tough time succeeding at it. We do not hear about the many applicants who apply to the show but don't get the help they asked for. The nearest presenters come to acknowledging the inadequacy of trying to help one family at a time is when faced with a disaster like Katrina. More typically, viewers are encouraged to weep cathartically at the decency of individual benefactors and the great good fortune of individual recipients, while the system that produced these asymmetries remains unexamined. Similarly, although *School Pride* attempts the renovation of an entire public school, because it is RTV it has to happen in one week with volunteers who are supervised by a TV design team that includes a photogenic SWAT commander and a former Miss USA, participants whose skills appear to be more telegenic than practical. Not surprisingly, the volunteers end up doing little more than literally papering over the cracks and one can't help seeing their largely cosmetic improvements as a metaphor for the more systemic underfunding of public education.

Ministering

Producers and hosts are more comfortable underlining ethical implications and the valuable moral lessons that can be gleaned from each episode.[20] *Home Edition* immediately began with the notion of the deserving poor, in contrast to the light-hearted, urban frolic of the likes of *Queer Eye*.[21] The fact that applicants want only what is best for their family deflects charges of narcissism leveled at other reality shows. Those being helped on *Home Edition* or on surgical makeovers are hardworking, uncomplaining, and rather modest types who are not personally very ambitious. They tend to work in worthwhile but low-income service sector jobs such as teaching, nursing, or firefighting, and they are often rewarded for helping other people despite their own need. Similarly uncomplaining workers appear in shows like *The Secret Millionaire* and *Undercover Boss*. These, too, are profiles of ordinary people working hard and trying to advance even though they face hardship. If producers reward those who are industrious and themselves help others in need then their virtue makes for effective drama, but it also compounds the unarticulated presence of widespread social need. Occasionally producers reward someone who has succeeded in getting their family out of serious poverty, but while the families they rescue are technically homeless for a brief spell, *Home Edition* generally ignores the many long-term homeless whose numbers could be seen as a comment on the moral failure of a neoliberal market economy. These invisible citizens remain the uncanny, the unmentionable, and apparently the unworthy.[22] Their absence reminds us how under capitalism the private dwelling is closely linked to identity and rights: if an individual has no home address, often he or she cannot get a job or much other bureaucratic help. The homeless are therefore at once invisible (bureaucratically) and exposed (on the street). They forfeit the basic right to privacy by having to live out their existence always in public. The chosen TV family, in contrast, relinquishes their privacy voluntarily. They are not the very poor or embarrassingly desperate. They have fallen into financial difficulties because of circumstances outside their control and their situation is something for which the audience can feel immediate sympathy.

Producers get to cherry pick who to help in accordance with televisual rather than social needs. One woman who was single-handedly looking after several severely disabled children is described by a TV designer as "the jackpot of worthiness"—a jackpot presumably because of the financial windfall for producers. But the language also reflects the low odds for those who apply for help.[23] There is a logical correlation between subject misery and commercial profit. Sometimes the producers' desire to feature the most extreme disability rises almost to the point of absurdity: for example, in the Llanes family the father, two daughters, and grandmother are blind, the son is deaf, and the only other family member, the mother, is battling cancer (aired 9/17/06). But whereas the 1950s *Queen For a Day* and its Applause O Meter encouraged audiences to support simply the most pathetic case without knowing much about their character, the situation here is given a more affirmative and less maudlin spin in that those selected appear to have some considerable moral virtue as well as indefatigable optimism. The idea is that they will "pay it forward" by subsequently helping someone else; a term popularized by science fiction writer Robert A. Heinlein in the 1950s but is particularly current in the age of Oprah and of diminishing social services.

Yet, though every ending is indeed happy, not everyone chosen is necessarily as virtuous as they appear on camera. Occasional reports surface that suggest that producers do not always properly vet their subjects or that they remodel them for television purposes. One recipient who was presented as a tireless mother of adopted children has a sizable police file (Debbie Oatman, aired 5/20/07).[24] Her ex-husband told local journalists that her main motive for adopting children—the basis for her receiving a home makeover—was the income it provided (Paul Grondahl, *Albany Times Union*, May 20, 2007). Then there is the case of the Leomiti family who, it is claimed, turned out the children they took in soon after *Home Edition* built them all a house. The children tried to sue *Home Edition* producers and ABC/Disney for not getting the home they felt they were promised and they were upset that the episode aired and continued to make money for ABC after they no longer lived there. However, the case was dismissed on the grounds that ABC did not promise them a home or owe them anything, a stark reminder that makeover subjects ought not to feel any sense of entitlement. On very rare occasions a prior criminal record is acknowledged and becomes part of the recuperative narrative. One episode featured a father who was arrested for stealing a car radio when he was 17 but who has since attempted to turn his life around (aired 1/14/07). In an obvious analogy, his legal rehab was rewarded by a home rehab for his family. A more famous rehabilitation was attempted by Martha Stewart, for a time the epitome of corporate deception and greed, who came out of prison and right into a new reality series that she and Donald Trump conceived while she was still doing time (*The Apprentice: Martha Stewart*, NBC 2005). Stewart was attempting to spin criminal notoriety into media cachet and to reclaim her brand. She almost entirely succeeded.

One well-known campaign for MasterCard bases its approach on a pious acknowledgment that "there are some things money can't buy" but meanwhile shows us how much pleasure can be had by purchasing "everything else." Both MasterCard and *Home Edition* engage with the desire for material gratification as well as the belief that there is more to life than material gratification. The reality series showcases those who place some values above the marketplace but whose ultimate embrace of material goods reassures us that they are also content members of a consumer society, not some overly pious or subversive element. The rule appears to be that people are helped when they have shown that they put love before material items; but then the reward *is* material acquisition and the recipients are very gratified by it. This is not as paradoxical as it sounds: the recipients don't reject consumerism but simply could not take part in it to the extent that they and everyone else would like. However, this transaction also inevitably (and inadvertently) points to an ultimate lack in consumer capitalism and the grand evasion at the heart of advertising, which is that those who promote products associate them with love and other strong values and emotions but that the products themselves can't deliver these. Some reality formats test which comes first, the emotion or the goods, by pitting one against the other to see how far market forces have come and to judge what should be, in Bourdieu's terms, *in*-alienable and not for sale; for example, *Joe Millionaire* (Fox, 2003), *For Love or Money* (NBC, 2003–4) and gamedocs like *Survivor, Big Brother,* and so on. Often money wins. But the ethos of wholesome makeovers is that, ideally, one shouldn't have to choose between love and goods. For those watching whose ship has not yet come in, the programming suggests that the love of family can and should compensate them—but they should still keep their eyes on the horizon.

As we have already seen, makeover shows infuse consumption with positive emotions as part of their re-personalizing of commerce. In the last century, mass production and distribution precipitated a transition from the personal interaction between producer and retailer or retailer and customer to a more aloof relationship between all three. Today, despite the recent rise of farmers' markets and other preindustrial models, most consumption in advanced economies takes place in front of disengaged and uninvested employees of large corporations or in front of icons on computer screens.[25] The TV makeover realigns provider and recipient into an emotionally charged and intimate transaction—a connection that suggests there is a neo-feudalism behind contemporary privatization. We witness the overt indebtedness of those who are saved and the consequent gratitude they owe to their protector, a contract that gratifies the known giver (Sears or whomever) and obligates the known recipient (the people we see on-screen). Families of contractors hug families they've helped, surgeons hug patients, CEOs from mortgage companies, insurance companies, or even university presidents appear on camera to grant deserving subjects a release from financial burdens, just, it seems, out of the goodness of their hearts. Public aid is required by legislation, is impersonal, and is as far as possible comprehensive and objectively assessed. Reality TV makes the most of the fact that private aid is voluntary, personal, subjectively selected, and under no obligation to be comprehensive.

Another sentimental model showcased on reality TV is that of individual "social entrepreneurship," whereby wealthy people directly decide where their money goes rather than entrusting it to some other organization. This conspicuous compassion illustrates another privilege of acquiring wealth, not opulent spending (*The Real Housewives, My Super Sweet 16* [MTV, 2005–08]) but the satisfaction of being a private or corporate philanthropist who earns deep gratitude and respect from others. On *The Secret Millionaire,* a wealthy individual goes undercover in a poor district in order to identify people who deserve their help. Whereas a bureaucrat would allocate funds based on need and entitlements, in this instance it is entirely up to the private businessperson to decide who receives what amount. At the end of one week, the benefactors reveal to others that they were only pretending to be poor but are in actuality very wealthy (how they acquired this wealth is not always clear, for *their* personal lives are not under scrutiny). The climax comes when they dole out their checks in person to extremely grateful recipients. A similar dynamic operates on *Undercover Boss,* though this time the transaction is not between strangers but between employers and employees. Under the pretence of making a documentary, a company head works in disguise alongside his or her employees for a week with an eye to improving efficiency and working conditions (assuming these are not mutually exclusive). The secret surveillance is framed as benign because it ultimately helps the workers and humbles the boss. It also, of course, provides great PR for business leaders and their companies. Indeed, the series announces in its opening segment that it is a response to images of corporate heads being "out of touch." At the end of each episode, the CEOs summon employees to the company headquarters where they reveal their real position of authority and, like a feudal lord, decide whom to reward for their hard work and fealty. This personalizes the relationship between HQ and ordinary employee not in order to alter the power hierarchy but to legitimize it. Reform is made through an executive order, not government regulation. Although the executive response is seen as decent and even sentimental, it is also a rational business initiative and, again, great advertising. From the recipient's viewpoint, neither on *Undercover Boss* nor on *The Secret Millionaire* is there any (open) resentment of the disguise or surveillance, nor of the economic disparities it reveals, only profound gratitude for the charitable check or promises to improve working conditions. Once again, the dramatic interest is more intense when we are given one individual helping other individuals than if we were observing government bureaucrats dispensing standard aid to thousands. Privatization and drama are mutually supportive.

Reclaiming the American Dream

One of the most effective aids for pushing through marketization and other legislation supporting corporate power and growth at the top is the self-consciously entitled and undoubtedly hegemonic "American Dream."[26] Retold by virtually every American president in key addresses down through the decades, this is the great origin story that holds together America's collective imaginary, and its handmaiden is television.[27] Since it began broadcasting, television is where this vision has been defined and showcased and today we see the concept being reinforced in a number of reality formats, particularly the makeover variety.[28] In essence, the Dream implies that the United States offers considerable social mobility so that anyone can be rich or powerful—but especially rich. Or, at least, almost anyone can attain the social markers of a nice private home and secure family life, so long as they apply some individual effort. The reality is that in the United States wealth transmission has for some time been quite static and economic opportunities not as common as people think.[29] But that is the key point: what people think. The mediation of the American Dream through media-advertising flattens a basic feature of contemporary America, which is the steep hierarchy in wealth and the stability of income disparities.[30] Although there are numerous self-made billionaires and other bootstrapping notables, very few of those born into the lowest quintile in the income spectrum move upward and few of those in the top quintile move downward. A similar pattern occurs in contemporary Britain and other developed nations,[31] although in America the income disparity is particularly stark and the gap between rich and poor is currently unprecedented (Lardner and Smith 2007).

Meanwhile, the American Dream holds out hope and creates sympathy for those who really do have and hold wealth (hence, perhaps, the lower classes' reluctance to heavily tax the very wealthy). Collectively, the Dream may be America's most powerful political delusion and one of its media's greatest creations. Hardly a day goes by without the phrase "the American Dream" appearing in some US media product.[32] But makeover programming provides the perfect distillation. In episode after episode this phrase is reverently invoked; in some instances, it is linked to recent immigrant families but in most cases it is the shared aspiration of those who have lived their lives on American soil.[33] One could say that from its inception reality TV has engaged with the concept of the American Dream and its relationship to American identity. When the documentarian Craig Gilbert produced the prototype of *An American Family* (PBS, 1973), its Californian location was deliberately chosen to represent the last frontier for capitalist expansion, just like the old West. In this case, the chosen family appeared to be enjoying all the material trappings of the Dream without any need for outside help. An associate producer is quoted as saying: "We were looking for a family that . . . . you see on a television commercial, in a pretty house, that has the best of what this country can offer materially" (Ruoff 2002, 15). In one pointed montage, visuals of the mother loading up her giant shopping cart are juxtaposed with a classroom discussion of the Reconstruction period, which her son ventures opened up the opportunity for everyone to achieve "the American

Dream." Whether or not this was true of the Reconstruction period, it was certainly the case that in the 1970s middle-class whites were enjoying their greatest income growth, and though in this documentary there were some hints of fraying at the edges there was no sign of the middle-class crisis to come.[34]

As every American schoolchild knows, the privately owned home is a central component of the American Dream and so it comes as no surprise that the phrase is often heard on *Home Edition*. However, its use here is ironic if we know the history of the concept and its original author's intentions. The idea of the American Dream began as cry for the maintenance of an egalitarian society that would sustain a large and resourceful middle class; whereas it is trotted out here during what looks like this class's demise. The series holds on to the phrase as a sacred credo but assimilates viewers into seeing aid coming from benevolent corporations, a scenario that does not at all align with the original vision. Actually, not much is commonly known about the history or ideological function of "the American Dream," despite its frequent invocation. It is not generally known that the celebrated phrase was popularized by James Truslow Adams in a history entitled, rather grandly, *The Epic of America* (1931).[35] A Book-of-the-Month Club selection and a best seller in its day, the book is now largely unread. Most people assume the phrase has an earlier origin, but though Adams looked back to explain the Puritan doctrine of hard work, he was also writing in a particular historical moment. He composed his narrative in a time of economic crisis, right after the stock market crash (1929) and before Roosevelt's New Deal (1933–37). His account can therefore be seen as a sort of pep talk, a rallying of national spirits by going back to what built America and made it great. And what, to Adams' mind, made it great was something he repeatedly termed the American Dream. Adams was a member of the American elite, a graduate of Yale with experience as an investment banker and political appointee,[36] but (and this is significant) he stressed that the dream of advancement was, at its best, shared and mutual. Those who use the phrase glibly in years since may need to be reminded that Adams had in mind the establishment of a particular social structure that offered an alternative to European hierarchical class-based societies, a new nation where "no dead hands of custom or exaction" would push people back into their place (69). The core idea was a meritocracy and equality of opportunity that would allow a large middle class to flourish, and indeed its flowering was a noticeable achievement of twentieth-century America. However, many of today's rescue makeovers signal perhaps the most significant political development of the current era, which is the steady evisceration of the class Adams hoped would greatly expand.

The vision of a meritocracy in which success is earned through individual effort and talent is showcased on series like *American Idol, Top Chef, Project Runway* and other career competitions where everyone supposedly has an equal chance (though of course those selected for TV are a tiny percentage of the population). On *Home Edition,* however, subjects are at the mercy of dark forces beyond their control and their need for rescue is a significant departure from the vision of a level playing field toward a more fatalistic and aleatory model of selection and luck. Unlike other charitable organizations such as Habitat for Humanity where "sweat equity" is required, *Home Edition* families contribute only their ritualistic emotional labor. Some are active initially in seeking help: indeed, many applicants have to be pretty enterprising during the application process (Ouellette and Hay 2008, 53). Other families are simply nominated. But once chosen, every family remains mostly reactive.[37] The greatest agency they are allowed is when they ritualistically yell "Move that Bus!," a moment that is cued only when sufficient suspense has been built and the cameras are poised for the big money shot.

Adams' Dream is distorted further because on reality makeovers advancement is strongly wedded to individual consumption rather than egalitarian reform. It is easy to see in US history a major shift from an early Puritan focus on attaining salvation to a later more secular emphasis on attaining wealth. But there has been another equally significant shift from communitarianism to an individualism expressed through consumption.[38] After industrialization and intense market competition, after the excesses of the '20s and the insecurity of capitalist investment, Adams felt compelled to impress upon his 1930s readers that the American Dream is

> not a dream of motor cars and high wages merely, but a dream of social order in which each man and each woman shall be able to attain to the fullest stature of which they are innately capable, and be recognized by others for what they are, regardless of the fortuitous circumstances of birth or position.
>
> (404)[39]

He cautioned that if the Dream were defined by business interests then the citizen would be reduced to a consumer (as was being championed by Henry Ford). The ordinary person, "goaded" by advertising was, he felt, already "getting into a treadmill in which he earns, not that he may enjoy, but that he may spend, in order that the owners of the factories may grow richer" (407–8). Adams' fears were fully realized midcentury when the Dream came to signify the very lust for individual consumption that he had opposed. Levittown and Chevrolet, the suburban home and this year's automobile, these came to represent the achievement of the Dream—though in trying to bring the vision back to social justice Martin Luther King Jr. (1968) famously drew on the trope to point out that opportunity had not been extended to all.[40] For most of the twentieth century, the concept of the American Dream became a powerful driving force behind a consumerist, free market economy and one could argue that a major consequence of Adams' invoking this vision was, ironically, to diminish it and to help mask inequality while still keeping up consumer demand. In other words, faith that the Dream existed took attention away from reform. As the cultural historian Lizabeth Cohen (2003) has documented in her study of the politics of mass consumption, after World War II a "Consumer's Republic" arose in which the democratic and egalitarian nature of US society—in contrast to Soviet communism—was measured by how much people had to spend on consumer items. It was taken for granted that mass consumption was synonymous with social equality and the achievement of the American Dream (125). Though lack of opportunity remained, Nixon, among others, insisted that consumer choice proved political freedom, most famously in his kitchen showdown with Khrushchev in 1959 (126).

Despite income statistics, faith in the American Dream survives today as a national belief, even a sort of religious faith that, like other religious beliefs, supports the political status quo by attributing lack of success to individual failure. A show like *Home Edition* does not blame those who have not succeeded but nor does it challenge the basic faith that opportunity does exist.[41] The somewhat paradoxical statement on the part of TV presenters that, thanks to them, some families have now (by proxy) achieved the Dream casts a romantic glow on the proceedings and it would seem churlish to break the spell by asking why so many cannot make it on their own. In particular, recent home improvement shows gloss over the fact that the American Dream of home ownership has had a ruinous impact on the global economy because it is *not* supported by a robust middle class. Given that the push for as many Americans as possible to own a home forced millions around the world to suffer various degrees of hardship due to an overextension of credit to homeowners who had to default on their mortgages, the quick fix being offered by upbeat reality shows is beginning to look increasingly desperate.

The Magic Kingdom and Beyond

The fact is that reality makeovers are always part fantasy and that much of this fantasy is inspired by the commercial world. These shows reflect not so much real life as they do advertising—for ads work, too, by conjoining the everyday and the fantastic. One fantasy shared by advertising and TV makeovers is that in the world of desire the usual financial constraints do not apply and every wish can be granted. As a realization of this fantasy, TV makeovers feature a huge and sudden influx of goods seemingly out of nowhere, a largesse that mystifies and fetishizes the production of commodities. Drawing on Marx's early observation of industrial fetishism, Baudrillard notes how today's abundance of goods

> continues to be experienced as a daily miracle, in so far as it does not appear to be something produced and extracted, something won after a historical and social effort, but something *dispensed* by a beneficent mythological agency to which we are the legitimate heirs: Technology, Progress, Growth, etc.
>
> ([1970] 1998, 32; author's emphasis)

Actually, it may be more accurate to say that most people forget this "daily miracle" but that makeover programming awakens us to the wondrous nature of our consumption. Part of the fantasy is what Gareth Palmer (2007) refers to as a "magical market" where love trumps finances. The paid professionals who participate in TV makeovers reiterate how morally uplifting it is to be involved and their appearance on the show is portrayed less as a career break or commercial opportunity than as an inspirational social project. On *Home Edition* the fact that most members of the design team have their own media/entertainment background and ambitions is never mentioned.[42] To reinforce that they are helpers rather than TV employees, each is asked to personally commit to the project as though they had some choice in the matter. They demonstrate this initially by participating in a ritualistic sports huddle on the way to the scene, as part of a wholesome and manipulative attempt to move the audience and get it primed for the emotional journey ahead.

A "fairy-tale ending" is how makeover producers, hosts, and recipients frequently describe the journey's end. According to the *Extreme Makeover* website, "lucky individuals" are given "a truly Cinderella-like experience: A real life fairy tale in which their wishes come true, not just to change their looks, but their lives and destinies."[43] This simile is given substance (of sorts) when the Cinderella coach actually makes an appearance during an *Extreme Makeover* wedding episode set in Disneyland, a location that has copyrighted its ability to "make dreams come true." *Extreme Makeover* is from Disney-owned ABC, as is *The Bachelor* (ABC, 2002–), which promotes a similar fairy-tale narrative and also the occasional Cinderella carriage. But all image makeovers essentially reenact the iconic scene from Disney where the poor and bedraggled Cinderella is suddenly provided with a stage coach, ball gown, and all the accessories for a milestone entry into the social sphere.[44] Jennifer Pozner dismisses *The Bachelor's* fairy-tale motif as "the saccharine coating that masks the genre's chauvinistic and anachronistic ideas about women and men, about love and sex, about marriage and money" (2010, 46). It works because the fairy-tale romance is an old story that is still compelling and still generates a strong, perhaps irrational, emotional response.

Today, the adjectival phrase "fairy-tale" indicates a happy ending, something that is better than expected, not the more grim (or Grimm) versions involving hobgoblins, evil witches, and moral ambiguity that were subsequently sanitized by Walt Disney. When owners of new homes or bodies report that their transformation is a dream come true—perhaps *the* central trope of all makeover programming—their enthusiasm does have some validity to the extent that surgeons or designers have indeed made real the imagined life promised by decades of media-advertising. This consummation reflects the strong nexus of consumption, entertainment, and American innovation that the mid-western conservative Walt Disney was anxious to promote in his film productions and even more overtly in theme parks (Wasko 2001; Nadel 2005) where he attempted to brand American reality— and in some ways to brand reality as American: America representing the best of what is possible for humanity. On makeovers, as with Disney's theme parks and animations, there is more evidence of magic than of industry, and viewers are encouraged to dream and submit rather than protest or agitate. So often is Disney's "dreams come true" slogan invoked on RTV that it was probably inevitable that a show called *My Yard Goes Disney* (HGTV, 2011) would appear to finally make the branding explicit. In this series, coproduced by Disney Parks, a family's garden is transformed into a mini Disney theme park, thus extending the brand further into the private sphere and in the process showing some promotional footage of a variety of Disney parks. Thus a producer in Disney's "Broadcast Marketing" division enthuses about what a great time he has had working on this showcase.[45]

Other analogies between TV makeovers and fairy tales (Disneyfied or otherwise) have been suggested: some scholars have noted the shape shifting (Bratich 2007), the resolution of trauma (Heyes 2007), the moral lessons (Bratich 2007), and the exoticism and clear moral lines that appeal to youth audiences (Palmer 2008, 12). Another advantage might be atemporality. Traditional fairy tales are usually set in some unspecified faraway place and time and makeovers, too, are timeless in many regards. Most episodes float in an immediate but atemporal zone with no reference to contemporary events that could date them, or devalue reruns. The fairy-tale analogy is therefore a matter not just of engaging the audience's imagination but also of keeping business options open.

We have witnessed so far a good deal of sentimentality, ethical rumination, and suggestions of magic, but do TV makeovers go so far as to associate corporate aid with a supernatural or religious authority? Are television's transformations so rapid and flawless as to appear miraculous? Perhaps the best candidate for investing makeovers with something like a religious significance is the surgical makeover, for more than other service providers the surgeon has power over nature and, ultimately, over life and death. As they stand in long robes under the illumination of powerful lights it is easy to see the surgeons as playing God, however humble their demeanor. Toby Miller (2008) refers to a 2006 Kaiser Foundation study of American reality TV that found that on-screen surgeons are presented as performing miraculous feats without any remotely critical perspectives. These "deities in scrubs," as Miller calls them, appear as magicians whose work is beyond ordinary understanding (128). Indeed, such is their power that they promise to prolong youth and/or alter the Creator's original design to produce "natural" results. "We gave her a beautiful, luscious natural mouth," one doctor boasts (*Extreme Makeover*, aired 2/5/04). Most crucially, the surgeons' skills allow them to take on one of religion's primary functions, which is overcoming the fact of material deterioration. Much religious doctrine has to do with the relations between the material and the immaterial: with policing the boundaries between the two, setting priorities, and ultimately managing the transition from one to the other at the point of death. All major religions have in common a prioritization of the immaterial (spirit, soul) over the material (body, materialism), the fundamental aim being to give meaning to the deterioration of the body and its disappearance following death. In Christianity, divinity finds flesh in order that others might transcend the flesh by being resurrected into a new life. Many traditions deny that physical decay is the whole story or even worthy of attention and counter with the existence of some spiritual being housed within the body that is released at the moment of death. Modern surgery offers an entirely different approach by doing everything it can to prevent death and, in the case of cosmetic surgery, by preventing signs of decay as a precursor to death. The body, in other words, is no longer a vessel but a raison d'être.

Noting the tremendous economic and psychological investment we now place in it, Baudrillard contends that the body "has today become an *object of salvation*" that "has literally taken over that moral and ideological function from the soul" ([1970]1998, 129; author's emphasis). Actually it is, as he also points out, a resacralization after many centuries of the body being regarded as subversive of spiritual values, as the site of weakness, vice, and sin (often associated with Woman). There are, no doubt, several reasons for this preoccupation with the body. For one thing, tending to the body is encouraged in consumer cultures because it generates all kinds of business, whereas many organized religions either downplay or repress the body and with it all forms of materialism. From Buddha to Jesus, religious founders have shown little support for storing up "treasures on earth, where moth and rust consume" (Matthew 6, 19). One could conclude then that, given the demands of a consumerist economy, the soul simply had to go.[46]

Advertising-inspired makeovers certainly give the body its due and, without going so far as to claim that these entertainments rival religion, it is interesting to trace their debt to sacred narratives. At base, all makeovers share the religious faith in the ability to improve and to renew. More specifically, in many style and especially surgical makeovers each subject goes through distinct stages that mimic the central narratives and rites of Christianity: confession, sacrifice, rebirth, and final revelation.[47] To begin, they must frankly confess their inadequacies before a sympathetic and wise authority. Surgeons become confessors and judges who, as Virginia Blum (2003) observes, take on the priestly function of distinguishing the normal from the aberrant and reasonable expectations from immoderate cravings (274). Much the same could be said of the style experts who assess the sartorial worth of each subject and force them to acknowledge their stylistic shortcomings.[48] In each case, subjects confess by disrobing or robing and thereby putting their sins on display. In both secular and religious makeovers, the acknowledgment of imperfection and the willingness to hand oneself over to discipline and surveillance is the necessary first step. Next comes the willingness to sacrifice and to undertake a journey without loved ones (the *Pilgrim's Progress*) since the televised regime on both style and surgical makeovers requires the relinquishment of family support, of privacy, of all kinds of volition. After a suitable period of days or weeks, made-over subjects are "born again" into a new life, a rebirth that is particularly marked when patients emerge from the deep sleep of a surgical operation.[49] The sociologist Zygmunt Bauman (2007) regards cosmetic surgery as a prime facilitator of the notion of serial rebirth that he finds prevalent in today's "fluid society."[50] He notes that for those who can afford it, surgery "has turned into a routine instrument of the perpetual remaking of the visible self" (101), thus allowing people to have a series of different identities or "lives." It is worth pointing out that if the end result of this surgery were a spiritual transcendence into an *after*life this would be considered a medical disaster (i.e., fatality). Instead, the makeover subject reemerges firmly grounded in, and often more at home in, materiality: The Word (as media image) has become flesh.[51]

Once reborn, the patient must undergo a recovery phase with its attendant discipline and continuing sacrifice. Instead of religious fasting there is dieting, exercise, and other bodily mortifications. There is also a social iso-lation that in some ways resembles a religious retreat. After this the subject is ready to test the extent to which they have been "saved" from previous inadequacies as they dutifully perform the rite of the Reveal, a term that may retain some of the religious associations of a revelation. Not unlike revival-ist meetings where participants are spiritually transformed on stage for the edification of themselves and others, fundamental change is made into an entertaining spectacle and an encouragement to onlookers who may like to try it themselves. Such display also has commercial possibilities, then and now. For as Jackson Lears (1994) suggests, nineteenth-century evangelical revivalists "played a powerful if unwitting part in creating a congenial cul-tural climate for the rise of national advertising" by popularizing the notion of dramatic self-transformation (57). With makeover spectacles, something of the reverse is taking place.

Home Edition, like any makeover, similarly progresses through phases of confession and renewal, but it has been less shy than other series about explic-itly invoking religious beliefs. For years this series has aired on Sunday nights, which for the majority Christian audience is a day on which they might expect spiritual instruction. Indeed, many *Home Edition* families appear to be rewarded for their professed religious faith. In some instances, the crew actually constructs a religious site within the private home; for example, one house incorporated a small private chapel (aired 3/12/06) and another boasted a Hindu altar (aired 9/3/06). Numerous other families simply state the importance of religion in their lives, especially as a way to cope with, and compensate for, hardship. Once rescued, many thank God as well as ABC for their good fortune, and it is sometimes suggested that those who produce the show are in fact working for both.[52] In one episode, when producers found deaf parents of a blind as well as autistic son, host Ty Pennington remarks with a straight face: "I'm just reflecting a light" (aired 11/7/04). On complet-ing another home, he remarks with equal solemnity, this week "we saw the power of faith" (aired 3/12/06).

Needless to say, none of this religiosity is puritanical or antipathetic to the overriding consumerist message. If there is professed to be a sense of spiritual renewal this works in tandem with consumerism—to the point, sometimes, of ecstasy. Another structure that all makeovers draw upon is the salvation narrative. As consumers, people are lost and then found. They have faith and then all is somehow provided. "Oh my God!," they exclaim, as they reverently enter into a new consumer paradise. In one unforgettable *Home Edition* episode, a gospel choir in full robes sang its way through the shop-ping trip to Sears, its members shouting out the chorus of "Shopping!" with as much enthusiasm as the more conventional "Hallelujah!"(aired 10/14/07).

On many style makeovers, too, there is an almost religious fetishizing of goods and services that suggests a transfer of power from spiritual to commercial authority. Consider the prestige given to the plain old industrial notion of the "product." On *Queer Eye*, when the presenters refer to products (pronounced *pro*-ducts) they do so with an awe that inspires reverence. The style expert Carson Kressley drops the phrase "haute couture" as a shibboleth that seems to encapsulate his expertise, his philosophy, and even his raison d'être. On *What Not to Wear*, the fashion "gurus" urge acolytes to "give yourself over to us mind, body and wardrobe" (so much for the soul) as though initiating them into a cult. Some resist at first, but eventually everyone comes to see the light and ends up a believer. The fact that they were reluctant before only increases the triumph of their conversion (as the prodigal—or rather frugal—daughter). This sacralizing of the material realm may signal the increasing encroachment of the market into the most intimate areas of life.

> Our deepest personal connections are increasingly dominated by market transactions, whether it's through surrogate motherhood, the sale of one's DNA, the booming trade in sex for hire, or the commercialization of religion and spirituality. Little remains sacred, and separate from the world of the commodity. As a result people become ever more desperate to sacralize the profane consumer world around them, worshipping celebrities, collections, and brand logos.
>
> (Schor and Holt 2000, ix)

With this shift in authority, consumer growth no longer faces the disapproval and principles of austerity promulgated by low-consumerist organized religions—a frugality that Max Weber famously argued (*The Protestant Ethic and the Spirit of Capitalism* [1905] 1992) was essential to the growth of early capitalism but appears less helpful now in its later stage of market expansion. Instead, love is expressed through material means and faith is rewarded on this level.

Yet, while the magic of the makeover can be seen to be borrowing from the drama of the religious realm, important distinctions remain. Makeover TV may share religion's interest in improvement and renewal, but not in an inner, incremental change due to spiritual discipline. A closer analogy is the quick fix of advertising, a ready solution that is possible because salvation is based upon a preoccupation with, rather than transcendence of, the material realm. At most sub-religious, makeover programs subdue or discipline the body not for the sake of the sprit but for the sake of the *body*. Prior to the twentieth century, religious instruction insisted that "self-improvement" meant spiritual development, which in turn meant reducing attention to one's physical appearance, to one's personal "vanity," and focusing more on serving others.

Whereas, as Jean Kilbourne ruefully remarks, "These days, self-improvement seems to have more to do with calories than with character, with abdomens than with absolutes" (153).[53] In other words, today self-improvement is less concerned with doing good than with looking good.[54] Certainly, looking good is a major component of reality TV and will be the main topic of the remaining three chapters, in which I will first examine the stylization of clothing and then move on to the stylization of the flesh.

CHAPTER 5

Retail TV

Imperative TV

Previous chapters have examined the promotion of capitalism from the perspective of corporate America. Now it is time to analyze, from the consumer's perspective, how commercialization impacts the individual. We know that all commercial television supports consumerism in a fundamental way by creating an audience for advertising, but an increasing number of series thematize an essential and often underrepresented activity that on reality television (RTV) is made dramatic and life changing, which is the act of shopping. This chapter will address the TV style makeover and its portrayal of consumption as a creative and symbolic act central to a market-based understanding of human relationships. As scholars begin to pay closer attention to a postmodern and subsequently postfeminist use of strategic and often high-end consumption to create a sense of self-empowerment (e.g., Tasker and Negra 2007), TV makeovers provide the very model for this kind of practice and its extension to both male and female consumers. They reinforce that the body is a medium that represents us to the world and presents the world to us, and that this communication is becoming thoroughly commercialized. It is not a new thing for women, especially, to be regarded as objects to be assessed on the (marital) market. But while feminists have worked to detach a woman's worth and social value from her physical attractiveness, a more recent postfeminism has attempted to yoke them back together using a discourse of self-empowerment that ultimately works for none better than those who profit financially from catering to the desire for maximizing one's physical status. And the postfeminist woman is rapidly being joined in an ever-expanding marketplace by the metrosexual man.

Makeover programming, I argue, very specifically reflects and supports the ethos of advertising. Consistent with advertising rhetoric, style makeovers are upbeat and solution oriented: everything can be broken down into problems with solutions one can purchase. Like advertising, the implication is that life is largely outer-directed and that improving appearance will yield inner results. Also consistent with advertising is that any sociopolitical context is greatly curtailed or simply lopped off. Makeovers back the idea that there is ample consumer choice but, in some ways, they exaggerate individual agency. Consumer advisors treat subjects as almost blank slates and ignore their ordinary budgetary or time constraints. Since the client is not paying for the advice, these experts are lent some considerable power, with the result that the acts of consumption they recommend are presented in a wholly positive light.

Style makeovers appear to be predicated on a reflexive, post-traditional society as described by sociologists such as Giddens, Beck, and others, but are especially indicative of the rise of the expert class and of the cultural intermediatory as observed by Bourdieu, Rose, and Featherstone. Consumer choice is professed to be key to self-identity, to social well-being, to professional and romantic empowerment, but these programs suggest that the marketplace is now so complex that we need to turn to those who know its codes. Both the complexity of the market and the skill of those who negotiate its complexity therefore demand respect. More pragmatically, reality TV needs to establish such expertise in order to create hierarchies that will generate predictable tension and drama. Modern consumerism is a story of both freedom and control, and of control because of freedom. By instructing subjects in appropriate forms of consumption from a wide array of choices makeover experts are seen to empower, enculturate, and discipline them. But there is another strain of programming, more evident in the last few years (perhaps not coincidentally during a recession), that uncovers a consumption that is pathological and out of control. This type of programming, which I will examine more closely in the next chapter, takes a more forensic approach to what can go wrong.

First, however, it is important to underline how many RTV formats demonstrate the joys of improving one's consumption through the benign discipline of a variety of guides. There are the friendly though mocking helpers and temporary best-friends-forever in style makeovers; the surrogate neighbor and instant community organizer in home makeovers; or the white-coated authority and god-like magician of surgical makeovers. Their exhorting viewers to improve, and the offer of largely consumerist solutions for their perceived lack (whether it be a stylish outfit or a gym workout), is part of the larger contemporary phenomenon of what I refer to as imperative TV (Deery 2006), programming that urges us to improve ourselves and our situation, usually by keying improvement to the purchase of goods and services. On talk shows and news programming, on shopping channels and infomercials, we are constantly being urged to shape up and to make more of ourselves: not by governments, family members, or friends, but by representatives of large commercial agencies.[1] This call to change is fundamental both to the economy it legitimates (hyperconsumerism) and to TV's function within this economy (promoting goods and services).

Reality makeovers are prime examples of imperative TV. Their emphatic message is that we need to improve our house/ car/ wardrobe/ body—and thereby ourselves—and that anyone can accomplish this feat by purchasing the right goods and services. The linking of improvement to consumption certainly must be gratifying for advertisers who have spent billions establishing this link. On style makeovers, in particular, shopping is front and center. Every episode centers on visiting retail sites, an iteration that goes beyond promoting specific products to establishing an entire ethos of consumption as life affirming, creative, and essential. If the economic point of television is to commodify leisure time, then makeovers aim to further commodify other discretionary time by encouraging people to shop, shopping still being commonly regarded as a major "leisure" (not work) activity. On TV makeovers, shopping has many dimensions: it can be a bonding experience, an entertainment, an art, even a form of science. It is hinted that not shopping appropriately and wholeheartedly is tantamount to being not only materially but also morally lacking. Making the most of one's self becomes a moral imperative, so that what might be interpreted as selfless sacrifice is transposed into the socially irresponsible. A mother who spends more time and money on her children than on herself is interpreted as actually being selfish or lazy because, makeover hosts will insist, it is also one's duty to make an effort to look good to others. Caring about others means caring about how you appear to them. It also signals an appropriate amount of respect for yourself: for example, there is no sympathy for someone who claims to be exhausted or on a tight budget. The makeover reflects a wider "solicitous society," solicitous because it tells us it cares about our welfare and solicitous because it is constantly making demands of us (Baudrillard [1970] 1998, 170). Remarkable though largely unremarked, this prodding and nudging establish a peculiarly intimate, even presumptuous, relationship between television and the viewer.

As the sociologist Nikolas Rose observes, in the management of everyday life it is today's media that has taught us how to "translate the enigmatic desires and dissatisfactions of the individual into precise ways of inspecting oneself, accounting for oneself, and working upon oneself in order to realize one's potential, gain happiness, and exercise one's autonomy" (1996, 17). One could pinpoint this further by underlining that this self-scrutiny is stimulated not just by the media but by the media's *commercial* role, by its alliance with advertising messages that are designed to highlight dissatisfaction in order to sell solutions. As John Berger (1972) put it, the advertiser steals our love of ourselves as we are and offers it back to us for the price of the product they are pitching (134). But—and this I believe is also keyed to advertising—Rose (1996) goes on to make the crucial point that the Foucauldian, decentralized authority of today's experts (whether clinical psychologists or style "gurus") is all the greater because it appears to be wholly in our service and in fulfillment of our own desires. Members of secularized, postindustrial societies have been freed from the arbitrary prescriptions of religious and political authorities.

> But we have been bound into relationship with new authorities, which are more profoundly subjectifying because they appear to emanate from our individual desires to fulfill ourselves in our everyday lives, to craft our personalities, to discover who we really are.
>
> (Rose 1996, 17)

For makeover experts, we might say that identity is a technical problem for which they have a solution because they claim they possess a calculus for determining the market value of individual appearances and for translating material into social codes.

A very popular and cost-effective subset of reality TV, style makeover series include *A Makeover Story* (TLC, 2000–05), *60 Minute Makeover* (ITV, 2004–), *How to Look Good Naked*, *10 Years Younger*, *Queer Eye*, and *What Not to Wear*.[2] The style makeover is also a strong element in other formats such as *My Fair Wedding*. None of these are consumer programming in the sense of offering consumer advice on how well a technical product works or how fairly it is priced (as in *Consumer Reports* or *Which?* magazines), but only in that they establish the power and effectiveness of consuming. Many series claim to go deeper than product information to therapeutically realign people with goods so that they will be psychologically and socially more productive. Collectively, these shows underline how "Knowing about consumption is inseparable from knowing how to live" (Redden 2007, 160). Largely evading the determinants of class, what we see on style makeovers are subjects appearing to amass instant cultural capital in what Pierre Bourdieu ([1979] 1984) would term the "embodied" (personal appearance/ body) and the "objectified state" (furniture, pictures) (243).[3] Unlike the slower accretion outlined by the French sociologist, American TV producers suggest that in the course of just one episode learning how to choose a jacket or prepare a crème brulée nullifies, at least temporarily, inconvenient constraints such as degree of formal education or socioeconomic origin.

Shopping as Art and Entertainment

On style makeovers, an enjoyable and productive day shopping reveals much about the power of commerce. Shopping as entertainment is a particularly strong motif in *Queer Eye* and *My Fair Wedding*, whose common goal appears to be making potentially agonizing decisions into an amusement. On *My Fair Wedding with David Tutera*, the eponymous designer answers the bride's request to help her plan her wedding in a couple of weeks. He arranges for retailers to offer a selection of goods or services so that the bride can visit each business to sample and express her preference. Tutera then chooses what will appear in the wedding, keeping the bride and the viewer in suspense (though since he generally seems to honor her preference the suspense is diminishing). A similar visiting of retail stores occurs in *Bridalplasty*, where brides choose their favorites from a series of requisite wedding items, but the suspense is who will win the final competition and get to keep the items she selected.

Both *My Fair Wedding* and *Queer Eye* elevate the mundane act of entering a retail store. Each relentlessly cheerful episode makes shopping a breeze and its powers to transform automatic. Normal socioeconomic constraints are sidestepped so that the mood remains buoyant and the presenters fairly sizzle with the upbeat, can-do attitude of American pragmatism and its popular translation in advertising rhetoric. Those being tutored in consumption are able to experience the joy not only of acquiring particular objects but of shopping in general as they skip happily from one store to the next, finding everywhere just the right thing. Some *Queer Eye* episodes featured specialized and even unique retailers as the presenters initiated the less experienced shopper into high-end commerce; for example, early episodes featured New York City family stores or small boutiques, whose name gets at least a few seconds of exposure. Later episodes shifted to suburban retail chains, whose well-known architecture and signage is used to promote the retailer-as-brand offering customers a sanctioned array of choices. In either case, production and location costs are low. On *My Fair Wedding* the acquiring of goods and services becomes a valuable experience in itself, which anticipates and maybe even rivals the Big Day (more on this later). The pleasures encountered in these retail experiences are in line with the steady historical expansion of the notion that shopping is, indeed, a form of entertainment and even of theater, ideas that emerged with the rise of the great city department stores in nineteenth-century Europe and America. Indeed, "Retail Entertainment" is, today, a formal division of Sony (Gabler 1998, 201) and the Build-a-Bear company describes as "entertainment retail"[4] stores that offer mall shoppers the chance to build and then buy a customized bear. This process extends production into the point of consumption and attempts to make shopping a fun and creative activity, albeit through customers using mass produced components in a linear process that ultimately mimics factory production. Some sites of production are also turned into an entertainment experience, as with factory tours of breweries or, again, teddy bears (e.g., The Vermont Bear Company factory is as much a tourist destination as a site of manufacture).

Even on a less light-hearted series such as *Home Edition* the presenters ritualistically head to the nearest Sears store—which thanks to capital con-solidation is always around somewhere (or at least producers must make sure there is a branch nearby). Though not a major focus, the shopping trip is framed as a huge and joyous spending spree—everything being free of charge. The recipients themselves are absent, but on their behalf presenters and vol-unteers run wildly throughout the store to gather anything they might want. Cute shots of them posing and playing with products reinforce the idea that shopping is fun. On these visits there is more of a carnivalesque license than on shopping series like *What Not to Wear*, where there is a limit on the expen-diture ($5,000 or £2,000). On *Home Edition*, the presenters' job is to shop and shop big, though for some reason it is all done in what seems like five minutes, so they have to grab everything in haste as though on a game show. After the frantic assembling of items, there is footage of multiple shopping carts racing out the door and right by what is ordinarily the financial bar-rier of the cashiers, off to heal the stigma of family members who are not able to properly consume on their own behalf. One episode of *Top Chef* enacted another consumer fantasy when the competing chefs were told to spend the night in a Target store and take whatever they wanted from its shelves. In this instance there weren't any cashiers and the only limit was time, since their task was to prepare a meal for the store's morning shift—thus the fantasy was revealed to be a marketing strategy used to advertise that some Target stores now offer fresh produce.

Like building one's own cuddly toy, RTV series create emotion and authenticity by personalizing the act of consumption within the context of mass production. Whereas for many people shopping is a solitary act, on *Queer Eye, My Fair Wedding*, or consumerist docusoaps like *The Real House-wives*, shopping is a time for social bonding: bonding with goods, bonding with people, and bonding with people by bonding with goods. Consump-tion, therefore, becomes a form of mediation since it mediates our role in society and between people. On RTV people are shown shopping together as a social act or presenters energize an individual's relations to things by providing a supportive and temporary social group of assumed intimacy. For example, once the bride-to-be on *My Fair Wedding* opens the door to her home she often professes a love for her wedding planner that seems to over-shadow her relationship with the groom. In return, as they walk through the wedding plans together, his sensitive customization of goods and services further bonds the pair. As planner, he refers with some sense of ownership to "my bride" and plays a prominent role at the wedding ceremony that is now part private and part a TV show: in one episode Tutera officiates at the wedding and in another he walks the bride down the aisle, all this after knowing her for no more than a few weeks. Here goods enter into and help create social networks and are given value by the emotions that circulate through them, however temporarily. Certainly, advertisers have been impressing upon us for decades that buying goods is a way of expressing love, of affirming relationships, of showing that you care: famously captured in the persistent emotional pressure (or blackmail?) of Hallmark's 1944 slogan "When you care enough to send the very best." Shopping, therefore, is something we neglect at our peril.

Another way to sell consumption is to portray everyday life as an art form, which means that the business of furnishing and decorating this life becomes a prestigious matter, even a creative accomplishment. The aestheticization of the everyday (Featherstone 1991; Jameson 1998) was in previous eras invoked as part of a self-conscious breaking down of the barrier between high art and everyday life, as promulgated by Dadaists and surrealists as well as by the likes of William Morris and the American Arts and Crafts movement. The idea of turning one's own life into a work of art was also passionately embraced in the late nineteenth and early twentieth centuries by artists, intellectuals, and dandies from Wilde to Bloomsbury. But it is in the late twentieth century that the aestheticism of both person and environment became strongly linked to consumption, to what Featherstone refers to as "a life of aesthetic consumption" of mass-produced objects (1991, 67). "Design For All™" is a notable marketing strategy from US big-box retailer Target, whose employment of high-end designers and architects like Michael Graves is just one highly publicized example of a larger trend of artists being incorporated into the realm of advertising and commercial design, a trend that has set the stage for making mass production seem more playful, more customized, and more stylish than before. Over several campaigns, television ads for Target have played with the notion that ordinary, mass-produced items, such as detergents or mops, can become objects of aesthetic admiration. Apart from the design strengths of any single object, their collective and dynamic arrangement in advertising campaigns suggests that mass production and utility can be twinned with creativity and play—all in an effort to connect every possible commodity to desire and entertainment. This, too, is the realm of makeover television, which, as a popular contribution to image culture, works diligently to connect design and style to everyday consumption and to associate even mundane commerce with creative entertainment as part of a larger stylization of life.

Coming Out of and Rearranging the Closet

Making shopping entertaining may ease anxieties and thereby break both social and commercial barriers. A prime example of this is *Queer Eye*, a series that helped expand the market for male products by using its experts' otherwise marginal (gay) status as a badge of their expertise in certain stereotypical areas of consumption: notably clothing and décor. This claim to expertise conforms to a broader gendering of space whereby interior design is coded as being feminine or gay, and exterior design (construction, architecture) as masculine. The majority of viewers of lifestyle and other kinds of reality programming appear to be female: one survey suggests by a 2:1 margin (Hill 2007, 66–7). But while it also attracted female viewers, *Queer Eye* reached out to men as viewers and as consumers. Its gay presenters went ahead into the, for straight men, somewhat mysterious realm of décor and "beauty products" and came back to advise other men, naïve and uncertain holders of masculine identity who have much to do in order to catch up with women in terms of body insecurity and subsequent consumer spending. This new being, captured by the marketing term "metrosexual," is concerned with grooming and style to an extent traditionally coded as feminine or gay—and is in some respects a mainstreaming of the older notion of the dandy or flâneur (Miller 2006).⁵ *Queer Eye* was pioneering in conjoining "male" with "beauty product," and it appears that straight men are now buying beauty products in greater numbers than before, this in addition to the increasingly significant "pink economy" of gay consumers. None of this is to suggest that a market expansion was engineered by one show alone, though some studies suggest that *Queer Eye* did have a measurable retail impact (Cava 2004; Florian 2004).

On *Queer Eye* the gays weren't outed, but their subjects were. The Fab Five were open about their gay identity and, in fact, riffed off this characterization endlessly. It was the straight subjects who got to feel what it is like to be brought out into the light of public scrutiny. It was their closet that was opened and exposed. In this queering of reality, heterosexuality is an inadequacy if not a handicap and gay cultural capital confers a superior status, at least for the duration of the program. The conventionally marginalized are turned to for advice—though only in certain areas: for example, they do not advise straight men on buying trucks or power tools. There has been some debate in scholarly and journalistic quarters about whether this series reinforced or broke stereotypes of gay men and the degree to which it supports heteronormitivity (e.g., Clarkson 2005; Sender, 2006; Di Mattia 2007; Kavka 2008; Lewis 2008). Some have characterized the series as a form of gay "minstrelsy," where a few narrow stereotypes are trotted out for the amusement of a heterosexual audience (Sawyer, quoted in Sender 2006, 133). Certainly, by being associated with this kind of programming, any gay identity comes close to being seen as merely a "lifestyle" choice (Miller 2006, 115), a notion that conservative opponents have often invoked to deny homosexual identity, and therefore rights, under the law. As in other media-advertising, the gay presenters on this series are notably asexual. As Rosalind Gill (2007) notes of advertising: "it often seems as if gay masculinity is primarily a style identity, not a sexual one" (101). Gay men are allowed to exist on network television only if they never actually engage in the practices that define their sexual identity (101).

Other repressions are more technical, for in the attention economy of television production what advertisers buy and broadcasters sell is time. On RTV, time compression serves to amplify the excitement and effectiveness of retail shopping. *My Fair Wedding* magically condenses what normally takes months (arrangements for a wedding) into a few weeks. *What Not to Wear* transforms lives after a mere week of instruction and shopping. On *Queer Eye*, the pretense is that it all happens in one day (in actuality it takes three). There are even makeovers that last a matter of hours, as in *Ambush Makeover* or *60 Minute Makeover*. But in all makeover formats there are at least two levels of compression. In the first place, events are compressed into a tight schedule in real time and things happen in less time than they would normally take. Then there is the second compression due to editing. This shaping of time serves to heighten the power of both television and of shopping, for subjects are moving at the speed not of everyday life but of advertising. The quickness of the transformation adds to the magic and authority of the expert intervention, but even more fundamentally the pace is rapid because, in that core principle of capitalism, time is money and must be maximized. The acceleration on makeover shows reminds us that transforming time (TV content) into money is the basic function of all media and that on a mass medium like television time's value remains high.

On competitive shows like *Top Chef* and *Project Runway* or on makeovers like *Queer Eye* the directorial stylization highlights haste. Instead of walking, people are constantly running around in a dizzying exaggeration of normal activity, thus demonstrating the busyness of business, the dance of commerce, the energy of consumption.[6] On *Top Chef* and *Project Runway* a ritual part of the competition is a timed excursion to a store to gather ingredients for creative projects. The stores get a plug and are seen as offering a range of goods whose quality is a significant part of the creative project. On style makeovers, the time compression amplifies another benefit of buying mass produced goods in retail stores, which is that they are instantly available, prêt-à-porter, with no need to wait for craft or construction. The fast pace also minimizes any scenes of buyer's remorse or a deflationary gap between an object's advertised promise and its real performance. Of course, when it suits, RTV is also known for its stretching of time in order to milk the money shot. On many formats, the contrast between the speed of a creative project and the slowness of the reveal becomes a crucial nodal point. Most extreme are the delays in revealing judges' decisions. For example, on *Project Runway* the authoritarian hostess Heidi Klum stalls at judgment time to pronounce the crashingly obvious. She asserts very deliberately just before the end of every episode: "There are two of you left. One of you will be out. [pause] And one of you will be in!"—as though the simple math were a revelation to her. Meanwhile we are treated to another commercial break and many close-ups of two competitors sweating.

Identity Prêt-à-Porter

Shopping is portrayed as fun, creative, and efficient. But on style makeovers subjects consume and are consumed in a process that highlights the extent to which consumer culture is also a primary site for identity construction, an emphasis that lends shopping a certain gravitas. To say that this is a novel association would be an exaggeration, for anthropologists have observed in a wide variety of pre-industrial settings that the circulation of goods goes beyond satisfying material needs and is a primary way to communicate one's social identity.[7] In many contexts goods are used to constitute "an intelligible universe," to "present a set of meanings more or less coherent, more or less intentional. They are read by those who know the code and scan them for information" (Douglas and Isherwood [1979] 1996, ix). What is unprecedented and more characteristic of advanced industrial economies is the level of consumption and the number and variety of consumer items that offer more than simply the means to survive. What is pronounced is the relative importance given to an "expressive" over a "functional or instrumental" use of goods (Lury 1996, 80).

Since the observations of Barthes ([1957] 1972) and Baudrillard we have come to recognize consumer items as signs organized into cultural codes. This applies to bodies also. Placing the body's semiotic function in the context of a consumerist society, Baudrillard observed that the modern situation increasingly shifts the emphasis from the body's concrete use value (energetic, gestural, sexual) to its exchange value as "a mere sign" ([1970]1998, 132). The boon to consumer culture is that this shift prioritizes consumption over production and offers latitude in interpretation, an interpretation that advertisers are happy to assign. This semiotic approach is implicitly ratified by the discourse of style makeovers, which implies the dominance of culture over economics (Slater 1997, 32). As one style expert reiterates, you cannot just ignore your consumer choices and say you are not communicating anything by them. "Everything you put on your body is speaking and you have to control the message" (Clinton Kelly on *What Not to Wear*, aired 12/21/10). While goods and appearance have always signaled status to some degree, now the relation between status and consumption is becoming more unstable, negotiable, and, according to these programs, altogether vital.

So the question soon arises as to whether people are using consumer items to express a core and stable identity or are creating and re-creating their identity as they consume. In the postindustrial context of the 1980s and 1990s, sociologists such as Anthony Giddens, Zygmunt Bauman and Ulrich Beck have argued that an erosion of traditional authorities and normative structures like community and organized religion has resulted in individual subjects having to form their own identity. For Beck (1992), the fluid self born of a "risk society" of institutional and economic instability provides each of us an opportunity, or a burden, to manage our own performance. In a process of individualization, human identity is transformed "from a 'given' into a 'task' " (Beck and Beck-Gernsheim 2001, xv). Instead of having an ascribed identity, the contemporary citizen must come up with a narrative of his or her own making, one that may need regular updating. Giddens describes it as inhabiting a culture of multiple choice where we build our identity from a choice of standardized options (1991, 5), similar to *Baudrillard's* structuralist image of a "calculus of objects" ([1970]1998, 27). But Baudrillard is more critical and argues that with mass consumerism we differentiate ourselves according to a horizontal system that "eliminates the specific content, the (necessarily *different*) specificity of each human being, and substitutes the *differential* form, which can be industrialized and commercialized as a distinguishing sign" (Baudrillard [1970]1998, 93; author's emphasis). So while our consumption "personalizes" us, being personalized isn't the same as being a person and ultimately it entails conformity to a system or code (Baudrillard [1970]1998, 92–3). While it is a truism that individualism is revered in consumerist cultures, the result is what we might term *mass individualism,* the paradox at the heart of consumer culture whereby one is expected to express individuality by acquiring mass-produced goods. On the rare occasions when makeover subjects admit to creating their own (and therefore unique) clothing, they are roundly mocked (e.g., *What Not to Wear,* episode aired 12/21/06). Their proper job is to choose from the already mass produced.

Not wishing to enter into a debate about the merits of competing claims about the stability/ instability or superficial/ core nature of individual identity, I offer two observations: first, that an alterable identity based on appearance (and with or without an immutable core) suits commerce and, second, that TV makeovers work to reinforce this malleability. Whether or not it is accurate to say that traditional authorities no longer play a prominent role in most people's (as opposed to most scholars') lives is also up for debate. Certainly there might be serious objections to the apparent discounting of factors such as gender, race, or class among those who describe unfettered self-fashioning by subjects who begin to resemble nothing so much as the conservative conceit of the "sovereign consumer" (an autonomous individual who makes free choices without sociopolitical constraints).[8] But this is what we see in TV makeovers, where consumers appear largely detached from sociopolitical underpinnings and constraints, and where it is assumed that one's social identity can be fairly easily managed and in large part managed simply by shopping. Gender dictates some choices, but much else seems up for grabs. The experts' confidence that they can select items for subjects they barely know suggests that identity is being aligned with the goods' symbolism more than vice versa. This supports Zygmunt Bauman's somewhat provocative claim that when people, today, make shopping choices, "What is assumed to be the *materialization* of the inner truth of the self is in fact an *idealization* of the material—objectified—traces of consumer choices" (2007, 15; author's emphasis). In other words, the process works from the outside in, with consumer choices coagulating into an individual identity. In any case, the question of whether or not a few days of shopping can genuinely define or express anyone's identity is not the TV producers' concern. What is their concern is marketing the potential for change through consumption—a change that is rapid, visible, relatively cost effective and therefore works for the medium and its investors.

Nevertheless, one of the clearest indicators of the influence of consumer society on everyday experience is the notion of defining one's identity in terms of a lifestyle or lifestyles. As early as 1933 American sociologist Robert Lynd identified the emergence of the "commodity self," by which he meant the self-image people began to construct in an initial stage of mass consumerism when material acquisitions became part of what Stuart Ewen refers to as one's "identity kit" (1988, 70). But the mainstreaming of the notion that one's life—like a product—can have a style, or be styled, is a fairly recent one and its heavy promotion by advertisers indicates that it has significant commercial advantages. It is economically important because a lifestyle doesn't just happen but is created through considerable expenditure and labor. Nor is it fixed, for it can be added to or modified without limit, with obvious benefits to the economy. Coming out of the affluence (for some) of the 1980s, the concept of a lifestyle was an attempt by advertisers to give a holistic interpretation to an assemblage of goods and services and to categorize consumers as groups. Psychographics employed VALS (the values, attitudes, and lifestyles system), for example, to try to estimate consumption patterns.

What Baudrillard referred to as a consumer's "repertoire" of goods ([1968]1996, 195) was seen as communicating a group (or multiple group) identity, creating a voluntary identification with some collectivity with which one may or may not ever come into physical contact. As David Chaney (1996) defines it, "lifestyle is a patterned way of using or understanding or appreciating the artefacts of material culture in order to negotiate the play of criteria of status in anonymous social contexts" (43). This is where advertising comes in, as a primary method for attaching symbol to good and for providing a repertoire of life narratives. The 2009 film *The Joneses* depicted a new specialty called "lifestyle marketing" in which people are hired to pose as an affluent family that promotes various products simply by having others emulate its lifestyle. Style makeover series perform a similar demonstrative function. Today, there are no longer sumptuary laws[9] enforcing social identity but we can recognize what John Hartley (2008) refers to as "vestimentary media," meaning social communication via apparel or by extension other items (56), managed today not by the church but by commerce.

As others have noted, makeover television brings to the fore a growing socioeconomic pressure to work on "the enterprising self" (Rose 1996), to market (promote) the self in order to advance in rank (be promoted). This is crucial in a post-Fordist era of flexible capitalism where managing one's image is part of the work that the "belabored self" (McGee 2005) must take on in order to prevent unemployment and obsolescence—though, ironically, most of those involved in RTV production are subject to just such an insecure and contingent market (Wernick 1991; McGee 2005; Sender 2006; Hearn 2008; Ouellette and Hay 2008; Weber 2009). If, in addition to jobs, relationships are less lifelong than in the past, then spouses as well as employees may feel obliged to retool and augment. In either case, what is not so often remarked upon is how this self-scrutiny illustrates how public relations (PR) concepts have become part of the basic tactic and idiom of popular discourse. The term "image" as used in public relations has become an increasingly common way for ordinary individuals to think of their public identity and today most people under thirty are consciously managing some kind of online profile. We can think of this and other forms of self-promotion as a "self-branding" (Hearn 2008) and as an instrumental response to contemporary employment contingencies, although, however it is described, impression management is hardly a new idea and stretches from the Greek Sophists to Machiavelli to Dale Carnegie. The pressure to project an attractive personality was also seen as paramount (and by some limiting) in the mid-twentieth-century workplace, as in Whyte's "organization man" (1957).

As indicated, some elements of contemporary makeovers can best be characterized as postfeminist, in that there is an intense focus on consumption, particularly of and for the body, as a key to individual empowerment and the promotion of a self-monitored sexualization in all spheres, including professional life. In makeover discourse, there is much talk of agency and freedom but these are ultimately contained by larger power relations, not least of which are commercial forces that tie personal expression and autonomy to a highly consumer-oriented lifestyle (Gill 2007; Tasker and Negra 2007). Postfeminism of this order works very harmoniously with media-advertising and with TV makeovers whose subjects are granted the "freedom" to focus on being sexually desirable objects, expert consumers, and monitors of the self, a perspective that shares with postfeminism and with neoliberalism a dismissal of collective concerns or actions in favor of an emphasis on private advantage. For example, on *What Not to Wear* there is a great insistence that the career-minded woman must also be sexually attractive (This is the converse of those who are scolded for not taking their professional life seriously enough and for going to work dressed like a too vulgar "hoochie mama"). The presenters dismiss the concerns of young doctors, lawyers, and scientists that paying a lot of attention to how they look will reduce their professional standing and cause them to be taken less seriously—or, more pragmatically, that it will take too much time away from their work. These women are encouraged to see wise consumption as important work and to have faith that looking physically attractive is a power they can harness in almost any career setting. Those who have philosophical or pragmatic objections to this attention to shopping must be brought around in a process that verges on moral as well as sartorial reform (environmentalists, academics, and frugal sorts are particularly recalcitrant). In other words, individuals are not just being made over, they are being made over *as consumers* and it is their attitude to consumption that is being revamped.

Consumer Training

For some time, the elite have had "personal shoppers" and for even longer the noveaux riches have had less formalized aid from people willing to help them spend their money (as in Moliere's classic portrait of *Le Bourgeois Gentilhomme*, 1670). But today's reality makeovers promote shopping as a profession, or at least an area of expertise, and so elevate its status along with other areas of the domestic and the everyday that once might have been considered trivial or below formal scrutiny but that are now becoming professionalized and therefore commercialized. In many instances, this involves professionalizing labor that was previously unwaged and performed by women, everything from decorating a room to organizing a children's birthday party. The "ordinary expertise" (Lewis 2008) of style makeovers can be seen as emblematic of a larger "new paternalism" (Lasch 1979) in which loosely credentialed, self-styled authorities help to classify, select, and circulate goods and services on behalf of uninitiated clients. Sometimes the expert's influence is extensive, or at least they convince clients that it should be. Take the rather high-handed, high-end providers of home décor on *Million Dollar Decorators* (Bravo, 2011–), one of whom rather grandiosely declares: "I'm not a house designer. I'm a life designer!" This appearance of the shopping expert conforms to a larger privatization or corporatization of private life and to what I have characterized elsewhere as the *professionalization of social relationships* (Deery 2006). This is a model whereby one pays for everything from "personal trainers" to "life organizers" rather than look for familial or other forms of non-billable advice. It is extended on reality shows that offer professional advice on parenting or family relations (*Supernanny, Nanny 911, Pregnant in Heels* [Bravo, 2011–]), advice on mating (*Millionaire Matchmaker* [Bravo, 2008–]), on weddings (*Whose Wedding Is It Anyway?* [Style, 2003–]) or on home cleaning and organization (*Clean Sweep,* TLC, 2003–05; *The Life Laundry,* BBC Two, 2002–04). The recipients of this advice appear to be socially isolated and so enter into a commercial network where one professional can lead to another (e.g., matchmakers bring in therapists). We notice, too, how many of the affluent on RTV are seen with their paid assistants (*The Real Housewives*), some of whom become an ersatz family (*Bethenny Ever After*). New, sometimes alarming, job titles emerge like "maternity concierge," which according to Rosie Pope of *Pregnant in Heels* is a person charged to see to the needs of wealthy, pregnant clients, something that might ordinarily be performed by family and friends. In one memorable episode in this series, an affluent Alpha couple engage Pope to help them effectively "brand" their baby (their words) in order to set him up to be presidential material some day, a process that includes hiring a focus group to help choose the baby's name (the couple go on to ignore this expensive input). But this is only a particularly stark example of a whole cadre of coaches and improvement experts who have come forward to advise clients, conduct seminars, and form professional associations such as the International Coach Federation and, of course, the only-to-be-expected National Organization of Professional Organizers.[10] Some of these new cultural entrepreneurs work for commercial entities while others list themselves as "Residential Organizers" who advise ordinary folk at home. Reality TV focuses on the professionalization of private life and alerts viewers to the many types of service available, but whether we are to admire or pity those who engage these professionals is not clear. Many viewers of *The Real Housewives,* for instance, report feeling sorry for those who don't appear to have real friends except those they pay for, as in the retinue of assistants and hair stylists.[11]

According to de Certeau, the expert has become so common and so influential a role in today's society "to the point of becoming its generalized figure" ([1980] 1984, 7). The rise of the retail expert might be attributed to, among other things, increased amounts of highly specialized knowledge, increased expectation of information access, and the proliferation of consumer choices. Returning to Beck, it may be that today we need experts as "answer factories" to help us resolve the tyranny of possibilities that reside in the overtaxed individual's hands (Beck and Beck-Gernsheim 2001, 7). What makeover TV makes clear is that now people pay upfront for almost everything from store-bought goods to store-bought social services. The result is that all kinds of social contacts are increasingly commercialized, from the brief paid-for greeting of the restaurant host to the wedding planner or life coach who becomes an intimate and professionally accommodating companion, all as agreed upon in a contract and for a specific and billable period of time. Personal life has become a large public, in the sense of commercial, affair and as Micki McGee (2005) observes, it is largely through the cultures of self-improvement that "values from the competitive world of the marketplace have been transplanted to the personal world of intimate life, and vice versa" (176). Personal life takes on the values of marketplace and the marketplace becomes focused on personal life via a new class of experts who mediate between goods and consumers.

TV's "fashion instructors" demonstrate their understanding of the geometry of the individual body and espouse almost mathematical principles regarding its dimensions or x, y and z co-ordinates. But while they analyze shape they do so according to cultural standards that determine what is best accentuated or hidden. Clothing experts are anxious to impress upon us that fashion has universal rules, even laws, a notion already indicated by the common parlance "fashion police": also the name of a series hosted by Joan Rivers that critiques celebrity style at red carpet events (*Fashion Police*, E! Channel, 2010–) and a metaphor invoked by the series *Style Court* (Style Canada, 2003–05). The host of *How Do I Look?* (MyStyle, 2004–09) began one episode by riding in a "fashion police" car and, after storming a house armed with a hairdryer, arrested a "fashion felon" during a hand-held filming that clearly mimicked the prototypical RTV series *Cops* (Fox, 1989–) (aired 5/27/07). In the case of *What Not to Wear*, policing is translated into highway code, with interstitial shots featuring road signs bearing rules like: "No miniskirts after 35." One episode devoted to making over a Ph.D. candidate inspired the hosts to actually get out a blackboard in order to write out fashion rules and then quiz the subject. The young woman, remarkably, took the whole thing seriously and (though a philosophy student) never thought to question the rules these presenters set up as absolute (aired 1/4/08). According to her instructors, style is tailored to each body type, for which there are set rules, but the one thing that is universal is that every person must maximize their physical attractiveness; they cannot aspire to looking less attractive for any reason.

How we treat the body, how we dress or undress it, what we pierce, ink or mutilate, these practices all indicate core beliefs of a culture and consequent power relations: it all comes down to who gets to do what to whom. Ordinarily, telling someone what to wear can be seen as a fairly trivial form of authority, although it is a fundamental form of control when exerted by government or other forces as a form of discipline (army), or discipline and punishment (prison). We consider it less disciplinary when private commercial forces tell us what to wear, presumably because the choices are wider, the dress codes less strict, and the intent not one of punishment or strict uniformity. In American and other advanced economies, citizens appear to be far more tolerant of commercial authority than that of their elected government when it attempts to perform a similar role. Reality makeovers demonstrate this tolerance by empowering commercial agents to survey and discipline subjects in ways that would be seen as highly objectionable, as well as illegal, if performed by noncommercial, governmental forces. On *Queer Eye* there is, technically, a home invasion as a style swat team storms through the door to surprise residents in their own home. Once inside, the presenters sometimes chuck items out of a window or throw things around, actions that would ordinarily cause someone to summon the police. On *What Not to Wear* subjects are secretly filmed, ambushed, and then, without their prior permission, publicly criticized and mocked, again on film. The hosts also engage in trespassing when cameras enter the subject's private home without their knowledge or permission (with friends or family as accomplices). Even when the preparatory surveillance is not secret it is deceptive, for there are different forms of public. For example, some subjects know they are in public (walking down a street) and even that are being interviewed by someone with a camera, but they don't know this material will be shown on national TV (much bigger public) and that their viewing of this tape will also be shown in an inner and immediate public of friends and coworkers. Interesting in light of these heavy-handed approaches is Martin Robert's assertion that *What Not to Wear* can be seen as "a cop show" with the successive stages of law enforcement "from surveillance and arrest through interrogation, conviction, and release to ultimate rehabilitation" (2007, 234).

Once subjects sign on for the makeover, the regime is strict and the ridicule free-flowing. On *What Not to Wear* the first demand is that the subjects stand in a tight space surrounded by a 360-degree mirror exposing them from every angle (in the United States they are wearing their own inferior outfit; in the United Kingdom they are in their underwear). By interrogating and breaking subjects down into parts, the stylists aim to break down their confidence or illusions about how well they look. After being shown the error of their ways and being schooled in fashion principles through the use of mannequin templates, subjects are sent out to see if they can replicate what they have been taught (an Old Navy ad campaign in 2010 showed people actually competing to be a mannequin). The training is ambitious because the aim is to mold them into good lifetime consumers. *Queer Eye* made some attempt to impart similarly lifelong lessons, but when it came to their subject's new wardrobe and décor almost everything was selected by the experts. The trainee-shoppers on *What Not to Wear* are granted more agency, but only as shoppers: they have to *spend* money and spend it on *clothes* (no slipping off to a bank to open a savings account!). On one episode that perhaps academic readers can relate to (aired 6/25/04), Assistant Professor Mirella Streuck took a break from shopping to sit down and read a book. This, for the shopping experts, is an unconscionable offense, and so they immediately pounced on her and dragged her away to do more shopping.[12] As Alison Hearn (2008) underlines, *What Not to Wear* makes it clear that shopping is work (499). Many trainees report that they find shopping a chore or a cause of anxiety and after a pattern of low consumption and frugality in the past some appear to feel guilty or apprehensive about spending large sums of money. This attitude obviously has to be corrected and the therapeutic value of shopping made clear. In this regard, the style makeover simply accentuates one of the primary functions of all commercial media, which is subjecting the public to what Jurgen Habermas calls "the soft compulsion" of constant consumer training ([1962] 1991, 192). Some anxiety must be relieved by the fact that in this instance the media producers are providing the spending money and absolutely require the subjects to use it all. But the job of the presenters is also to impress upon subjects how empowering, strategic, and liberating clothes shopping can be. Expenditure in this area is portrayed as less of an indulgence than a sober investment, an investment in social as well as material fabric.

What Not to Wear more clearly defines and exploits power differentials than do other style makeovers. The tone can be playful and the authority subject to self-parody, but producers and presenters do control much of the subject's actions and behavior. We note immediately that the show's title is negative and repressive. On *Queer Eye* previous consumer choices are critiqued and casually discarded. On *My Fair Wedding* the planner largely spares the subject his reaction to her bad taste (he rolls his eyes only in front of the national audience in a take outside the house). But on *What Not to Wear* the tossing out of the subject's prior wardrobe is a central dramatic moment, even to the point of becoming a literal tug-of-war between subject and presenters. The latter, with the power of the camera and studio location on their side, are quite merciless. They smile as they capture an item cherished by its owner and seem to enjoy ritualistically tossing it into a large trash can. Generally they throw out just about everything the subject owns. A similar pattern of discipline and punishment emerges on *Made* (MTV, 2003-), another self-improvement series that calls on the sudden intervention of an expert to help transform high school students into singers, athletes, cheerleaders, or something else that will change their current image and standing. The new recruit usually feels overwhelmed but learns to buck up and follow the expert's regime in order to achieve results. Only rarely does any resistance outlast the makeover show. One such incident was when "Plum," a subject on *How Do I Look?* remained wholly resistant to change, was throughout unimpressed and unappreciative, and to the end bitterly criticized the friends who nominated her for a wardrobe makeover.[13] Another unusual degree of resistance is displayed by a subject on *What Not to Wear* (aired 12/21/10) who, as a law student, begins by talking about invasion of privacy and then goes on to dispute the experts' right to "trash" subjects and their clothes. She does finally come around and show proper deference, but for a while her lack of respect for the whole process threatens to bring the format down (at one point the usually easygoing host actually has to leave the set because he is so offended by her disrespectful attitude). However, these scenarios are very much the exception—at least on episodes that make it to air. Generally, the final reveal is a triumph during which audiences can enjoy the overcoming of doubts and completion of a task: this is essential because if viewers witnessed only instructions and not the final results the program would likely lose its status as a pleasurable entertainment.

The reveal also reinforces that the accordance of physical attractiveness is a social act that depends on (or springs from) a larger validation than can come from just the individual. Stylists make much of their attempt to match dress to individual bodies, but there are overall patterns and parameters. For instance, presenters invariably instruct their female charges that femininity means sacrificing comfortable for less comfortable clothing. This means high heels and tight belts trump comfortable shoes and jogging pants, and we don't need the presence of corsets to understand how historically this pattern of favoring restrictive clothing has also restricted women's social mobility. But neither history nor feminist thought is part of the curriculum here. Nor is therapy a predominant motive, for, if it were, producers would not display the humiliating "Before" stage to the world.

Watching shoppers toe the line on style makeovers can be seen as a micro-cosm of how consumerism disciplines and socializes elsewhere. Put simply, if they are living in an advanced capitalist economy then citizens are required to shop. If they don't do so regularly and in great numbers, their economy will collapse. Hence, it wasn't much of an exaggeration for leaders like Blair and Bush to assert that shopping is one's patriotic duty in the aftermath of an attempt to destroy a center of trade. Highlighting the socialization that this mutual dependency brings, Baudrillard observed some decades ago that "Consumption is an active, collective behavior: it is something enforced, a morality, an institution. It is a whole system of values, with all that expression implies in terms of group integration and social control functions." He points to the need for "social training in consumption," which he compares to the training of nineteenth-century industrial workers in matters of production ([1970]1998, 81). This recognition that industrialization requires the pro-duction of consumers as much as products can be traced to Henry Ford, but it is even more the case in today's consumerist economies. The ultimate cul-tural achievement of these shopping series is, therefore, the reinforcing of our identity as consumers and their instruction in better fulfillment of this social role. And while other social institutions contribute to this training, it is easier to observe the process on a television show where, for economic and dramatic reasons, the parameters are so fixed and the control so visible. Ordinarily, con-sumer culture is more seductive and it relies more on the "soft" and co-optive power that political scientist Joseph Nye (2004) describes as "the ability to shape what others want" (7).

CHAPTER 6

Mixed Blessings

Retail Rite

Consumption that is effective, disciplined, and appropriate will produce noticeable improvements in the self—this is the central claim of television makeovers. But there is also programming—prominent in the last half decade—that depicts high consumption or overconsumption: either spending that is lavish but socially sanctioned or spending that suggests a much more troubled relationship between the consumer and the consumed. This darker material, most of it launched during a recessionary cycle, portrays not the drama of successfully harnessing the power of commodities but the morbidity of letting consumption get out of control. This chapter will begin with an analysis of programming that encourages viewers to enjoy the ritualistic, the theatrical, and the fantastic dimensions of high consumption, especially as seen in the largely feminine ritual of the big wedding. Fundamental to the propagation of the community and, in some discourse, to notions of a secure state, this rite is also a prime example of what I refer to as "event spending." After sampling the recent outpouring of shows with wedding content, I go on to consider programming more often coded as masculine, in which buying beyond one's immediate needs is validated because it is educational, has historical and patriotic significance, or is a skillful sport. The chapter will conclude with programming in which overconsumption is pathologized and has distinctly negative consequences. The focus throughout will be not the immediate commercialization of content (as with product placement) but how this content represents the relations between the consumer and the consumed.

What is arguably the most important ritual in contemporary consumer culture has often been overlooked by social scientists, economists, and cultural historians. Yet for most people their wedding is the biggest consumer event of their lives, more lavish than any other life passage (birth or death) and, after home buying, their biggest financial outlay. Not because there is any legal requirement to spend lots of money, only social pressure that, thanks in large part to the promptings of media-advertising, encourages people to feel that on this occasion they have a license not only to marry but also to spend. At this one cardinal event, the fruition of years of consumer training, one's choices of goods and services carry enormous social significance. Weddings, in fact, are noteworthy for providing an intense version of several consumer patterns, among them, positional consumption to establish status; an infatuation with goods accorded a deep symbolic meaning; the substitution of goods for people; and the pleasure of excess.

Today, expenditure on weddings is a sizeable and growing segment of most developed economies and is a particularly important part of the small business sector which tends to be local, family owned and, in the case of wedding services, often headed by women. In the United States and elsewhere, spending on weddings has risen exponentially in recent decades (Otnes and Pleck 2003, 2) and now supports a myriad of specialized goods and services as well as another class of consumption experts referred to as wedding "planners," "consultants," or "coordinators." These organized as a profession in the middle of the twentieth century and have since contributed greatly to the enthusiasm for expensive nuptials. In this they had a great deal of help from film, television, specialized magazines, and of course advertisers. In dramaturgical terms, weddings are virtually guaranteed to provide a satisfying ending, as writers have long recognized, but the real payoff is how much business they generate—both on and off screen. Long a topic of film, weddings now appear in a growing number of television formats. There are even whole channels devoted to this theme: in the United Kingdom, Wedding TV launched on Sky (satellite TV) in 2001, and in the United States, Wedding Central (cable) began in 2009. Meanwhile, so many wedding programs currently appear on WE channel that some have suggested it be renamed *Wedding* Entertainment rather than *Women's* Entertainment. A wedding is an obvious topic for reality television (RTV) given that it inevitably comes with heightened social significance, in-built drama, and its own conventional liturgy/ script. Things began simply enough with a chronological narrative on *A Wedding Story* (TLC, 1996–), where each episode focuses on the romance of a happy couple as they prepare for their big event. But newer formats began to focus on the wedding as a huge consumer event and explored opportunities for the extremism and excess that is characteristic of RTV. The wedding theme mutated so that series began to specialize in just one iconic commodity; for example, *Say Yes To Dress* (TLC, 2007), which then inspired *Amazing Wedding Gowns* (WE, 2009-), *Say Yes To Dress: Big Bliss* (TLC, 2010–) for plus sizes, *Say Yes To Dress: Atlanta* (TLC, 2010), *Say Yes To Dress: Bridesmaids* (TLC, 2011–),

Girl Meets Gown (WE, 2010), and *Amsale Girls* (WE, 2011). There are also wedding versions of other formats such as cooking shows (*Amazing Wedding Cakes*, WE, 2008–).

A wedding is where ordinary life is expected to coincide with dream and fantasy. It is a quintessential instance of the extra-and-ordinary experience of RTV, an occasion when ordinary people experience being extraordinary and are catapulted out of the mundane without any producer needing to prompt them. Weddings are a great subject for reality television because they show that it is possible to be factual and fantastical, authentic and dramatic. The two most entrenched aspirations that ordinary people have for their wedding are the fairy-tale ending and the celebrity event. Both are conceits largely created by the media, both promise a temporary elevation of status, and both require big spending.

The wedding fairy tale is of someone finding her prince and becoming a princess on her wedding day. The primary progenitor of this modern legend is Walt Disney, particularly his 1950 version of *Cinderella*. Though advertisers have linked weddings to Cinderella from the beginning of the twentieth century (Otnes and Pleck 2003, 28), it is the Disney imagery that has solidified this transformational tale and bride after TV bride refers to wanting her event to be like this heroine's. More than once in Britain this narrative has been realized before an audience of several millions when young women plucked from relative obscurity don a beautiful gown and ride in a decorative coach from a church to the palace of her prince, most recently in the royal wedding of 2011 (also described more than once as a great reality show). Reinforcing this link between weddings, princesses, and Disney, just before this wedding in London, Disney seized the opportunity to release a "Royal Edition" DVD of *Cinderella* in the United Kingdom.[1] The Walt Disney Company is also itself in the wedding business and sells signature "fairy tale" weddings (most often the Cinderella version) at its resorts and cruise ships, in packages that include carriage rides and a (dangerous sounding) "spontaneous" fireworks display. To date, tens of thousands have got married in Disney resorts, perhaps with the help of Disney's chief wedding planner, who is none other than David Tutera, the "fairy godmother" of *My Fair Wedding*. On *Wedding SOS* (Slice TV, Canada, 2007–) the "fairy godmother" metaphor is extended when a wedding planner steps in and grants a couple three wishes (accompanied by graphics of a magic wand). As in fairy tales, they have to choose their wishes wisely if they want pull it off in the end and have a wedding ceremony. Without benefit of television, brides can also purchase certified Disney wedding dresses from certain retailers. For example, the advertising for one prominent salon hits all the usual notes (magic, fairy tale, princess, Cinderella):

> Dreaming of a fairy tale wedding? Alfred Angelo can make dream weddings come true with a magical collection of Disney wedding dresses or bridesmaid gowns for your Cinderella moment. Alfred Angelo has a variety of Disney wedding dresses from the princess inspired gown collection, so you can be the belle of the ball.[2]

It is hard to think of another consumer mythology that has such purchase.

A wedding encapsulates the belief that high expenditure increases one's status just by displaying the right props. Translating this feeling of importance into the hierarchies of media culture, many couples today talk about wanting a celebrity wedding. Their dream is of being the star of their own show and so they arrange a theatrical spectacle that they hope will impress their audience (guests). Perhaps for the only time in their lives, their performance is filmed by professionals who follow them around and then produce a record of their turn in the spotlight: indeed, weddings were one of the first occasions that ordinary people photographed or videotaped. In other words, many weddings are like RTV to the extent that they are about ordinary people wanting to have an audience and be a celebrity, even if only for some equivalent of 15 minutes. The bride and groom approach their ceremony as a stage production that they hope will get good reviews, so having their wedding featured on a television show is simply the logical next step. Some TV couples arrange for a red carpet and photo shoot, or even a step-and-repeat banner imitating commercial staging. Ordinarily, such a banner would be a backdrop for the display of sponsor logos, its purpose being to promote brands during red carpet pseudo-events when celebrities or VIPs pose in front of it. "Step-and-repeat" comes from the Photoshop term for the duplicating and spacing of an object. In this instance television is also validating and replicating itself because it shows people on TV wanting what they've seen on TV, for others to see on TV. The couple accept the validation of media-advertising by imagining that their event is sufficiently important to attract sponsorship—which of course RTV, but not usually private weddings, does attract.

Weddings illustrate the mass individualism I identified earlier since this rite involves a good deal of custom and customization. Whatever the ceremony, just about everyone will have a white dress, a gold ring, a tiered cake, an abundant display of flowers, and a professional and public reception. Great reverence is given to these conventional items, yet each bride strives to express something of her individuality in her choice of details, as in what kind of flowers or cake. (Even the royals can bend tradition as when Prince William asked for a cake to be made of his favorite biscuit, the iconic British McVities Digestives, an informal but also quintessentially nationalistic choice). Brides tend to call it "my day" with a strong emphasis on the possessive. This is the only time some people will be able to afford the luxury of highly personalized consumption (e.g., initialed goods) and it is an advantage for television producers, too, because it gives people a reason to watch each unique episode. Of course there is also a sentimental motive for the couple stressing the uniqueness of their event because it asserts there will be no repeat due to divorce or death (unless there is a renewal of vows, a great reason for more spending later).

There used to be religious prohibitions on excess and luxury, including lavish spending on weddings (Otnes and Pleck 2003). Defined as spending above one's station, "luxury" was considered a sin and a rebellion against the proper social order and was legislated against in ecclesiastical courts until the Reformation (Slater 1997, 69). Today's RTV producers bank on creating interest by highlighting extremes, hence many series look not just at weddings but at very expensive weddings, leaving it up to the viewer to judge whether the expenditure is impressive or excessive and the events spectacular or just people making a spectacle of themselves. Either reaction keeps people watching. Extravagance appears to be the main theme of *Platinum Wedding* (WE, 2006–), *My Big Fat Fabulous Wedding* (VH1, 2007), and *Big Fat Gypsy Weddings* (Channel 4, 2010; TLC, 2011). The very title of *Platinum Weddings* speaks to a society of inflation where gold is no longer supreme. The official website entices us with:

> Imagine a wedding day in which no detail is too miniscule, no wish is too extravagant and no request is unattainable. It's a dream come true for any bride-to-be. Join WE TV for the ultimate wedding show that captures the drama and decadence of wedding planning on an extraordinary budget![3]

During each episode the cost of various elements is displayed on-screen and as the spending mounts (sometimes approaching a million dollars) there is no overt criticism from the voice-over or participants but rather an air of entitlement and lack of budgetary concerns. Cameras dwell lovingly on every detail and offer viewers the pleasure of both specificity and abundance in a complex choreography of goods and services. The tagline for the series is "The perfect wedding is priceless." The idea that a wedding has to be "perfect"—meaning with limitless spending—is a notion that has been pushed by the wedding industry since the 1920s (Otnes and Pleck 2003, 18). Here the amount spent does rather seem the point, whether viewers think it is impressive or obscene. The grand affairs of *Platinum Weddings* or *My Big Fat Fabulous Wedding*, where consumption is both high and temporary, resemble a potlatch display (Mauss [1950] 1990) that proves the couple's wealth and status by how much they spend on entertaining guests, with little thought of thrift or conservation. Hotel ballrooms are turned into themed palaces with great temporary constructions that, once the wedding is over, are torn down. This is also the trend in RTV where designers demolish whole houses, throw out entire wardrobes, or update otherwise perfectly functional furniture and appliances. Drama and design together accelerate planned obsolescence.

Wealth Voyeurism

Reality TV offers viewers a form of what I would characterize as wealth voyeurism, seen not only in extravagant weddings but in a whole stable of shows featuring wealthy lifestyles and high-end, hedonistic consumption. There is more lavish event spending in *My Super Sweet 16* and *Outrageous Kid Parties* (TLC, 2011) and hosts of high-expenditure Bravo TV shows with *Million* in the title, from *Million Dollar Listing* (2006) to *Million Dollar Decorators,* this in addition to the I-married-money series like *Football Wives* (VH1, 2010), *Basketball Wives* (VH1, 2010), and the long-running *Keeping up with the Kardashians* (E! 2007–). Bravo makes this voyeuristic stance explicit on its website for *Million Dollar Decorators,* where viewers are invited to "peep" and "oogle" photos of luxurious homes, described as a form of "real estate porn." Another unmistakable example of wealth voyeurism is *The Real Housewives* franchise, which invites viewers into the land of McMansions, designer labels, and Range Rovers, or shows that whet our appetites for expensive goods like haute cuisine (*Top Chef*) or haute couture (*Project Runway*).

Displaying the wealthy on screen is of course far from new, but it may have a more direct economic impact when it involves real people and real products that viewers, too, can purchase (as opposed to costumes in fictional drama). Certainly some RTV viewers respond directly (online) by asking where to buy the same items as those modeled on television and broadcasters oblige by offering such information on their websites: for example, a Bravo "Guides" site shows you in which high-end stores the "housewives" shop. The consumer theorist Juliet Schor (1999) identifies as an increasing trend in American society the "vertical desire" for the goods of those much higher on the social scale—as seen on TV—rather than the more traditional, horizontal desire for one's neighbor's goods seen in real life. The media's mainstreaming of luxuries results in a trickling down of formerly exclusive upscale brands in what I'd call the Godiva effect (after the mass dispersion of a formerly exclusive chocolatier's brand). With weddings, it is easy to see ordinary people fulfilling this vertical desire and aspiring toward a wealthy lifestyle if only for one day: already limos, personal makeup artists, and large receptions are fairly minimal expectations and displaying these repeatedly on television will likely reinforce this expectation. On *Bridezillas* (ITV, 2001; WE, 2004–), one bride-to-be unabashedly borrowed another's wealthy trappings when she knocked on a stranger's door in an affluent suburb and asked if she could pose for her wedding pictures both inside and outside this home (the initially reluctant homeowner agreed once payment was mentioned). This example is just a more intimate and ad hoc version of the renting out of all kinds of impressive lifestyles that for weddings are customarily available for a fee.

Some RTV series mine drama from a situation where conflict between desire and budget is unavoidable. This is the central dynamic in *Rich Bride, Poor Bride* (WE, 2006–) where usually a spendthrift bride has to be reined in by a worried groom. But even here overspending is indulged and forgiven because it brings such joy. In the final segment the now married couple recount how much they went over budget but they usually agree that they are worth it. Other series focus on budget constraints when buying a specific item, most notably the wedding dress (*Say Yes to the Dress, Girl Meets Gown*). One of the viewing pleasures of these shows is the sheer abundance of choice as sales staff walk through rows and rows of voluptuous material. The quantity is impressive but the dresses are each different in one detail or another, so we are to admire both the ingenuity of designers and manufacturers for producing so much variety and the match-making skills of the retailer who brings object and consumer together. Viewers share the perspective of the retailers whom they get to know over time and identify with their efforts to triangulate between a bride, her family, and the business. These staff members are portrayed as feeling an almost sacred duty to make the bride happy, no matter the impact on sales and commission. Sometimes the depth of the bride's desire or the pathos of her situation will cause the retailer to lower the price so she can be united with the dress of her dreams if she cannot otherwise afford it. As a love object, the wedding dress appears often as a substitute for the absent groom who in most wedding shows figures in a secondary, auxiliary role, more or less as a prop. Indeed, many TV brides seem to have a more intense relationship with wedding commodities than with their future spouse. What we witness again and again is the bride "falling in love" with the dress and ignoring the budget once she finds "the one" (a ritualistic phrase heard on almost every episode). Her rapturous joy at having realized her dream makes looking at the price tag crass, so whoever is paying usually accedes, after some suspenseful deliberation, however strict the budget going in. The socially sanctioned extravagance of a wedding suggests that there ought to be an *affective override* of financial concerns. Indeed, wedding goods and services have a notoriously high markup because providers know that on such an occasion customers are not always focusing on price and in fact might be seen as failing, romantically and socially, if they do. One could argue that the orthodoxy of romantic love and the love of goods arose around the same time in the nineteenth century and that a romantic consumerism has grown stronger and more profitable ever since (Otnes and Pleck 2003, 11). Thanks to advertising that has long used it as an appeal, romance is now thoroughly commodified and commodities have been imbued with romance.

With spending ability comes power. In *Whose Wedding Is It Anyway?* we occupy the perspective of wedding planners and admire their professionalism as they negotiate with difficult clients, vendors, and unforeseen circumstances (usually the weather). In this case, the clients are paying for everything themselves and so their wishes must be granted as far as humanly possible. The converse is *My Fair Wedding* where the producers are paying (largely by brokering television exposure for donated goods) and so the subject surrenders quite a bit of autonomy. Similarly, in *For Better or for Worse* (TLC, 2003–05) an engaged couple agree to hand over their planning to family, friends, and the show's wedding planner in return for a $5,000 wedding. In *Don't Tell the Bride* (BBC Three, 2007–) more drama is generated by power differentials tied to money. This time the soon-to-be-married couple sign a legal contract in a lawyer's office stipulating that, in return for their wedding expenses being covered, the groom must plan everything and tell the bride nothing. The couple can't even see each other for a month before the ceremony. As the wedding day unfolds, it falls to the bride to judge how much her groom's consumer choices express his love for her and his knowledge of her desires and preferences. Again, spending signifies and expresses love.

Being a princess for a day and imitating the wealthy can go to some people's heads and this stepping out of bounds is turned into another television entertainment and more negative form of affective override, most notoriously seen in the long-running *Bridezillas,* whose mocking title (bride plus Godzillas) and lively non-diegetic commentary cue us in to the attitude we are supposed to adopt as the bride plans her wedding: horror and disgust, mixed with some amusement, at her self-importance and vulgar behavior. Repeatedly we hear phrases like "But I'm the bride so you have to!" or "I can be as late as I like since it's my day!" Most charitably described as "high maintenance," these women often don T-shirts with "Bride" printed on them, but the way they repeatedly demand respect only emphasizes their inability to earn it. It soon becomes clear that being a self-anointed princess takes priority over any other relationships, as the bride-to-be mistreats and alienates everyone from the long suffering groom to her own family and friends. The bride's insistent claims that she is a queen or princess is undermined by her most unregal behavior. Generally the featured bride is someone from a lower-class background who appears to be making up for her lack of status and autonomy in everyday life by throwing her weight around for this period. These brides have rented all the trappings of a more elite lifestyle but can't quite carry it off. While the first US series featured quite affluent New Yorkers who had no idea they were to be portrayed negatively and were horrified to learn once filming was over that the title of the series had changed from *Manhattan Brides* to *Bridezillas,* subsequent seasons have featured more working-class couples who may be lured by vague promises that they will be "generously compensated."[4] This is, of course, the catch-22 of reality programming: that it would like to grant access to the lives of the wealthy and the elite but that anyone who would agree to be televised is, by definition, not one of these. The really wealthy have little incentive to take part in this kind of programming (except an occasional subset who hunger after fame) and so producers have to settle for, at best, an ersatz elite who *appear* to be of this class or are on the fringes of it (*Real Housewives*). That is, reality TV hits real limits in class representations that fictional programming can ignore.

Nevertheless, there is much drama to be had in exposing those who can't quite pull it off. This is why weddings are attractive to producers because they can combine lower socioeconomic status with big expenditure, out of which drama almost inevitably erupts. *Bridezillas* provides a caricature of the consumer behaving badly, though one could argue that it is not entirely fair to mock those who stress about pulling off the perfect event that media-advertising set them up to expect. Clearly these young women are frustrated when the dream does not materialize as advertised. But they are also part of a much older comic tradition. Usually overweight as well as overbearing, they are the descendents of the unruly harridans who have been mocked throughout Western literature, a popular example being Noah's wife in English medieval mystery plays.

Trade Shows

Another category of reality programming is not about event spending or about voyeuristically gawking at the lives of the wealthy or pseudo-wealthy, but is about the process of buying and selling goods. These "trade shows" don't feature the impersonal, anonymous consumption of fixed price goods in a shopping mall but more dramatic interpersonal negotiations that reveal the afterlife of objects once they've been sold for the first time. This is not about consumption intended to satisfy basic needs but about buying and selling for the hobbyist in a developed economy.

A striking development in recent RTV has been the attention to the activity of collecting, as seen on the History Channel's popular *American Pickers* (2010–) and *Pawn Stars* (2009–), and the Discovery Channel's *Auction Kings* (2010–). Collecting and antiquing are elements of consumer culture that merit more attention. Again, one theorist who did pay heed to them was

Baudrillard in *The System of Objects* ([1968] 1996). In this work he associates antiquing with an obsession with authenticity (80), which one could argue makes it akin to RTV for those who seek a similar authenticity in its depiction of real life. For the individual consumer, collecting is an activity that confers legitimacy on what might otherwise be seen as superfluous. This aggregative consumption produces added value given that a collection is often worth more than the sum of its parts. Collectors are also quick to claim that their collections have historical and educational value, which turns desire into need and whim into a buyer's pride for recognizing an item's importance to a collection. Collectable items are elevated in status, so that "junk" or "secondhand" becomes "memorabilia" or "antique" (even when new, items categorized as "collectibles" are sold as having instant historicity). Although there is something of a difference between collectable (adjective) meaning something that could be collected (from fine art to shaker furniture) and a collectible (noun) meaning something produced in order to be collected and often of lesser status (Hummel figurines, Hess trucks). In either case, collecting spurs consumption because a collector feels obliged to buy objects that may be of little interest in themselves, but, as part of a collection, have what Baudrillard calls a formal rather than a real interest ([1968] 1996, 112). A collected item is, above all else, a structuralist object that takes its meaning and value from the fact that it is part of a larger assemblage relative to which it is both similar and different.

What are known as "pickers" fill a particular niche in the commercial ecology, which is to search for old or abandoned objects in private ownership that can be sold for a profit in a retail store. Those who possess these items may be collectors themselves, or they may be closer to hoarders who simply accumulate a large amount of stuff. But once placed back into a retail environment the items are bought by collectors. The job of the picker, therefore, is generally to transfer objects from a disassociated accumulation into an ordered collection. *American Pickers* is a popular series that follows two male partners who ply this trade by traveling all across America and putting objects back into circulation after being outside the market often for generations. The series focuses on the finding of objects, not their retail sale. The partners re-purpose objects by making the previously functional into the artifactual. For example, some of the most frequently purchased items on this series are old advertising signs and strongly branded objects. The pickers are always eager to dust off these (literal) signs of commerce and aestheticize them because apparently there is currently a consumer demand for such things. The reference (advertised item or company) may now be nonexistent, but this legacy advertising (my term) now advertises a previous era and at the same time encourages reverence for advertising itself. It is a striking example of the importance of sign value over functional value when the formerly instrumental becomes purely decorative. Advertising that was used to fetishize other objects now becomes fetishized itself. Baudrillard describes this transcendence of mere functionality as transforming "the everyday prose of objects . . . into poetry" so that they "become the mental precincts over which I hold sway, they become the things of which I am the meaning" ([1968] 1996, 93, 91). No wonder then that people invest so much, and not just money, in their collections.

On the television series, pickers are portrayed as curators and conservers who bring to light the historical worth of objects, something one might expect from a series that appears on the History Channel. However, it is history lite. Shows about pickers and pawnbrokers are part of a larger rebranding of formerly more educational channels that the development of RTV has greatly facilitated, including the shift in 1998 from The Learning Channel to just TLC or Bravo's move from arts programming into RTV, a move that is associated with the dilution of the public service tradition in Europe. The History Channel is currently branding itself as providing history through commodities and, of course, is itself turning history into a commodity. The channel's current slogan, "History. Made every day," is candid about history being something the programming creates. It also suggests a populist revelation of history through everyday objects, which perfectly describes the RTV series we are examining. Its historicity is, paradoxically, why this kind of programming does not date. Episodes are rerun frequently because historical knowledge doesn't date like news information. As Bernard Stiegler has underlined when discussing one of the media's most important functions, its technical exteriorization of memory, "the value of information as commodity drops precipitously with time (in contrast to that of knowledge, which remains constant or increases over time)" (Stiegler 2010, 78).

In every introduction to the *American Pickers* the claim is that "We make a living telling the history of America one piece at a time" and the programming does glance at history in the form of pop-ups that display some facts about an item under negotiation, particularly when and by whom it was manufactured. Both buyers and sellers also exchange information informally in conversation and self-consciously declare how important it is that they educate each other. The featured business is called Antiques Archeology, which suggests more educational respectability than mere trade. And on *Pawn Stars,* in the unlikely setting of a Las Vegas pawn shop, viewers are similarly given factual nuggets about every item under consideration and in many instances hear from an expert who is brought in to authenticate and describe an item's historical significance. Very often on both *American Pickers* and *Pawn Stars* the historical information is a celebration of America's manufacturing past and there is great reverence for brands like Harley-Davidson, Remington, Colt, and numerous other smaller companies that are now defunct. Pickers and collectors are conscious of restoring not only particular objects but also national pride; hence they are not just pickers but *American Pickers* (the current website has the TV duo in an *American Gothic* pose, spade in hand).[5] Also it is not just history but commercial history that is being accorded worth.

Pickers and pawnbrokers inhabit a largely masculine world, as an unmistakable counterpoint to the feminine wedding and docusoap formats examined above. It is certainly no secret that the History and Discovery channels are geared toward a male demographic. *American Pickers,* for instance, is presented as a rugged alternative to the image of antiquing as an activity of older women and gay men. The website declares: "This isn't your grandmother's antiquing. . . . If you think the antique business is all about upscale boutiques and buttoned-up dealers, this show may change your mind—and teach you a thing or two about American history along the way."[6] Whereas retail shopping is often coded as feminine (the mall), this is portrayed as a different kind of shopping requiring different rituals. Both those collecting and those buying are predominately white men, or more specifically older white men, and there is more than one elegiac suggestion that these figures, too, are "national treasures" whose oral knowledge and informal preservation of history might die with them.

The pickers and pawnbrokers we get to know on television have in common an interest in objects conventionally associated with masculinity, such as machines, tools, guns, military paraphernalia, toys, and transportation: what are known in the trade as "mantiques" (cf. *Queer Eye* beauty products). Another niche category is "petroliana," meaning gas station and oil company memorabilia that apparently some men like to collect (this gendering is assumed but is not explained). One could see this emphasis reinforcing the vision of the TV broadcaster that history is masculine and is about men's stuff. But perhaps predictably, since RTV producers are always looking for the next twist, it was not long before other series appeared that provide a feminine variation on this successful programming. TLC launched a series called *Pawn Queens* (2011–), about what is claimed to be America's first female-owned pawn store (but with background male partners). The store is run by women who are far more photogenic than their male equivalents in other shows and drama comes from the novelty of their presence in a man's business. Female owners are also featured in *What the Sell?!* (TLC, 2010), a series about an antique store that is really about the family dynamics of those who own it and the fact that they are women, whereas the male ownership of the other businesses is normative and unmarked. Then there is *Sister Pickers* (Lifetime, 2011–), which features attractive female hosts (transplants from *Home*

Edition) who travel around in tight shorts looking for old objects that they (or their male handyman) can turn into decorative pieces (not unlike the hosts themselves). Unlike their male counterparts, these women show little or no interest in either knowing or preserving the historical significance of the objects they aim to repurpose into tables or lamps. At the time of writing, none of these feminine variations have done as well as the masculine originals.

While "bargain hunters" is a phrase also used to describe female consumers, on *American Pickers* the shopping-as-hunting involves a good deal of muscular activity. The men dig and dive into piles of objects and drag out heavy items. Sometimes they and the seller agree on a price due to an arm wrestle or some other physical competition. We see this aggression expressed in the titles of other series, such as *Storage Wars* (A&E, 2010), *Storage Hunters* (truTV, 2011), *Auction Hunters* (Spike, 2010–), and *Auction Kings*, where there is highly competitive bidding among men, resulting in triumphant victors and chagrined losers. Whereas elsewhere we witness young women aspiring to be princesses and stars, these men mimic warriors or frontiersmen who travel through a largely uncharted territory where prices are not fixed and have to be assessed on the fly. This requires quick and decisive action, as well as courage, skill, and a somewhat combative attitude: one picker even refers to himself as the super-hero Spiderman as he scales another unsteady pile of goods. Moreover, that *Pawn Stars* is set in Las Vegas underlines the gambling that is at the base of much human commerce where negotiation relies on poker faces, keeping cards close to the chest, and taking chances. This, too, is often coded as masculine behavior.

Most of these recent series feature self-made and minor entrepreneurs from modest backgrounds. This is in contrast to the much earlier and more genteel *Antiques Roadshow* (BBC One, 1979–; PBS, 1997–), which in both British and American versions guards its distance from trade as a matter of prestige. Whereas the latest batch of RTV programming very much focuses on price and profit, when on *Antiques Roadshow* a market price is assessed there is often a coy suggestion that profit is not a concern since no one is actually going to sell their cherished heirloom. They are merely being informed about how much they should insure the object for (and indeed the series is sponsored by insurance companies). But, at the same time, much of the program's drama and suspense comes from the revelation of this price. So market value does matter. *Pawn Stars* or *American Pickers* typically exchange less prestigious items hauled from the backyards and barns of ordinary, rural folk. But the personal, ad hoc nature of this exchange raises ethical issues. A hefty profit makes for good drama, but some viewers express concern about the ethics of this kind of trade and, by extension, about the deception and antagonism at the heart of capitalist systems. *American Pickers* especially has come under fire (at the broadcaster's website) for what some see as the overly predatory nature of the featured business and its profit taking from elderly sellers. Other viewers argue that maximizing profit is just basic capitalism and that the buyers have all kinds of costs and overheads that must be taken into account.[7] The position of the buyers is not helped by the dramatic structuring of the program that has them appear in separate interview mode during a transaction gleefully relaying how much more an item is worth than they intend to pay for it. We are reminded that trade, just like drama, makes the most of gaps in awareness. Nevertheless, the opportunity to have these same pickers come to your home and examine your collection is now being framed as a prize a viewer could "win." In other words, the user-generated participation, which profits those who produce the program, is again framed as a privilege. The lure for both pickers and sellers is, of course, being on television and therefore acquiring or touching celebrity. What is being sold on *American Pickers* or other trade shows is not so much an object as a television show; otherwise the economics are unrealistic (e.g., driving all across America in a van looking for a limited number of objects with small profit margins). It turns out that even the realistic looking pawn shop on *Pawn Stars* is now as much of a television set as a regular store and is today visited as a media-generated tourist destination as well as a working business. The power of mediation is that it subsumes other businesses into its own (pawn stores into television sets) and transforms outlay into profit, as when labor is eagerly contributed for free.

Desperation and Addiction

Reality TV was not immune to the recession that hit the economies of America, Europe, and the Pacific Rim around 2008. A good example of its impact is the *Real Housewives* series. When the economic downturn occurred, it became clear that several participants portrayed in this series were living beyond their means and a sizeable portion have gone on to declare chapters 7, 11, or 13 (various forms of bankruptcy). The women usually try to keep news of their financial embarrassment off camera, but it is fodder for much tabloid and online speculation and now the topic increasingly appears on the show itself. Yet few appear to have significantly modified their extravagant lifestyle and some at least seem addicted to spending even when bankrupt: for example, one woman's way of coping with bankruptcy was not to seek a job but to have a feng shui expert come in (no doubt for some hefty fee) to realign the energy in her house. Of course, unlike most RTV participants, these women are paid a negotiated amount for being on the series and as we have seen most use the television exposure to promote their own businesses. The show, in other words, in part creates the lifestyle it portrays, even if this wasn't the original intention. Even more specifically, the women afford their lifestyle in part by selling the props of this lifestyle to others (clothing, jewelry, cosmetics, design, real estate). While their affluence was supposed to be the show's selling point, it turns out that many are nouveaux riches *manqués* whose current deflation could be read as emblematic of a larger socioeconomic disparity between appearance and reality, between getting and spending, that greatly compromised the US and other economies. More directly attuned to the recession is the unglamorous docusoap *Downsized* (WE, 2010–), in which a formerly comfortable middle-class family struggles to make ends meet with coupons, food stamps, and semi-successful attempts to raise money (from home businesses to kids' lemonade stands). In contrast, though they have been scrambling to supplement their husbands' diminishing incomes, the "housewives" are not yet portrayed as desperate.[8]

This is not so in another kind of reality TV, where the desperation for goods and services is the show's focus and participants are made to fight it out to win a prize. Again, the big wedding provides a good example of a much sought after trophy promoted by media-advertising. First, there is the mild competition of *Four Weddings* (Living, 2009–; TLC, 2009–) where participants pay for their weddings but compete to win a honeymoon by attending and then criticizing each other's ceremonies, usually the sign of a badly behaved guest (they give each other marks out of 10). Other more extreme formats are even more pronounced tests of what people will do to grasp the tantalizing images of media-advertising. On *Bride vs. Bride* (WE, 2006–) two couples in full wedding dress battle through nuptial-themed games, usually involving a great deal of messy food and drink. The climax requires the two brides to tear apart a giant wedding cake in order to find the grand prize. *Last Bride Standing* (SunTV, 2009–), a Canadian show reminiscent of depression era dance marathons, has for the last few years required brides-to-be to stand in their wedding gowns with one hand on a wall to see who is the last to collapse. It takes days (with short breaks) but they hang in there because the survivor wins a free wedding. Also about physical endurance is *Shedding for the Wedding* (CW, 2011), which combines the popular weight loss format (*The Biggest Loser*, NBC, 2004–) with the wedding theme, so of course the couple who shed the most weight wins a free ceremony, a process that involves much interpersonal strife and desperate tactics. However, perhaps most bizarre of all was the idea of melding weddings with war to give us *Wedding Wars* (VH1, 2011), where (with perhaps ill-judged sponsorship by e-harmony.com) contestants undergo deprivation in a jungle setting in order to have a chance at winning (yet another) "dream" wedding. More reliable is the nightmare they enter when ten couples compete in a ruthless *Survivor*-like competition whose military allusion is actually not too farfetched since the contestants engage (metaphorically) in cut-throat competition, back stab-bing, and all kinds of aggressive behavior. Neither physical hardship nor loss of reputation matter, such is the social pressure to achieve an elaborate wed-ding. Also astonishing is the melding of surgery and wedding competition in *Bridalplasty*, a series I will examine in the next chapter, where women com-pete to win a big wedding as well as cosmetic surgery along the way to make them the "perfect" (meaning physically perfect) bride. This raises the stakes so that now people may feel the need to budget for surgery, too, as part of their wedding expenditure.

Another extraordinary form of consumer behavior is what a TLC series has dubbed "extreme couponing," where (mostly) housewives amass sufficient coupons to leave a supermarket with hundreds of dollars' worth of groceries and 90 percent or more in savings (*Extreme Couponing*, 2011). This super-consumption suits a recessionary environment though the end result is still the amassing of lots of goods, not avoiding shopping. Frugal couponers are model, almost mythical, consumers in that they give evidence of the adver-tiser's long-standing claim that spending money means saving money. The practice is presented as giving housewives a sense of accomplishment and ele-vating shopping into a skillful and strategic activity. Beyond this television show, some couponers are involved in online networks that share informa-tion (for free). Other couponers offer workshops and guides for a fee.[9] This activity could be seen as the organization of consumer labor, or as a fur-ther commercialization of consumer labor for those who purchase DVDs or attend workshops hoping to learn about how to save more money. Consumer knowledge, it turns out, is commodifiable by consumers too. On TV, the couponers appear to work independently. But what is not entirely realistic is how the cashiers and store managers apparently don't mind spending hours processing one shopper's coupons as other customers look on and applaud. Then there are the consumer's hidden costs that are bracketed off to make the purchase moment more dramatic; for example, the expense of having to buy multiple copies of newspapers or pay for printers and computers to produce coupons, never mind transportation and storage costs.

Once purchased, items are brought home to extensive and highly orga-nized storage areas that the housewives display with great pride for the cam-era. As Virginia Heffernan (May 1, 2011) notes of this series in the *New York Times*: "Where a hoard is disgusting and proof of pathology, a stockpile is as orderly as a grocery store, and proof of sound home economics." Yet some darker elements do emerge that bring to mind larger public health and policy issues. For one thing, it is not clear if these shoppers need all the items they stockpile, unless the "need" is a psychological one, to shore up their ego or stave off fear of a crisis (some rather defensively claim that they give what they don't use to charities or the military). Certainly the extreme couponers depicted on television display some compulsive tendencies and seem to experience a kind of addiction: some are described as "chronic couponers" who are "deal dependent." They are seen shaking nervously before the hit of the final receipt proving their savings and then they become visibly ecstatic as they exit the store—until the anxiety of preparing for the next big shop sets in, usually in the parking lot. When they clear out the store's entire supply of some item or monopolize a cashier for a long time these consumers could appear selfish or antisocial. Then we note that much of what they have coupons for is highly processed and unhealthy (snacks and sugary drinks) and no one seems concerned about environmental, social, or health costs. We see one couponer driving around a neighborhood snatching newspapers from people's driveways. She claims she does this only at houses she knows are empty and in foreclosure, but of course we don't know if this is the case and wonder why a foreclosed homeowner wouldn't cancel a paper subscription or why this woman moves around quite so furtively. In addition, viewers have made allegations online that the savings on the television show are dramatic because some of the women are committing fraud by falsely using coupons for products other than those the manufacturer specified.[10] Some of those accused have engaged in this viewer discussion and reply that they have a right to beat the system if the computers let them through. Retailers and television producers have admitted no guilt. Nevertheless, reality TV now faces the charge of being not only inauthentic but also fraudulent.

Unsanctioned Excess

There appear to be different dramas for different consumer profiles. Couponers appear to have a touch of OCD and are compulsive, organized, and disciplined. Other series focus on those who are compulsive, *dis*organized, and *lacking* in discipline. Some behavior is regarded as a mild psychological disorder, a sign of laziness and turpitude, but other practices are treated as requiring full psychiatric intervention. In what we might call de-clutter shows, spatial disorder is seen as a sign of a mild to moderate psychological disorder. On *American Pickers* buyers often have to persuade sellers to let go of their things, but the latter usually have enough land, barns, or trailers to house their stuff and are left in peace. Other shows intervene to de-clutter homes that are so full of things that they are messy and partially nonfunctional. In *Clean House* (Style, 2003–) and the very similar *Clean Sweep*, TV presenters organize, discard, or sell items in a yard sale. A similar de-cluttering occurs on *The Life Laundry, Neat* (HGTV Canada, 2004–) and *Mission: Organization* (HGTV, 2003–09) and is part of the preparation for selling a house in *House Doctor* (Channel 5, 1991–) and numerous such shows, so apparently lack of clutter has a market value. More focused on cleanliness and hygiene is *How Clean is Your House?* (Channel 4, 2003–09; Lifetime 2004–05), a program that was sponsored by manufacturers of cleaning products and offered residents a fresh, and in this case clean, start. For those who don't live in the country with barns and other supplementary spaces, there is also the option of renting space somewhere else. This curious practice of paying to house items that apparently you don't need (or at least not immediately) is perhaps the most definitive sign of a culture that accommodates and seeks to profit from overspending. Nothing speaks so loudly of the excess of consumption than this practice that gives rise to further commercial opportunities for those who rent out these spaces and for those who buy and sell their contents when the renters default. This capitalist niche is the premise of *Storage Wars* and *Storage Hunters* in which we watch people competing in auctions to buy the contents of a storage unit that someone else has abandoned or forfeited through nonpayment of rent. In this case, the de-cluttering is involuntary.

Another approach is to offer some kind of rehab for those who overspend and attempt to increase their consumer literacy. British TV, which has a strong tradition of consumer advice programming, recently offered *Superscrimpers: Waste Not Want Not* (Channel 4, 2011), which advises families how to spend within their means. More melodramatically, this pedagogic approach can take the form of a fiscal-and-parenting hybrid that aims to humiliate spoiled offspring. In Britain there is *Bank of Mum and Dad* (BBC Two, 2004; SoapNet, 2009) and in the United States *You're Cut off* (VH1, 2010–), both offering a sort of detox for young adults who spend enormous amounts of their parents' money on themselves and do little else. This scenario plays off a contemporary anxiety about older children continuing to live with and remaining financially dependent on their parents. On *You're Cut off* the participants (all young women) originally thought they were appearing on a more flattering RTV show but are tricked into a program where they are obliged to spend some weeks in a house with other spoiled offspring all of whom are cut off from their parents/ credit cards (it is difficult to know which is the more significant relationship). They have been sent there by their parents to be tutored in how to properly relate to money and at the end of the program the parents decide whether or not to take them back home. The show's host attempts to teach them to spend less, think about others, and, ideally, get a job. Needless to say, the drama is created by similar and conflicting material: each one of the participants complains about her deprivation and displays various degrees of laziness, selfishness, and rebellion against the program (both television show and rehab). They are shocked to have been pushed out of their private, affluent cocoon to face the horrors of having to take a public bus (a first for them) or work in a fast-food restaurant. Some do eventually display the desired behavior though the authenticity of their rehabilitation is difficult to judge, as are the motives or even credentials of those who conduct the program. Both of these parties are potentially quite mercenary.

Clearly we are meant to note that overspending has ethical and developmental consequences. But a more morbid picture has emerged in the last few years with *Hoarders* (A&E, 2009–) and *Hoarding: Buried Alive* (TLC, 2010–), series that move into a pathological and disturbing territory to examine how overconsumption can be not only profligate and wasteful but also deeply harmful to subjects and their relationships with other people. The amateur collectors on *American Pickers* can seem pathetic at times and occasionally we learn that their behavior may be compensating for some kind of trauma (death, divorce, warfare). But those who come into contact with them usually regard them as harmless eccentrics. Those whom producers select for a de-cluttering show like *Clean House* can be on the verge of making their environment unhealthy or nonfunctional, but both home and family interactions are still deemed to be within the realm of the normal. In contrast, producers appear to regard people as "hoarders" when their living spaces are so full they can't make use of them anymore and when their relationship with things seriously disrupts their relationships with people, becoming a centrifugal force that drives others away: sometimes family members move out or in extreme cases are forcibly removed (if dependent children). As Baudrillard observed, collecting involves having relationships with others, for example through trading or exhibiting, and so it "has a door open onto culture" ([1968] 1996, 111). Hoarding, on the other hand, shuts this door. There is no trading or display, only secretive and guilty isolation.

With hoarders, quantity destroys value. Most items are never used and their accumulation becomes physically and psychologically unhealthy or even dangerous; for example, hoarding can lead to unsanitary conditions or create a fire hazard or a space where people could get injured or crushed. Hoarders are most typically seen as overwhelmed and as attached to, but defeated by, their possessions. Their compulsive behavior has made what is ordinarily the sanctuary of the home into a dangerous and shameful place. Whereas style makeovers link spending with both professional and personal success, hoarding has the opposite effect. Instead of the reveal scene reintegrating the subject into the social group, there is a depressing unraveling of family and career. The subject is forced to see that they have prioritized consuming objects over people and that this is not socially acceptable.

These series work commercially if they attract advertisers, as apparently they do, but they delve into areas where consumption is a significant problem. So the question is do they fly in the face of the numerous other shows that ultimately promote consumption? The answer is not necessarily. Hoarding is a testament to the power of consumption. These programs impress upon us that shopping ought not to be trivialized but rather respected for its impact and consequences. On makeovers there is a scolding and even mockery of inadequate consumers, but with subjects deemed to be hoarders there is a more serious but also more professionally calm intervention by clinical psychologists who seem to go out of their way to acknowledge that the subject has a difficult addiction. Hoarders reciprocate by talking about their habits also in terms of addiction, though many reject the diagnosis at first and the label of hoarder. Nevertheless, while clinicians are seen to work professionally, there is no doubt that as TV entertainment these programs are in line with the freakish or abnormal behavior on display elsewhere, particularly, in the United States, on TLC (*My Strange Addiction* [2010], *Toddlers and Tiaras* [2009–], and (so far) *19 Kids and Counting* [2008–]). As anomalies, hoarders are not viewer surrogates or examples of what might happen to ordinary shoppers.

It is a dark curiosity that hoarders inspire. Theirs is not the high-end extravagance of *The Real Housewives* or the super-spenders of *My Super Sweet 16* where subjects claim their lifestyle is fabulous and viewers can choose to admire, envy, or loathe. The result of hoarding is not luxury and pride but dilapidation and shame. The piles and piles of unused, low-cost items do not impress others with anything other than pity and disgust. The kind of clutter seen on *American Pickers* is validated because it is old and possibly has historical value, whereas the hoarder more typically accumulates mass-produced chain store items, most often clothing that they never wear. Collectors can be congratulated for possessing some knowledge about their objects and their value, whereas many who hoard seem unaware of most of their stuff or what they paid for it. Part of the proposed recovery process is having experts assess the value of their hoard and converting some of it into saleable commodities. However, in an unusual move for reality TV, the fix is not guaranteed to be a matter of a day or a week. We are told that recovery may take months, years, or maybe never happen. A room or two might be improved before the film crew moves out, giving viewers some Before-and-After gratification. But the show's focus is not on the long and largely internal process of gaining mental equilibrium, it is on the stunning visual impact of the disequilibrium.

CHAPTER 7

The Body Shop

Real Estate

This chapter addresses one final and radical impact of consumerism, which is the turning of the material self into a consumer object with the help of cosmetic surgery. In the most intimate enactment yet of the commercial imperative traced throughout this book, makeover surgeries quite literally shape the body in conformity to the imagery of media-advertising to produce an unmistakable objectification, or more specifically, a commodification, of this material. The body and our perceptions of the body are always being shaped by culture, but the literalism of this procedure is striking. We have seen how makeover producers present surgeons and their power to transform as benign (Chapter 2), but this chapter will take a closer look at their practice to see how it impacts more than professional image. More scholarly attention has been paid to style than to surgical makeovers, but some analyses have looked at the latter for their gender implications, for issues of identity formation and normalcy, and for their ties to neoliberalism (Deery 2004b, 2006; Fraser 2007; Gailey 2007; Tait 2007; Jones 2008a, 2008b; Weber 2009). Continuing to focus on consumer culture, my discussion of these formats will be based on a comparison of home and body makeovers for the insight this yields into attitudes about the body's socioeconomic function and links between commodification and mediation. Drawing on earlier discussions in this book and my work elsewhere (Deery 2004b, 2006), I will read surgical makeovers through home makeover formats to underscore how the body functions under capitalism as a property, as an investment, and as a commercial prospect—not unlike a renovated house. Similar program techniques and rituals underline the notion that the body, too, is something one owns and inhabits. It can therefore be treated as something that one *has* rather than something that one *is*, a notion that is potentially libratory but not necessarily so. It used to be that the notion of having an "owner's manual" for one's body was novel and cute, but surgical makeovers suggest that this metaphor is losing its playfulness. The onus to work on one's body, and not just what covers it, is real. Now that we have options, now that surgery is being advertised, opportunities begin to act as pressures and the media are happy to oblige, both in creating pressure and in promising to alleviate it.

Once again, I will draw on Baudrillard for his insight into the link between body modification and consumer culture. What surgical makeovers make conspicuous is the pronounced link in consumer culture between body and identity and the turning of both into possessions. As Celia Lury (1996) observes: "consumer culture provides the conditions within which it is not just that self-identity is understood *in relation to* possessions, but that it is itself constituted *as* a possession" (8; author's emphasis); this is, after all, an era that has given birth to the notion of "identity theft." On reality makeovers we witness not so much theft as corporate sponsorship: identity is not stolen but is signed over and used to further commercial aims.

For some time, people have accepted the responsibility of maintaining and making fashionable their living space. Surgical makeovers mainstream the idea that we should do the same for our bodies—not just by arranging hair and clothing but by altering the body's very architecture. While some superficial body modification is as old as human culture (piercings, tattoos), recent technologies render the body more radically malleable than ever before. Thanks to surgical techniques, the body's flaws are fixable: therefore, says a consumerist society, they ought to be fixed. Exactly what motivates any given individual to request a surgical makeover is impossible to fully determine—even for the subject involved—but there is no question that media-advertising has already played a significant role before anyone lines up for their makeover audition. My aim in examining on-screen transformations is to follow the logic presented in each series and offer an interpretation of its cultural significance.

Although it has been exported around the world, the surgical makeover is another particularly American form of reality television[1] which appeals to this culture's intense and early interest in physical appearance, in glamour, in self-improvement, and in what amounts to a cult of youth. In other countries cosmetic surgery is less socially acceptable, as in many parts of Europe (Franco 2008), or people are more reserved when it comes to showing the body in general, as in China or other parts of Asia (Lewis 2011, 84).[2] My account will consider a variety of mostly American formats, including *Extreme Makeover*, *The Swan*, *10 Years Younger*, *Bridalplasty*, and the docusoap *The Real Housewives*. These programs put into popular view rarefied postmodern discourses about the fluidity of the self, about sex and gender, and about the self as a project; however, they are generally non-committal about whether this project involves multiple selves or the linear evolution of one core self.

Techno-euphorists can say all they want about going online and leaving the body behind, but TV makeovers drive home that the focus on the material body has never been greater, nor have our anxieties about this site, no matter how many glamorous avatars we create. The body matters and is being looked at from all sides in both academic and popular spheres. That it is a site of power and increasingly central to our sense of self-identity was underscored by second wave feminists in the 1970s and taken up by sociologists and philosophers in subsequent decades.[3] Most notably, Foucault's work was essential to keying the body to a decentralized, noncoercive but nevertheless fundamental power network. Today, there is some agreement that the body plays a pivotal role in revealing the relationship between social forces and individual agency (Blum 2003). Also that the body is shaped by, and helps to shape, its social environment; in other words, the body is in society and society is in the body (Shilling 2003). An awareness of this mutual constitution can now be found in fields as diverse as history, anthropology, sports and leisure studies, philosophy, theology, sociology, and cultural studies. Meanwhile, outside academia, looking after the body is a major sector in advanced economies: for example, health care, clothing, beautification, diet, exercise, and so on. Also profitable are segments of popular media such as women's/celebrity/fitness magazines whose commentary would suggest that body shapes and altering body shapes is a central cultural preoccupation, if not obsession.

Every culture has taboos and prohibitions about which body parts may be subject to another's view, when, and in what circumstances—taboos that are often understood as a matter of ethics but also signal underlying economic arrangements (e.g., the female body as property in capitalist patriarchy). On surgical makeovers, shots of nipples and genitalia are conventionally blurred but otherwise makeover subjects have to display and discuss with a doctor, while on camera, what they perceive to be their specific physical flaws. Ordinarily, this filming of a patient consultation would of course be judged highly unprofessional. The fact that the critique of the body comes largely from the subject herself, a lifelong witness of media images, rather than from another judge, is at this stage a fairly minor distinction. The scenario is uncomfortable for the patient and this is, of course, the point, for their humiliation is the price they have to pay for securing a media audience/surgery. The patients are exposed according to the producers' stipulations in a process that has no medical use or justification. The inappropriateness of this voyeurism was particularly flagrant on *Bridalplasty* when the surgery candidates had to bare all not only to the surgeon or anonymous others (TV audience) once the episode aired, but also to a small, face-to-face group of rival brides on the show. Having their disgraced body parts displayed as they sit in a known group has a particular note of impropriety and it made one candidate burst out with: "No one should have to do this!" accompanied by an awkward laugh. Sue Tait suggests that such sequences are in part designed to get viewers on board with the surveillance and its normative judgments in order to justify the upcoming surgery. The audience is "to share the candidate's assessing and disciplinary gaze and assent with the identification of the aberrant features of the displayed body. This ostensibly 'proves' that surgical intervention is warranted . . . " (2007, 125). That may be the plan anyway.

The Temple

The typical makeover has a female patient seeking help from a male surgeon.[4] His bending over her mute and supine body in the operation room brings to mind the old narrative of the male scientist dissecting Nature depicted as a female body (Merchant 1980). Or his incisions could be seen in purely sexual terms as a male penetration. A more specific account which dominated Western thought for centuries is Aristotelian reproduction. Without benefit of empirical research, this most influential natural philosopher forthrightly asserted that during reproduction the male shaped formless matter that lay within the female and so he was likened to, among other things, a carpenter creating objects out of wood.[5] So here we have at least fragments of the tropes of body as house and male as builder embedded in early Western patriarchal thought. In the case of the modern makeover, the surgeon resembles a builder not of another body within a woman's body but of the woman herself. Indeed, one of the most striking and repeated images on televised surgeries is of the male surgeon marking up with ink areas of the patient's body that he will be work upon, like a carpenter marking up a piece of wood before he cuts into it. Aristotle's account reflected the tradition of according superiority to form over matter, to intellect and skill over dull substance. The modern makeover does not deviate significantly from this account.

The extent to which the body is something we inhabit, like a home, or something that is more inherently part of who we are, is a question that has exercised philosophers for millennia and kept psychologists and social scientists busy in more recent decades.[6] Obviously, I don't aim to resolve the issue here but simply wish to underline that on TV makeovers having an unattractive body is portrayed as equivalent to inhabiting an unattractive house, so the correct articulation is "I *have* an ugly body" rather than "I *am* ugly." It is perhaps not a coincidence then that some titles invoke the analogy between houses and people, as when *Trading Spaces* (TLC, Discovery Home, 2000–08) becomes *Trading Spouses* (Fox, 2004–07) or when these realms are conflated in *Renovate My Family* (Fox, 2004), *Property Virgins* (HGTV, 2006-) and *Date My House* (TLC, 2008). That the body is a structure and even a home of sorts is reflected in common phrases such as "feeling at home in one's body," or assessing someone's authenticity or sanity by asking if "anyone's home." Regarding the body metaphorically as a building is, in fact, a very old idea. St. Paul famously instructed early Christians that the "body is a temple of the Holy Spirit." Remarkably, it was this early religious leader who also raised the notion of the body as a property and transferable commodity. He did so to reinforce the obligation the Christian should feel to God to keep his or her body pure. "You are not your own; you were bought at a price. Therefore honor God with your body," Paul admonishes (1 Corinthians 6:19–20). The price was Christ's sacrifice of his life which transferred ownership of each person's body to God, the ultimate landlord. Of course what makes the body distinct as a habitation is that it is permanent and inseparable, until death that is. After initially inhabiting another body (our mother's), being born means inhabiting our own, and only our own, body: this is the condition of being alive and is the most fundamental experience of everyday life. Inhabiting this body means we always have a particular perspective, literally and physically, because we see out of two eyes in a singular location and, more metaphorically, because of the experience and culture in which this body lives. Hence in English and other Indo-European languages, the body is the first reference point for understanding and measuring space: for example, the thumb gives us the inch and the foot the measure of one foot.[7]

Yet while it is an intimate space, the body is also potentially a site of separation and alienation. Having a body is why subjects can be taken as objects or as things[8] and one could argue that this is the stance being advocated on TV shows that solve problems by fixing the body's material and surface—a glib conclusion, perhaps, but an understandable one. For example, during their initial consultation both surgeons and patients tend to distance themselves from body identity and personal biography by agreeing on the importance of general principles of design such as proportion and symmetry, as one would when working on an architectural project. We saw in style makeovers a similar invocation of principles in order to impress upon subjects that there can and should be an objective assessment of body topology. This is even more the case in surgical makeovers where redesigning the body is presented as an objective task based on neutral factors such as geometric space and proportion, a sublimation most noticeable on *Extreme Makeover* when a photo of the patient's body is displayed like a blueprint, either static on the UK edition or rotating against a geometric grid in the American. In both instances, graphics label problem areas that need to be fixed, an early mapping which reinforces the idea that the person has become part of the object world. In actual fact, surgery is a violent act involving the breaking, tearing, and sawing of human bone and tissue, but on makeover shows clean spatial graphics largely overshadow blood and gore. Contrast this with procedural crime dramas such as CBS's *CSI* (2000-), another popular strain of television that focuses on the narratives that bodies reveal but that relies on sadistic violence and trauma. The surgical makeover focuses on more containable abstract images which suggest that its procedures are almost a matter of mathematical measurement and redistribution of mass: for women, the redistribution involves smaller waists, larger breasts, smaller noses, bigger lips, while for men the results are "stronger" chins, wider chests, and straighter noses. In addition, one effect of surgery is to make these bodies more like buildings by being static and taut.

In common parlance, patients employ phrases such as "getting work done" or having "a nose job" to euphemistically attach their cosmetic surgery to the more impersonal notion of commercial construction and there may be a form of relief or even liberation in this transaction as depicted on television makeovers. For seeing their body as an object to be worked upon perhaps removes culpability from these subjects, especially as their assessment of their body's flaws is not challenged by sympathetic doctors who simply ratify that their concerns are justified and deserving of attention. Hosts on house makeovers are often careful to avoid blaming inhabitants for the dilapidated condition of their home, stressing financial and time constraints for lack of upkeep and repair. Similarly, blaming subjects is not part of the discourse of *Extreme Makeover* or *Bridalplasty*. Patients simply hand over their body as an unsatisfactory project for someone else to fix. Surgeons say little about the reasons for excess flesh: they simply suck the offending matter out (avoiding phrases like "you are fat"). However, culpability does emerge on *10 Years Younger* where being put on public display in a glass box has a whiff of the village stocks. This time subjects are held accountable for their state of disrepair: usually the problem is lack of prevention (sunscreen) or bad habits (diet, smoking). Blame and personal accountability are at the forefront of weight loss programs such as *The Biggest Loser*, programs that do not resort to surgery and instead encourage people to modify their bodies themselves over time. Programs that focus on surgery incorporate diet and exercise guides to some extent, but their emphasis is on promoting the rapid transformation achieved by putting one's body in someone else's hands, and the magic happens when the patient is not even conscious of being worked upon by others (under anesthetics).

Property Values

The comparison with home makeovers also brings into focus the extent to which the body under capitalism becomes a property, meaning a place that is generally private and privately owned though available for various forms of economic exchange. Privacy is a legal concept that is historically relative and culturally specific. It is something that can be lost or surrendered.[9] In most cultures and in most places, the body is the most intimate and private of spaces. But, as with home makeovers, body makeovers temporarily disband the owner's customary rights and privileges: in both instances, subjects hand over or lease out their space to others who benefit financially from the transaction. This is only a particularly stark illustration of the way in which the relationship between individuals and their bodies is, today, being managed in consumer society where the body is treated as a property in which one can invest both economically and psychologically. Individuals meet capitalist objectives by focusing on the property's competitive market assessment to produce an instrumental relation to the self. We noted in the previous chapter the imperative to work on the enterprising self: seeking surgery is often part of this reflexive economy.

That beautification is a sober investment rather than a personal indulgence is a persistent message of the surgical makeover series. The calculating nature of this investment is captured by Baudrillard's observation that, today, individuals are told it is their responsibility to put on a planned or "synthetic" narcissism ([1976]1993, 111–12) in order to index the body to "the code and the norms of a society of production and managed consumption" ([1970]1998, 131). The focus on the self is synthetic in that it is not spontaneous but is deliberate and managed for strategic ends. It is a matter not of pleasure but of work, in a process that involves a self-objectification and staging of one's body. Tying what he calls "the beauty imperative" to market capitalism, Baudrillard observes a contemporary "*turning* the body to *advantage* by way of narcissistic reinvestment" ([1970]1998, 133; author's emphasis). No one calculates more closely how to make the most of this synthetic narcissism than the women of *The Real Housewives* franchise, whose extrovert behavior exposes the more muted transactions occurring in a series like *Extreme Makeover* or *The Swan*. On *The Real Housewives,* making the body look good is a serious business and while cosmetic surgery is not a central narrative focus it is a vital element in the lives of those being filmed. It appears that most of the women have had some "work" done and increasingly they acknowledge this on camera. Unlike the modest "ugly ducklings" of charitable makeovers, the housewives rely fairly heavily on cosmetic surgery to advance their ambitions, which for many of these women is circumscribed by the finding and keeping of a wealthy husband. For others, an attractive body is also good for their professional careers (e.g., models, realtors, marketers, designers). In either case, these women recognize that body upgrades are essential for maintaining their market value and so for them cosmetic surgery is calculated and routine. In one scene, a husband rewards his wife for having her breasts augmented by surprising her in the recovery room with a gift of diamond earrings. Drowsy but gratified, she gets the message and says (with a laugh of sorts) that she should have cosmetic surgery more often, presumably because of the immediate financial gain.

So much is surgery normalized that one mother and daughter go in for a cozy surgery together (Lynne and daughter in *The Real Housewives of Orange County*) and another woman has almost a drive-thru experience when she has her fourth breast augmentation at a "Same Day Surgery" clinic in a strip mall (Danielle in *The Real Housewives of New Jersey*). The casual nature of the clinic and its setting is one reason why other medical practitioners look aghast at some cosmetic surgeons because they don't legally have to operate within hospitals and can conduct business anywhere. Several other *Real Housewives* women are filmed having minor cosmetic procedures as a fairly regular part of their lives and sometimes they bring friends along as though on a shopping trip. Botox parties are especially popular, both in home and work settings: for example, Vicki (*The Real Housewives of Orange County*) thinks it a nice reward for her employees to have a surprise office Botox party where she coerces them into getting injected, while also acknowledging that having an attractive appearance is good for (her) business. This brings office management into a new (and possibly illegal) area. But her intentions are pure to the extent that she, like the other women in this series, are convinced that working on physical appearance is a sound investment in one's financial future and so she is mentoring others in how best to succeed. Some of the housewives openly discuss how much they paid for various procedures and whether it was a good deal. Certainly they are not shy about displaying the results.

For many of these glamorous, sexualized, postfeminist women, turning their bodies into objects of desire is their chief career and it is their success at this self-commodification that allows them to spend most of their lives consuming other goods and services. Those who secure and rely on a wealthy husband's money are shown working hard to "maintain their body" and keep their side of the bargain. They may not work but they "work out," a distinct form of labor usually undertaken by those who don't otherwise have to exert themselves manually. In societies of abundance, part of being beautiful is being toned and slim. This signals discipline and has become an indication of prestige, of success, even of class. *The Real Housewives* series do not depict charity makeovers but those who are able to afford surgery (mostly thanks to their husbands) and who come across, for the most part, as irredeemably superficial and hollow. Their harping on about how it is their choice to trade physical attraction for money (or, less bluntly, achieve a "successful" marriage) hardly masks their subordinate position or the fragility of that marital arrangement. For all their faith in improvement through consumption, there is still an unease and a defensive attitude about their body's status as a commodity, even if within a marriage contract. The specter of being a "prostitution whore"[10] looms over these well-groomed and surgically enhanced women who are in many ways caricatures, but, as caricatures, effectively illustrate some of the negotiations, ambivalences, and even hypocrisies of many other contemporary women and men who similarly invest in their body's appearance. In one sense it seems these women trade their bodies for real estate and in this way one property is exchanged for another. The wealthy husbands become a means to an end, the end being a luxurious home. At least this is where editors often focus their attention; for example, outside shots of each opulent dwelling is ritualistically used to identify the person who will be featured next. Only to the extent that they are wedded to the house (as a signifier of economic position) are they "house-wives," for certainly there is little evidence of the housewifery that is traditionally associated with this term given that many of these women employ nannies, maids, and personal assistants. However, as the various series have evolved, an unintended consequence of the franchise's success is that several of these women are growing more financially and socially independent (for them it appears the two are connected).

Commodification

The human body is more than a collection of bones, fat, and tissue. As we have seen, much of its significance lies in its role as a social sign and it is as a sign that it enters into various economic circuits (even by default, for not opting for cosmetic surgery can also become a social statement).[11] An interesting thing about the body is that it can be an object and a subject at once (Falk 1994, 1) and when we associate this dualism with the notion of media consumption, curious relations arise. Physiologically, the body is first and foremost a site of consumption, meaning that one of the body's main functions is to consume food in order to create matter and energy. But on surgical makeovers, even more radically than on style makeovers, it is the body that is being consumed: consumed by viewers as a mediated object but also by the participants themselves who, once transformed, become consumers of an image of themselves which is being sold to viewers. The body is consumed and can stimulate consumption. Of course, treating bodies as transferrable commodities is not a new concept: both ancient slavery and "the oldest profession" attest to that. It is a practice fundamental to most stages of patriarchy, where women are legally owned and traded as commodities between father and husband (as in the marriage ritual of "who giveth this woman?").[12] Though this gendered transaction is often overlooked in economic accounts, Luce Irigaray, for one, ranked it as absolutely fundamental; rereading Marx in the 1970s, she stated plainly that "[t]he society we know, our own culture, is based upon the exchange of women" (1985, 170). In countries that today produce and view reality makeovers, the notion of the female body as an exchangeable commodity is not so overt or legally enforceable. However, on surgical makeovers we do see a curiously regressive picture as female bodies are passively transferred among mostly male authorities who impose tight restrictions on their behavior. Some *Extreme Makeover* episodes make over engaged couples who aren't allowed to see each other again until the veil is lifted at their wedding ceremony, a flirtation with the strictest of patriarchal practices. This arrangement was taken up by *Bridalplasty* where it became the series-long narrative. In this format, several brides-to-be live in an isolated environment and compete to win surgical procedures (provided by a surgeon from *The Swan*) and the grand prize of a complete surgical makeover and elaborate wedding. After being transformed, the winning bride is revealed to her groom only at their wedding ceremony when she emerges from behind a curtain and walks up the aisle in a totally opaque veil. The climax of the event is the reveal of her new body rather than the exchange of vows; hence the minister obligingly halts the religious rite in order to make the most of the TV moment when the male first sees his new bride after four months apart. Normally the bride is a reproductive commodity in that she will bear children, but here she has acquired value also as a media commodity. With all eyes and cameras on her, she is escorted up the aisle by a senior male relative as is traditional, but "who giveth this woman to be married to this man?" could well be answered by the television producers and their advertising support.

On *The Swan* even the subject was not permitted to see her transformed body until it was simultaneously revealed to viewers. Prior to the reveal ceremony, the show's "mirror police" forbade every candidate from looking in any reflecting surfaces on penalty of being thrown out. When she is first allowed to see herself in a staged ceremony in front of a mirror, each subject's re-imaging of her new body is, in Foucauldian terms, a quite literal internalization of the mechanisms of surveillance and the gaze of the Other (Deery 2004b). She is now not only an object, but "an object of vision: a sight" (Berger 1972, 47), a sight that seems to both fascinate and alienate her. The fact that her body is the product of others' work is perhaps why the subject is not usually modest about expressing delight in how it looks: in praising her appearance she is praising those who created it. On the more punitive *10 Years Younger* subjects who request a makeover have to stand in a glass box in the equivalent of the town square while passing strangers (literally the-person-on-the-street) are polled about the subject's age and physical appearance.[13] Their appearance (i.e., market value) is assessed while on display, as though a retail object. To compound their status as a thing, they are deaf and mute while in the box and are unable to hear what these casual others are saying about them.

Here is how the *Queer Eye* website describes their style makeovers:

> With help from family and friends, the Fab Five treat each new guy as a head-to-toe project. Soon, the straight man is educated on everything from hair products to Prada and Feng Shui to foreign films. At the end of every fashion-packed, fun-filled lifestyle makeover, a freshly scrubbed, newly enlightened guy emerges—complete with that "new man" smell![14]

Each episode, we are told, boils down to a "one-hour guide to building a better man." This description of a person in terms of an industrial product like an automobile is intended to be comic because it is not exactly appropriate. But it is not entirely inapplicable either. The made-over person does resemble a product to the extent that his new identity is produced and produced by others. This is especially the case with surgical makeovers where some surgeons refer to the post-op body as, indeed, "the final product." Moreover, when these made-over bodies conform to a fairly narrow range of looks this homogeneity increases the sense that they have not been born but produced: like any manufacturing process, it is a matter of finding cheap raw material ("ordinary" subjects), processing and designing it in line with market forces, and then packaging the results.

On both home and body makeovers there is a similar carving of the narrative into the three phases of exposure, rehab, and reveal. During the initial exposure, the patients lay bare their personal site (body) in order to catalogue its problems, not unlike the assessment of the dilapidated home. After the structure has been redesigned (not, in the case of the body, demolished), the revelation of the new body is equivalent to the moment in home improvement shows when homeowners view what has been done to their home or room and involves the same mix of unfamiliarity and ownership, of distance and possession. There is the same proud display of the "new-and-improved" product and the same admiration for the workmanship and its impact on future lives. The subject's job is to simply stand on display and generate comments about how successful the project has been: in the United States everyone is "thrilled" and in the United Kingdom "gob smacked."

Like house projects, surgical makeovers create much of their final drama from time compression. Hence the timeline and form of surgery are designed to suit programming over individual needs. Several procedures are performed in one mammoth operation, which is more risky for the patient but more cost effective and dramatic for the producers, and subjects are chosen because their surgery is projected to require the budgeted recovery time of six to eight weeks.[15] This prioritizing of schedule over psychological well-being was revealed in a lawsuit concerning one candidate named Deleese Williams who was informed the night before surgery that she was being dropped from *Extreme Makeover* because producers had decided her recovery time would not suit their schedule. Meanwhile, her family had been encouraged to go on camera to comment on how unattractive she was, assuming she would soon be receiving aid. When this help did not materialize, her family was apparently guilt-ridden and embarrassed for having criticized her. Her sister, Kellie McGee, was struggling with bipolar disorder and she moved out of the house and committed suicide four months later. The law suit against ABC/Disney claims that the reality producers' decisions contributed to the suicide because of the anguish McGee felt for disparaging her sister's appearance (Bone 2005). After a year, both sides in the dispute reached a settlement for an undisclosed amount.

In any society, the treatment of the body indicates some of the ways power circulates. Foucault ([1975] 1977) crucially observed in the modern era a shift away from obviously coercive legal and militaristic control of the body to today's more commonly administrative, medical and psycho-cultural mechanisms. We witnessed the producers' attempts at coercion on style makeovers but on surgical makeovers their control tends to be more firm. On these shows just about all of the patient's movements are dictated in another example of private, commercial forces being acceptable where public and government overtures are not. Rather than formal, institutional restrictions, there is a therapeutic imperative distributed through private channels (media-advertising) urging the subject to conform. To a deeper extent than with shopping makeovers, this handing over of the body for surgery creates an alienation in the labor of self-reproduction. However, television shows such as *Extreme Makeover* and *The Swan* have also helped create a new relationship between patient and surgeon beyond the TV screen. When these series were being filmed they reflected the still authoritarian relationship between uninformed patient and all-knowing doctor where the patient does not question, negotiate, or critique. But since most of these shows have aired and the Internet has opened up further sources of information, patients are more likely to shop around for a surgeon who will best perform what they already judge needs to be done (Tait 2007, 126). Meredith Jones (2008b) observes that, in part because of information circulating through popular channels like reality television, cosmetic surgery patients are now more inclined to approach their doctors as customers looking for a good service provider. So the commercial basis of the transaction is more marked today despite the public relations exercise of makeover TV that tried to erase these finances. In an era when such surgery has become another thing you buy, surgeons report a loss of status but an increase in business (Jones 2008b).

Attractive bodies attract and very attractive bodies attract even more, so it is no surprise that media-advertising skews toward representations of ideal beauty. More than this, advertising enjoins us to aspire to achieve the extraordinary appearance it uses to capture our attention. As numerous studies have suggested, one of the strongest effects of the media's daily parade of ideal beauty is that this alters what viewers regard as normal and what they aspire to be.[16] That the logic of television prioritizes the superficial and the visual has had profound and still evolving cultural ramifications. For instance, if our models of ideal beauty were textual only there would be more room for our own standards and input (Blum 2003, 260), whereas a visual model fixes and imposes the image in exact detail. This opens up an almost infinite market for selling products to those who will never meet this image. On surgical makeovers we witness a diligent and procrustean chopping of bodies to meet a beauty ideal, but there is no suggestion that media representations should instead be altered. The previously unmediated become fulfilled not just by being mediated but by being mediatized, meaning conforming to media images. Surgical candidates appear to have little interest in media exposure as an end in itself, but this kind of programming teaches them, and by extension us, that being mediated can be very beneficial and life transforming and therefore something to be desired.

What particularly struck Fredric Jameson (1992) about Guy Debord's depiction of the "society of the spectacle" was the latter's observation that the ultimate form of commodity reification in contemporary society is the image itself (11–12). With surgical makeovers, the media image is reified in the subject and then resold as a TV image. In other words, if ever discourse impacted the material realm it is at this point, the human body. As Baudrillard observed, today we find not only "the forced extraversion of all interiority"—which almost any reality series pushes to the limit—but also the "forced introjection of all exteriority" ([1987]1988, 26), meaning the internalizing of media imagery. RTV makeovers don't just display the ideal bodies we see everywhere else in the media, they show people imposing this ideal on real bodies: so that they become a simulation of an ideal (Baudrillard

[1990]1993, 45). In some instances, as in MTV's *I Want a Famous Face* or TV Guide Channel's (nonsurgical) *Look-a-Like*, participants wish to resemble specific media products such as Brad Pitt or Pamela Anderson. Others wish to emulate an iconic figure who is not human, as in Cindy Jackson's 29 plastic surgeries to make her look like Barbie (Gabler 1998, 210). (Cindy, incidentally, is the name of a British version of the Barbie doll.) RTV's mainstreaming of surgical procedures that offer to real-ize a hyperbolic image raises the bar for what people are expected to do and to spend in order to achieve a satisfactory status.[17] Producers are tapping into a media effect (the near obsessive desire for an attractive body) within a media product (the makeover series) in order to create a media product of the body.

But it is not an internal feedback loop entirely. Nor is the significance of physical attractiveness an illusion arbitrarily impressed upon us by a cynical media simply in order to secure its own profits. People pay heed to media images, to what the culture deems attractive, because there are real-world consequences. We observe anecdotally and through more formal study that those who look attractive are admired and rewarded. Some of this response may be due to biological mechanisms and some to more socially constructed and culturally variant preferences, but whatever the origins of our attitudes there is little dispute that in real life being judged attractive has distinct advantages.[18] On the biological front, certain body types may be favored because they signal fertility and virility while, for example, symmetrical features may indicate freedom from harmful genetic mutations, traumas, or residual effects of disease (Sullivan 2001, 21). Sociological studies suggest that the physically attractive are more likely to be promoted and to achieve other forms of success in all stages of life.[19] In any case, whatever the validity of such results, the perception that appearance matters becomes important and largely self-fulfilling, a logic at least reinforced on makeover TV.

Gender Construction

One of the most compelling roles played by media-advertising is that of defining what is feminine or masculine, and it is striking how often female makeover patients report that they wish to be "more feminine," a concept that is almost always tied to being more "sexy." The men's desire for masculinity is generally more muted and indeed there is a possibility that their seeking surgical enhancement will be coded as feminine. Whatever the case, on-screen doctors treat anyone's desire to accentuate their gender as natural and are happy to support heterosexist and sexist norms. As Brenda Weber notes, they appear to support the idea that "sex or biology is malleable while gender is constant," and so the former is shaped to match the latter (2009,

170). One pragmatic advantage of invoking "feminine" or "masculine" in a surgical context is that if doctors and patients have a similar understanding of what this means then it will provide a commonly agreed upon diagram of what an improved body should look like, and so doctors, patients, and presumably viewers will be similarly impressed by the results. But two things are being communicated here: that being strongly gender-marked is a desirable goal and that this effect can be produced through fairly rapid and superficial changes in bodily appearance. As though upholding, and in fact enacting, Judith Butler's notion that biological matters, too, are culturally determined, surgeons redesign the patient's body in order to better meet their culture's gender template. This is a remarkable process since it is only in recent times that there been such an opportunity for a culture to not only interpret but also to physically carve the body and to do so radically, swiftly, and with reasonable safety. In this manner, discourse physically shapes materiality and, if we maintain a gender/ sex distinction, then cosmetic surgery imposes notions of gender (femininity) on to sex (the female body).[20]

The women on some of these shows emerge not just as feminine but as hyperfeminine, most notably on *The Swan* and *The Real Housewives* where the glamour version of femininity produces women who hark back to more patriarchal times: big hair, high heels, lots of "curves," and so on. These shows appear to offer enclaves of "enlightened sexism" where it is deemed acceptable to resurrect retrograde stereotypes and diffuse offense to more progressive viewers with mockery and ironic amusement (Douglas 2010). The matter takes an absurd turn when what seems like sexism is extended even to the design of teeth. *Extreme Makeover*'s Dr. Bill Dorfman is of the opinion that a woman gets what she wants by "flashing her pearly whites" and that a "feminine smile is bright, soft, and beguiling. . . . Not unlike a feminine-looking body, a feminine-looking smile is all about curves." Masculine teeth, on the other hand, should appear "more angular" with the central incisors "square, strong, and more powerful" than the surrounding teeth (Dorfman 2006, 15). If biology doesn't mark gender in this way, then the surgeon is there to help fix this oversight.

One main reason for the surgical redesign of the body is that it is a place that exists in time, and there are two things that we have always known about aging: that it is inevitable and that it is universal. Both of these facts enhance the profitability of addressing nature's planned obsolescence. Fighting time's effects on the flesh is, indeed, a billion dollar segment of the "fashion-beauty complex" (Bartky 1990) in which scientific-sounding ingredients and techniques (with adjectives like bio and molecular) are marketed as powerful "defense" mechanisms, often incorporating but reengineering natural substances (Douglas 2000, 273).[21] For example, Garnier offers "Ultra-Lift⁶Pro gravity defying cream" (Newton, never mind NASA, would be impressed). But this is the essence of commodification: adding value by offering the techné (craft, technology) that works on and even against nature. In many consumer cultures women of any age, despite other accomplishments, are expected to look as slim and adolescent as when they first started out in the market (or as they never did). The fat deposits and stretch marks that are natural testaments to the nurturance of others are matters for self-loathing, while wrinkles are pathologized as a disease that must be cured. As its title suggests, *10 Years Younger* makes reversing the signs of aging its particular focus. On the British version of this format the host walks the subject through a gallery of blown-up photos each sitting on its own easel and each documenting the subject's gradual physical deterioration over time: as they penetrate this spatialization of time's passing, the sense of failure and public condemnation could not be more bleak. Aging, or rather allowing the signs of aging to go uncorrected, is treated as at least a misdemeanor if not a larger crime. But as Sadie Wearing points out, there is a contradiction about the attitude to aging in this and other makeover programming that reflects an ambivalence in postfeminist thinking. On the one hand, postfeminism suggests that aging need not mean loss of femininity, of fun, of self, and so on. But, on the other hand, it insists that people take on the responsibility of making the body look as young as possible by making the right consumer choices (2007, 286).

We have seen how makeover TV, in conjunction with media-advertising, supports what sociologists have identified as a shift in postindustrial society to where "The body is less and less an extrinsic 'given' . . . but becomes itself reflexively mobilized" (Giddens 1991, 7). The extent to which surgical work on this self is either empowering or a sign of victimhood has for some time been a polarizing topic and has given rise to some debate among feminist scholars. There are those such as Naomi Wolf (1991), Susan Bordo (1993), and Germaine Greer (1999) who assert that opting for cosmetic surgery cannot be reconciled with feminism and that the practice is little more than a reprehensible effect of patriarchy.[22] Even when an individual feels they are freeing themselves, "In fact, what is happening is a more intense policing of the body" (Banet-Weiser and Portwood-Stacer 2006, 263). Then there is Kathy Davis (2003) who argues that such scholars need to respect the fact that for any individual the option may be empowering and rational given the sociopolitical conditions under which they act. However, it seems the majority of scholars today have adopted a more mixed or ambivalent approach which recognizes both empowerment and oppression (e.g., Jones 2008b).[23] They are unwilling to dismiss cosmetic surgery patients as deluded or vain or victimized, but they underline that individual choice is constrained by the larger sociopolitical structure within which the decision to have surgery is made. As we have seen, makeover TV presents an upbeat narrative of individual empowerment with no serious acknowledgment of social pressures or constraints. Almost invariably TV subjects maintain that their surgery confers on them more "self-esteem," a term that is today very much in vogue (though, remarkably, only since the late 1990s; see Lunt 2008). This benefit is regarded as a deeply and individually empowering, though it could be considered a disingenuous claim since this self-esteem is so clearly yoked to the esteem of others (the reveal) and the frequent assertion that "I am doing it for myself" becomes almost meaningless since they are clearly improving their appearance in such a way as to better impress others. In any case, one of the problems with research in this area is that so much depends on self-reporting from patients and this can only take us so far. Even if this input is genuine and reliable, people tend to repeat the available repertoires (self-esteem, I'm doing it for myself) without necessarily realizing how they are being influenced and it is difficult to see how anyone else could prove influence either. However, this much we can say: that reality shows provide some insight into what people say (publicly) about why they want surgery, that they provide information about what surgeons can accomplish, that there appears to be an interest (on television and in real life) in accentuating sexual differences, and that according to both patients and surgeons these series have contributed to an increase in requests for various procedures. Deeper psychological or collective reasons why people elect for surgery are worth speculating about but are not easily proven.

Seeking surgery could, for example, be another form of compensation symptomatic of large sociopolitical trends. This was the opinion of Christopher Lasch and has been implied by others since. When studying narcissistic behavior in the 1970s, Lasch (1979) suggested that the focus on the self and on self-improvement was a reaction to the individual's feeling of helplessness in a wider sphere (in his own period, the failure to effect political change after 1960s and the ever-present threat of nuclear warfare). Lasch believed that the self-empowerment that comes from working on the self was acting as a palliative for larger forces bearing down on individuals which they could not alter. Noting the recent intense focus on body improvement, Anthony Giddens similarly traces its origins to a deeper unease and further institutional unraveling. "What might appear as a wholesale movement towards the narcissistic cultivation of bodily appearance is," he maintains, "an expression of a concern lying much deeper actively to 'construct' and control the body" (1991, 7). It may be that the body is targeted because it is a malleable material whose change is feasible and evident, and whose alteration produces both social and financial benefits. As we have seen, improving one's body can be presented as a pragmatic way to prosper in a climate of instability and job insecurity in which individuals are being urged to make the most of their own public relations. More broadly, it may be a comfort in a society of increasing complexity and risk to focus on something one can control. Sociologist Chris Shilling backs this up when he identifies a contemporary reaction where "if one feels unable to exert influence over an increasingly complex society, at least one can have some effect on the size, shape and appearance of one's body" (2003, 6). If we accept this explanation, then the accelerated embrace of cosmetic surgery is a sign of a cultural and political ill health that goes far beyond somatic concerns.

Whatever the reasons—and no doubt they are diverse and complex—what is clear is that record numbers of people in Western nations report dissatisfaction with their body image, even in childhood (Grogan 1999). In this context, TV's surgical fixes are likely to lead to increased pressure to change, which statistics suggest is already happening. As surgery becomes more widespread, we can speculate that the end result will be a form of commercial eugenics linking beauty, money, and rank even more firmly than in epochs past; for if, as these makeovers insist, we can fix our body image but we don't, then an unimproved body would signal either indolence or lower socioeconomic status. Beyond this, if the focus rests on body as the locus for change this inward turn promises to provide little political counterbalance to the prioritization of public image, whether of the individual or of larger social bodies, thus contributing to a future when both micro and macro politics could implode entirely to media-advertising and PR.

Conclusion

The hybridity of reality TV, its melding of the staged and the spontaneous, is what makes its form of public relations so galvanizing as an entertainment and as a social force. The formats examined throughout this book indicate, and extend, the degree to which commercially motivated discourse has come to dominate and to conflate public and private life, transforming the private from the intimate into the *commercial* and the public from the civic into the *publicized*. The pseudo-events of reality TV provide the quintessential example of mediation as consumption and consumption as mediation. They illustrate how the act of mediation commercializes its own content and, by extension, real life. Many series also insist that consumption is key to mediating social relationships. In particular, the rigid optimism of the makeover, a format that seems to have endless mutations, can be viewed as a compensation for (unstated) failures on local or national levels. If there is unequal opportunity or lack of social mobility, makeover experts assure us that the right consumer choices will earn a person more respect and better career prospects. If the government is not having much success at domestic or foreign nation building, then designers can build someone a nice home in an impressive time period and help restore collective self-esteem. The main thing, we are reminded, is to keep on consuming.

Notes

Introduction

1. I write in the context of major commentators such as Baudrillard ([1970]1998), Jameson (1991), and Featherstone (1991), who regard the prominence of both mediation and consumption as key to understanding contemporary or postmodern society.
2. Andrejevic links these trends to another form of convergence, that between leisure, labor, and consumption (2004, 53). This third conflation, while significant, is not my primary focus.
3. For simplicity's sake, I still employ the terms "television," "broadcast," and "air" to refer to the primary source for the material I am discussing, even though much of it is delivered digitally via cable or satellite and distributed in a more heterogeneous fashion than in the network era.
4. I will use "public relations" or "PR" as singular nouns.
5. Indeed, Baudrillard (1996) goes one further when he credits Disney with being the precursor of a recently begun process of turning all of real life into a giant reality show.
6. Perhaps not surprisingly, this has been my own experience on several occasions, but I have also heard others say it both in real life and on television.
7. *Cinema Verite* (2011) is a dramatized behind-the-scenes account of the PBS series *An American Family*, in many ways the most obvious forerunner of today's reality TV.
8. In 2011, US campaigns for Kraft mayo and Febreze fabric spray adopted RTV narratives and aesthetics.
9. Technologies of the self are, in Foucault's terms, the ways in which individuals experience, understand, judge, and conduct themselves.

Chapter 1

1. In 2010, the US expenditure on advertising was $131 billion and global spending on advertising is projected to exceed $500 billion in 2011. See http://www.bloomberg.com/news/2011-03-17/u-s-advertising-spending-rose-6-5-in-2010-led-by-television-internet.html (accessed May 15,

2011). Also: http://www.aaaa.org/news/agency/Pages/120610_groupm_forecast. aspx (accessed May 15, 2011).

2. I have written elsewhere about the particular dynamics of product placement in the commodity-starved, Spartan environments of gamedocs like *Survivor* (Deery 2004a).

3. The annual rate of growth of product placement between 1999 and 2004 was 16.3 percent (Lehu 2007, 34). Nielsen Media Research recorded more than 100,000 placements on US television in 2006, with reality shows like *American Idol* and *Home Edition* leading the way (Magder 2009, 152).

4. There are only a few notable exceptions to ad avoidance, such as the American Super Bowl, when many television viewers tune in to see the ads.

5. This "Antichrist" remark was attributed to the CEO of Turner Broadcasting Jamie Kellner (Donaton 2004, 2).

6. For an account of Hollywood's sometimes painful attempt to accommodate the grammar of advertising, see M.C. Miller (1990).

7. I compared infomercials and RTV in an earlier article, which I incorporate here (Deery 2004b).

8. The 2006 Pepsi ad featured an agent working for a can of Diet Pepsi and negotiating its role as a costar of a film with Jackie Chan. Available on YouTube: http://www.youtube.com/watch?v= pz-rnHqRtek (accessed June 7, 2008).

9. One of the earliest offenders, the Breakfast broadcaster GMTV, was fined £2 million by the British media regulator Ofcom.

10. Other countries that ban or restrict product placement on television are Austria, Germany, Norway, and Denmark.

11. The spoof entitled "Extreme Home Makeover: Indian Edition" is available at: http://www.youtube.com/watch?v= xJaZpeMmEfo (accessed March 7, 2009).

12. Home Depot went from 340 stores and $12.5 billion in sales in 1994 to 1,890 stores and $73 billion in sales in 2004 to $66.2 billion in 2009. For details of the company's growth history see http://www.homedepot.com/HDUS/EN_US/ corporate/about/timeline.shtml (accessed May 14, 2006). Similarly, Lowes went from $6.4 billion in sales in 1994 to $36.5 billion in 2004 to $47.2 billion in 2009: see http://www.shareholder.com/lowes/index2.cfm (accessed May 14, 2006).

13. For a Reality Blurred article on the campaign see, http://www.realityblurred.com/ realitytv/archives/industry_news/2005_Nov_23_wgaw_product_invasion (accessed April 16, 2007).

14. Stacy London has appeared in ads for Pantene, Dr. Scholl's, Riders Jeans and many others. Copresenter Clinton Kelly is a spokesman for Macy's and has a clothing line through the QVC brand Denim & Co. Kelly also wrote *Freakin' Fabulous* (2008), *Oh No She Didn't* (2010), and cowrote with London *Dress Your Best* (2005).

15. In recent years, Bayer has been accused of (among other things) knowingly distributing blood products with potential HIV contamination and marketing more than one drug with lethal side effects. The company has also been prosecuted

for the deaths of children who ingested a toxic milk substitute. So bad is Bayer's public relations that it has inspired an international organization called the Coalition Against Bayer Dangers that documents the many current complaints and lawsuits against this giant manufacturer. See http://www.cbgnetwork.org/4.html (accessed June 2, 2008).

16. For decades, Bayer's ads claim that "the ingredient in Bayer aspirin" performs such and such a wonder, implying that the Bayer brand has some USP (unique selling proposition). Actually, it has the same active ingredient as any aspirin: so it is true that it has real health benefits, but then so does any other brand. We are also informed that Bayer aspirin prevents more heart attacks than any other aspirin. Again true, but not the whole truth. Bayer aspirin prevents more heart attacks simply because it is the most commonly bought brand: a testament more to its advertising than to the product.

17. http://www.thefutoncritic.com/news.aspx?id=20041207nbc01 (accessed October 5, 2008).

18. The Delivery Agent platform enables viewers to purchase products they see on-screen by visiting a show's website and clicking on an online store or calling a toll-free number. See http://www.deliveryagent.com/about.php (accessed April 17, 2007).

19. I visited the *Home Edition* site during filming in Colonie, NY on 27 March 2007.

20. A *Fear Factor Live* theme park attraction was opened in 2005 at Universal Studios Florida (Magder 2009, 156).

21. For more on sponsorship in early television, see Barnouw (1978), Boddy (1990), G. Jones (1992), Marling (1996), Samuel (2002), Murray (2005), and Baugham (2007).

22. The most notorious case of sponsor rigging was the behind-the-scenes coaching of academic Charles Van Doren for the quiz show *Twenty-One*; see Stone (1992). The best known dramatization of this scandal is Robert Redford's 1994 film *Quiz Show*.

23. See http://www.toyota.com/about/news/product/2002/09/23-1-4runner.html (accessed October 17, 2003).

24. Linking mass production to home production is not new. In the 1920s, Heinz ran an early ad campaign that stressed that its canned products were made in "homelike kitchens" and depicted individual women preparing single dishes of food (Marchand 1998, 171).

25. By the beginning of *Home Edition*'s seventh season (2009–10), an estimated 500,000 Americans had helped with the show. See http://en.wikipedia.org/wiki/Home_makeover#Reaction_and_criticism (accessed June 15, 2011).

26. Available at http://www.o2mediainc.com/ (accessed March 15, 2011).

27. For studies of TV and the Internet see Brooker (2001), Spigel and Olsson (2004), Jenkins (2006), Ross (2008), Turner and Tay (2009), Kackman, et al. (2010) and Gillan (2011). Multiplatformicity is also becoming an important consideration in fan studies, as in Booth (2010). More specific examinations of the Internet and RTV include Tincknell and Raghuram (2002), Andrejevic

(2004, 2011), Holmes (2004), and essays in Ross (2008), and Kackman, et al. (2010).

28. Coactive describes the use of two or more devices at the same time.

29. For example, Holmes ponders where media scholars should now draw the line between text and reception (2004).

30. First there was *The Real Housewives of Orange County* (2006), then *The Real Housewives of New York City* (2008), *Atlanta* (2008), *New Jersey* (2009), *Washington D.C.* (2010), *Beverly Hills* (2010) and *Miami* (2011).

31. The Internet is generally regarded as a clear example of new media, though it encompasses many different possible relations between content-producer and content-seeker.

32. For overviews of new media and digital culture, see Lister et al. (2009), Creeber and Martin (2008), Gane and Beer (2008), Jenkins (2006), Manovich (2002) and Flew (2002).

33. In "The Work of Art in the Age of Mechanical Reproduction" Benjamin ([1936] 2006) writes: "the distinction between author and public is about to lose its basic character. The difference becomes merely functional; it may vary from case to case. At any moment the reader is ready to turn into a writer" (28).

34. In his seminal essay on "Encoding/Decoding" (1980), Hall suggested that there are three main ways for audiences to "decode" a text: the "dominant," where audience members accept the producer's preferred meaning; the "negotiated," where they inflect the preferred readings according to their own sociopolitical position; and the "oppositional," where they reject the preferred reading and recognize it as a hegemonic device that favors the ruling class.

35. The same categories of participation and interactivity can apply to online communication, though the potential for participation in texts or interactivity with texts or some combination of the two tends to be greater on the Internet.

36. Jenkins borrowed the term "poachers" from de Certeau ([1980]1984).

37. For an incisive discussion of recent fan activity and new media see Booth (2010).

38. Gillan (2011) does an excellent job of detailing how network producers and broadcasters have adjusted the production, scheduling, and distribution of fictional drama due to the availability of new platforms. In contrast, I focus on the distinctive environment of reality programming.

39. A 2008 Nielsen survey showed that 31 percent of in-home online activity occurs at the same time that the user is watching TV, which suggests that there is not necessarily a direct threat to TV ratings. See: http://www.reuters.com/article/internetNews/idUSTRE49U7SC20081103 (accessed November 3, 2008).

40. For an account of Jon de Mol's development of *Big Brother* and the Endemol RTV empire, see Bazalgette (2005).

41. Patti Stanger, for instance, is now in print media (with a coauthored book entitled *Become Your Own Matchmaker*), radio (XM Radio's "P.S. I Love You"), the Internet (the dating website, PSXOXO.com), DVDs ("Married in a Year" 2011), and, for good measure, she is also a 1–800-Flowers "Love Coach" and spokesperson for Sensa weight loss.

42. See http://www.bravotv.com/the-real-housewives-of-new-york-city/blogs/kelly-killoren-bensimon/isurvivori-housewives-style (accessed July 7, 2010).

43. An article in *The Telegraph* breaks down the profits for phone-in British quiz shows thus: out of a phone call that costs the consumer 75p, the TV channel gets 30p, the production company receives 15p, the phone companies 9.5p, the government (in taxes) receives 13p, and 7.5p is spent on prizes. Available at: http://www.telegraph.co.uk/money/main.jhtml?xml=/money/2007/01/26/cngame26.xml (accessed May 5, 2008).

44. Holmes (2004) cites an exception in a series (*The Salon*, Channel 4, 2003–04) where the participants read viewer online comments while still filming and incorporated viewer reactions into the television show.

45. The *Watch What Happens* Official Rules state that anyone who submits a comment agrees to grant NBC ". . . a worldwide, royalty free, perpetual, irrevocable, non-exclusive and fully sub-licensable license to use, reproduce, modify, adapt, edit, publish, translate, create derivative works from, distribute, perform, and display your Submission (in whole or in part) . . .." Available at: http://www.bravotv.com/watch-what-happens-live/official-rules (accessed May 3, 2011).

46. A rare example of unauthorized participation is when viewers have flown banners above the mise en scène of *Big Brother* with messages that influence the participants' beliefs and behavior. Amateur video and news reports are also becoming increasingly prominent in mainstream television news: for instance, since 2006 CNN has been using viewer "iReports" and most national and local news organizations use viewer photos or videos, usually before they can be vetted.

47. So bad was the publicity over phone-in profits and fixes that UK's Channel 4 declared that its eighth season of *Big Brother* would take no profits from viewers' text messaging.

48. See http://www.telegraph.co.uk/news/main.jhtml?xml=/news/2007/03/22/nquiz22.xml (accessed May 22, 2007).

49. One fan offered his *American Idol* site for sale: see http://marketplace.sitepoint.com/auctions/33922 (accessed April 11, 2008).

50. See Smith and Kollock (1999) for a useful anthology of essays on online community.

51. For a discussion of non-fans and anti-fans, see Gray (2003).

52. The first virtual party was held for *The Real Housewives of New York City* on May 5, 2009. It won the MMA Global Mobile Marketing Award and Mobile Excellence Awards.

Chapter 2

1. This quote comes from Jackall (1995, 380).

2. For a comprehensive historical overview of the PR industry, see Cutlip (1995).

3. One critic describes public relations as the nearly invisible Grey Eminence operating behind the scenes "with the ease of a Cardinal Richelieu and the conscience of a mercenary" (Nelson 1989, 19).

4. Public Information Officers are the PR specialists who work for local and state governments and legislators or who represent organizations like police and fire departments.

5. Some who teach PR have written textbooks and rather sanitized histories to prepare students to go into the industry (e.g., Cutlip 1994, 1995). Cutlip and Center's frequently published *Effective Public Relations,* a textbook first published in 1952, is self-described as the "bible of public relations." Its authors dismiss negative or critical accounts of PR as "jaundiced" (2006, 2), but actually they needn't be concerned as there are few substantial critical accounts available. A subset of PR is political marketing, but again most texts are written for practitioners; see, for example, Steger, Kelly, and Wrighton (2006), and Davies and Newman (2006).

6. The activity of public relations sometimes appears in accounts of the celebrity industry, as in Hartley (1992). A few critical accounts look at advertising and spin in politics; for example, Jackson and Jameison, *unSpun: Finding Facts in a World of Disinformation* (2007). A biting but somewhat less academic approach to PR is taken by Stauber and Rampton (1995) in *Toxic Sludge is Good for You* and Nelson (1989) in *Sultans of Sleaze*; see also Jowett and O'Donnell *Propaganda and Persuasion* (2005). An early study of propaganda was undertaken by Ellul ([1962]1965) and there has been some more recent work on political propaganda; for example, O'Shaughnessy (2004), and Secunda and Moran (2007). Jackall and Hirota's (2000) *Image Makers* focuses mostly on advertising and its history.

7. Dinan and Miller (2007) also edited a collection of essays on corporate PR. A few recent collections attempt to draw on social studies or rhetoric to theorize public relations for scholars in this field (i.e., those who teach PR), but they do not offer a critical stance on the industry and are for the benefit of PR students and practitioners (Ihlen, van Ruler, and Fredriksson 2009; Heath, Toth, and Waymer 2009). Coombs and Holladay (2007) look at the impact of PR on society, but, again, not from a critical stance.

8. Habermas expressed some concern about the degradation of the public sphere by PR in *The Structural Transformation of the Public Sphere,* where he observes that PR or "publicity" has come to play a vital role in politics by manufacturing and managing public opinion—which, given the lack of rational-critical deliberation, he dismisses as "nonpublic opinion."

9. The growth of commercial PR has been marked. In 1979, 20 percent of the top 500 British companies used PR consultancies. By 1984, it was 69 percent of the top 500 and 90 percent of the top 100 companies (A. Davis 2003, 28).

10. "Brand pushers" are individuals who are paid to say positive things about a brand in online conversations.

11. One collection of essays, most of which touch on some aspect of this issue, is entitled *How Real is Reality TV?: Essays on Representation and Truth* (Escoffery 2006).

12. Indeed, perhaps influenced by the success of reality TV, documentary today is more inclined to be self-reflexive and to foreground personal and subjective narratives than make broader attempts to represent a public sociopolitical reality or consult with fully credentialed expertise; see Corner (1996), Kilborn (2003), Biressi and Nunn (2005).

13. Even if there is no direct plug, being on reality TV can increase business because of the internal network that arises among the different local firms at the construction site (Dawn Wotapka, *Wall Street Journal*, April 6, 2010).

14. Pine and Gilmore (1999) contend that if you customize goods this turns them into a service and if you customize services this turns them into an experience.

15. *10 Years Younger* involves surgery only sometimes and only in its UK version.

16. Other surgical series offer a more ambivalent or even negative view but these tend to be less prominent than positive makeovers, either appearing on less popular channels or for shorter time periods. Examples are *I Want a Famous Face* (MTV, 2004–05), *Plastic Surgery: Before and After* (Discovery Health Channel, 2002–07), *Dr. 90210* (E!, 2004–), *body/work* (TLC, 2004–05), *Brand New You* (Channel 5, 2004–05) and the even more didactic *Say No to the Knife* (BBC 3, 2007) and *The Ugly Side of Beauty* (Channel 4, 2010).

17. 2009 statistics from the American Society for Aesthetic Plastic Surgery are available at: http://www.surgery.org/media/statistics (accessed September 10, 2010).

18. Information on the survey results is available at: http://www.prnewswire.com/cgi-bin/stories.pl?ACCT= ind_focus.story&STORY=/www/story/07–23–2007/0004630552&EDATE=MON+Jul+23+2007,+11:30+AM (accessed July 14, 2008).

19. A 2004 survey by the American Society of Plastic Surgeons revealed that more people were reporting favorable views of cosmetic surgery than ten years prior: the largest increase was among women, almost 50 percent of whom declared a more favorable attitude. Information available at: www.plasticsurgery.org (accessed June 23, 2006).

20. For more on the history of cosmetic surgery, see Haiken (1997), Gilman (1999), Blum (2003), and K. Davis (2003).

21. The term plastic surgery often encompasses both reconstructive and cosmetic surgery, but the former usually addresses more medically sanctioned needs such as repairing injuries or disfigurement, often in the attempt to improve functionality, whereas cosmetic surgery aims to improve appearance for aesthetic reasons.

22. On Channels 4's *The Ugly Side of Beauty* the doctor/host warns about the "horrors of botched surgery" and provides a link to a website that enables patients to check surgeons' credentials.

23. Dorfman solidified his ties to reality TV when he married *Apprentice* contestant Jennifer Murphy in 2006, in front of Donald Trump.

24. See gallup.com for annual results. In the survey taken in November 2008, 84 percent of respondents rated nurses as high/very high regarding honesty and ethics

while only 22 percent rated building contractors high/very high. Realtors scored 17 percent and advertisers 10 percent in the high/very high category.

25. For an account of the Mafia's illegal involvement in construction, see Selwin Raab, *New York Times,* June 1, 1990 (accessed September 10, 2010).

26. The popular perception that the Mafia are connected to the construction trade has come up on the *Real Housewives of New Jersey.* On declaring bankruptcy, one of the husbands, an Italian contractor (Joe Guidice), revealed that he received a large monthly "assistance" from unnamed family members and immediately viewers speculated that his "family" is the Mafia. See: http://www.nypost.com/p/news/local/deadbeat_reality_8f3qwDPV2oY8s9N51fL82I?offset= 160 #comments (accessed July 6, 2010).

27. See http://www.renovationpsychology.com/ for information on Renovation Psychology as promulgated by its founder Dr. Debi Warner (accessed May 9, 2009).

28. See Alure's website at: http://www.alure.com/09-emhe-ali-aet.html (accessed June 9, 2008).

29. The video on the website of one contractor, Alure, has one basic theme: that the *Home Edition* project was about teamwork and cooperation. Available at: http://www.alure.com/09-emhe-ali-aet.html (accessed June 9, 2008).

30. For accounts of the history of American broadcasting and the pull between private and public interests, see Barnouw (1978), Douglas (1989), Streeter (1996) and Ouellette (2002).

Chapter 3

1. Scholars are beginning to show some interest in RTV and nationalism (Kraidy and Sender 2011), but the inquiry is not yet extensive.

2. Volcic and Andrejevic (2011) note that in discussions of nationalism the commercial production of national identities has been largely ignored, except in a minor way when used for certain types of marketing and tourism (115).

3. See the Pew Center report of August 18, 2004. Available at: http://people-press.org/report/?pageid= 864 (accessed July 3, 2010). America's unpopularity was confirmed by a 2007 survey of 45 nations that found that anti-American sentiment was indeed extensive. See: http://people-press.org/report/478/bush-legacy-public-opinion (accessed July 3, 2010).

4. Gillan (2006) also establishes a link between the neighborliness depicted on *Home Edition* and a US foreign policy that portrays the nation as a good international neighbor.

5. The candidate's website declares: "George Amedore has made the American Dream a reality for thousands of families across the Capital Region." He vows "As your Assemblyman, I'll give Albany an 'extreme makeover.' " Available at: http://www.georgeamedore.com/ (accessed July 11, 2007).

6. Both Presidents Bush and Obama have also appeared (via a video link) on another reality show, the *Idol Gives Back* fundraisers (Fox, 2007, 2008, 2010). Columbian

President Alvaro Uribe appeared on the set of *Big Brother* to promote a series of constitutional reforms (Thussu 2007, 85). While in Poland one *Big Brother* contestant went on to win a parliamentary seat (Bazalgette 2005).

7. The term "nation" is also sometimes used (somewhat in jest) to describe a virtually mediated tribe or community who see themselves as a distinct ideological subset of the official nation, as in The Colbert Nation or The Fox Nation.

8. When the disaster was unfolding in New Orleans, Secretary of State Condoleezza Rice was reportedly shoe shopping in New York and most members of the Cabinet were on holiday with no immediate plans to return.

9. The Cheney incident occurred in Gulfport, Mississippi and footage is available at: http://www.youtube.com/watch?v= p3SemYQH-8o (accessed May 15, 2008).

10. See http://www.onlisareinsradar.com/archives/002503.php (accessed May 1, 2008).

11. The episode entitled *Home Edition: After the Storm* (aired 4/6/06).

12. Though he doesn't link home makeovers specifically to a post-9/11 culture, Rosenberg (2008) underlines that the home is commonly regarded as a place of security and protection in today's risk society.

13. Compare TV makeover speed with the government response to preventing or dealing with the 9/11 attack. The solemnly imparted advice from the newly created US Department of Homeland Security that one should duct tape one's home against some unspecified menace was of little use to anyone but stand-up comedians.

14. Michelle Obama addressed the WGA on June 13, 2011. See http://www.washingtonpost.com/entertainment/michelle-obama-addresses-hollywood-unions-urges-them-to-tell-military-families-stories/2011/06/13/AGRubUTH_story.html (accessed June 14, 2011).

15. Bush's speech is available at: http://georgewbush whitehouse.archives.gov/news/releases/2003/03/20030317-7.html (accessed June 16, 2010).

16. Nevertheless, one private security company generated such bad publicity over its shooting of Iraqi civilians that in February 2009, in a not-so-subtle rebranding exercise, Blackwater changed its name to Xe. For a critical account of Blackwater's ties to ultra right-wing "crusaders," see Scahill (2007).

17. On September 14, 2003, on *Meet the Press,* Vice President Dick Cheney assured host Tim Russert that "I really do believe we will be greeted as liberators" (Isikoff and Corn 2006, 208), while another chief architect of the war, Paul Wolfowitz, predicted that the Iraqis would be on streets cheering US troops (Ricks 2006, 96).

18. We can trace the origins of British PR to the Boer war in the late nineteenth century and the occupation of Ireland in the early twentieth century (Miller and Dinan 2008, 16–17). In the United States, public relations consolidated as a profession after the Creel Committee of World War I.

19. On May 1, 2003, after an unnecessary but televisual jet landing on the deck of the USS Abraham Lincoln (the ship was only 30 miles from shore), President Bush emerged in a flight suit to declare an end to major combat operations in

Iraq. Behind him was displayed a prominent and now notorious banner declaring "mission accomplished."

20. Rumsfeld affirmed in the "Information Operations Roadmap" (October 2003) that psychological operations, or PSYOP, are "a core military competency" in modern warfare.

21. A concern for business interests was certainly felt at the January 2007 Private Sector Summit on Public Diplomacy when the PR firms, lobbyists, and the State Department got together to discuss, in the words of Secretary Condoleezza Rice, how "to increase private sector involvement in US public diplomacy." The official report is available at: http://www.state.gov/documents/organization/82818.pdf (accessed April 22, 2008).

22. The same kind of language about selling the war and at the same time selling America or the Gospel of Americanism to the world was employed during the World War I Creel Committee (Jackall 1995, 357).

23. There are, today, indexes of nations as brands, as in the Anholt-GfK Roper Nation Brand Index (begun in 2005), which conducts global surveys in order to assess a nation's reputation.

24. The growth over the last century of corporate third-party influence on both British and American politics is uncovered in some detail by Miller and Dinan (2008).

25. The primary job of the Think Tank employee is not to do "research" so much as to circulate in the media whatever position they (and their funders) represent.

26. The fact that government agencies hire individuals to do PR work beyond war propaganda only comes to light occasionally, as when it was considered scandalous in 2005 that the conservative commentator Armstrong Williams was paid $240,000 of taxpayers' money to promote the Bush administration's No Child Left Behind education policies through an Education Department contract with the PR firm of Ketchum.

27. Gillan (2006) produces a detailed analysis of this episode that links camera work to ideological work.

28. The builder's enthusiastic call for a military parade is found at: http://www.extremeebheroes.com/parade.php (accessed June 19, 2008).

29. Fighting fires used to be a private for-profit service for which people paid individually, but it soon became clear that due to mutual dependency (your fire can spread to my house) it was better if it were publicly funded and universally available.

30. In actual fact, as Faludi (2007) and others have noted, many of the firefighters and police officers who died in 9/11 were the unfortunate victims of organizational incompetence and lack of proper equipment.

31. In a different context, Volcic (2009) employs the term "commercial nationalism" to describe the way in which national identification (including prejudices and stereotypes) is being exploited commercially on Balkan television. See also Volcic and Andrejevic (2011).

32. The promo for the hundredth show is available at: http://www.youtube.com/watch?v=1W-VCIhSd7k&feature=related (accessed June 18, 2008).

33. Reagan's deeply sentimental and now iconic campaign spot, written and narrated by ad man Hal Riney, is available on YouTube at: http://www.youtube.com/watch?v=EU-IBF8nwSY (accessed June 18, 2008).

34. Video available at: http://www.youtube.com/watch?v=DKVwNUzF5kU&mode=related&search (accessed July 15, 2007).

35. Looking at the creation of space as a way to understand larger social agencies is an approach that is becoming increasingly central to human or cultural geography, as well as to other fields, in the light of work by Lefebvre ([1974]1991), Foucault ([1975]1977), and others. Some of the seminal work in cultural geography has been produced by Harvey (1973), Soja (1989), G. Rose (1993), and Massey (1994).

36. A hundredth episode celebration (aired 11/24/07) featured brief updated glimpses of selected families from previous episodes, but generally the show's involvement with the new home and its inhabitants ends when filming ends.

37. Empirical effects studies indicate both less social engagement (Kraut et al. 1998; Nie and Erbring 2000; Shim 2007) and more social engagement as a result of Internet use (Kraut et al. 2002; Lee and Kuo 2002; Robinson, Barth, and Kohut 1997). Some of this depends on what kinds of Internet activities are engaged in and where (for example, at work or at home: see Nie and Hillygus 2002), and whether or not one thinks of online social networks as genuine communities.

38. Castells (2000) points out that we shouldn't discount geographic proximity even when it comes to the technical development, if not the implementation, of new media, and he cites the San Francisco Bay area as an example of face-to-face contact stimulating new ideas (67).

39. A flash mob occurs (first in 2003) when hundreds of people suddenly show up at a physical location because of instructions from some online source. Crowdsourcing (crowd outsourcing) is when a task is distributed among a collection of unpaid volunteers.

Chapter 4

1. These ideas are prominent in advertising campaigns in 2010. Target produces its mission statement on its website, a practice now common among major corporations. Available at: http://sites.target.com/site/en/corporate/page.jsp?contentId=PRD03-004325 (accessed August 15, 2008).

2. Caring capitalism is a phrase associated with Ben and Jerry's ice cream company and other socially concerned enterprises.

3. In Stuart Hall's schema, a dominant reading is one that conforms to the producer's preferred interpretation and goes along with hegemonic norms, in contrast to negotiated or oppositional readings.

4. Class is too large an issue to cover here, but we can observe that American TV does not have the British tradition of producing popular working-class dramas.

5. Transcript of a speech by the prime minister on the Big Society delivered on 19 July, 2010, available at: http://www.number10.gov.uk/news/speeches-and-transcripts/2010/07/big-society-speech-53572 (accessed September 14, 2010).

6. The distinction between tactic and strategy was underlined by de Certeau ([1980] 1984) when he described institutions and large enterprises as using systematic and long-term "strategies" to exert their influence in contrast to individuals and smaller groups who employ "tactics" or ground-up practices to poach, co-opt, or otherwise negotiate with these larger, established forces.

7. There has been a flurry of books with titles such as *The Market for Virtue: The Potential and Limits of Corporate Social Responsibility* (Vogel 2006), *Corporate Social Responsibility: Doing the Most Good For Your Company and Your Cause* (Kotler and Lee 2004), *Compassionate Capitalism: How Corporations Can Make Doing Good an Integral Part of Doing Well* (Benioff and Southwick 2004) and *Capitalism at the Crossroads: Aligning Business, Earth, and Humanity* (Hart 2007).

8. Classic "cathedrals of commerce" are the Woolworth building in New York and Wanamaker's in Philadelphia.

9. Otherwise very successful brands like Nike have been stung by ethical concerns regarding its labor practices.

10. Wal-Mart's "Giving and Community" page is at: http://walmartstores.com/CommunityGiving/ (accessed May 3, 2008).

11. The "(Red) campaign," begun by U2's Bono and by Bobby Shriver in 2006, encourages people to buy brands associated with this movement because some of the profits will buy medicine for HIV/AIDS patients in Africa. The (Red) Manifesto spells out the power of today's consumer: "As first world consumers, we have tremendous power. What we collectively choose to buy, or not to buy, can change the course of life and history on this planet." The (Red) Manifesto is available at: http://www.joinred.com/manifesto/ (accessed June 3, 2008).

12. The Pepsi refresh campaign can be found at: www.refresheverything.com (accessed August 20, 2011). Cohen appears on television ads to urge viewers to participate.

13. See http://abc.go.com/abettercommunity/index?pn=getinvolved (accessed November 3, 2007).

14. See http://www.fastcompany.com/social/2008/profiles/points-of-light-hands-on-network.html (accessed July 3, 2008).

15. See http://www.forallthewaysyoucare.com/ (accessed January 3, 2009).

16. The Ford competition is found at: http://www.fordvehicles.com/heroes/ (accessed May 5, 2009).

17. The Sears website is at: http://www.searsamericandream.com/about/index.html (accessed November 8, 2005). I discussed this site in an earlier article (Deery 2006) and this venture is also noted by Ouellette and Hay (2008).

18. Compare this with the potential for radical explosions on other types of reality programming such as talk shows: see Glynn (2000).

19. See http://abc.go.com/primetime/xtremehome/qa/forman.html (accessed June 16, 2008).

20. Usually *Home Edition*'s ethical message is fairly implicit but occasionally it can get downright didactic, as when one episode took on the issue of discrimination against those with AIDS and lectured the audience on proper attitudes (aired 5/20/07).

21. Even *Queer Eye* moved into this heavier territory toward the end of its run by helping some whose causes were seen as worthy rather than just fun.

22. Compare *Home Edition* with *Random 1* (A&E, 2005–06), which does engage to a limited extent with homeless people but on a very small scale. There is some modest aid but no life-changing rescue or attempt at helping more than one person get off the streets.

23. The "jackpot of worthiness" remark came from designer Preston Sharp on an episode that aired 11/6/05.

24. Reported incidents at Oatman's previous home range from domestic disputes to arguments with neighbors to car vandalism and one of Oatman's sons apparently turned her in to police for smoking marijuana.

25. My remarks throughout apply to an Anglo-American economy.

26. Since being coined, the "American Dream" has been passionately invoked by virtually every American president in key addresses down through the decades: most Democrats regarding it as a call for social support and equal opportunity (the egalitarian element) and most Republicans for individual effort and responsibility (rewarding individual effort).

27. Barack Obama's best-selling book *The Audacity of Hope* is subtitled *Thoughts on Reclaiming the American Dream* (2006).

28. For other analyses of possible links between makeover programming and the American Dream see Heller (2006). Some material in this chapter comes from my own essay in this collection but no other material from this collection is used here unless cited.

29. Today, social mobility is actually greater in those northern European countries whose class hierarchies new American immigrants were supposedly escaping.

30. In a representative survey of more than 5,000 Americans in 2005, Norton and Ariely (2011) found that respondents greatly underestimated the current level of wealth inequality and that their projections of an ideal wealth distribution were of a much more equitable system than is in fact the case in contemporary America.

31. For a graphic breakdown of social mobility in the United States, see Leonhardt and Werschkul (2005).

32. I mean this quite literally, for during this project I have become attuned to this phrase and hear it almost every day.

33. Among the immigrant families featured on *Home Edition* are the Llanes who came from the Philippines (aired 9/17/06), the Peter family who came from Guyana (aired 5/7/06), and the Pauni family who migrated from Tonga (aired 11/26/2006).

34. In this series, the enterprising father produced fairly spoiled and unambitious offspring.

35. Walter Lippman used the phrase earlier, in 1914 (Jillson 2004, 6).

36. Adams was born in Brooklyn on October 18, 1878. After studying at the Polytechnic Institute of Brooklyn (B.S.) and Yale (M.S.), he entered investment banking. In 1917, he undertook some government service as a Military Intelligence officer and was a US delegate at the historic Paris Peace Conference.

37. Heinricy (2006) links surgical makeovers to the American Dream but the analogy does not seem to be as pertinent as with home makeovers. She argues that patients earn their Dream by passive labor (their suffering) and the doctors through their active labor (performing surgery).

38. Heinricy (2006), who like others does not refer to Adams' book, focuses on the shift from salvation to materialism rather than Adams' emphasis on sociopolitical arrangements.

39. President Obama's 2008 inaugural speech addresses this point when he refers back to the aspirations of generations of immigrants who "saw America as bigger than the sum of our individual ambitions; greater than all the differences of birth or wealth or faction."

40. Levitt and Sons, builders, in many ways represent the American Dream mid century. They built the first of many new (white-only) suburban developments in Levittown, New York, in the late 1940s. By employing mass production techniques and non-unionized labor, they enabled thousands of Americans to own their own home. The company filed for bankruptcy in November 2007.

41. TV producers will happily push privacy and sexual envelopes but there are all kinds of sociopolitical taboos: for example, on American television characters will rarely denigrate the flag, seek an abortion, or espouse Fascism or communism.

42. Every member of the *Home Edition* design team has a media/entertainment background. Eduardo Xol is an actor, dancer, singer, and musician as well as landscape designer. Ed Sanders was an actor and television host in England before moving to the United States to do carpentry on *Home Edition*. Tracy Hutson worked as a model and actor. Carpenter Paul DiMeo (who, appropriately, comes from a place called Media, Pennsylvania), worked in theater as a stage designer and stage manager and now his Hollywood business renovates the houses of the stars. Preston Sharp is a furniture designer who also boasts a Hollywood clientele. Michael Moloney owns a furniture store and was a professional fashion model who first appeared on *Clean House* (Style Network, 2003–). Carpenter Paige Hemmis apparently aspires to be a stunt driver for films and advertising.

43. See http://abc.go.com/primetime/extrememakeover/show.html (accessed February 18, 2004).

44. A Chinese series modeled on *The Swan* translates as *Lovely Cinderella*.

45. The remarks of a producer in Disney's "broadcast marketing division" are at: http://disneyparks.disney.go.com/blog/2011/06/sneak-peek-my-yard-goes-disney/ (accessed June 20, 2011).

46. There have been valiant attempts to reconcile materialism and spirituality, more recently the American Prosperity Gospel of charismatic and Pentecostal Christians and numerous earlier Protestant sects that suggested that material wealth is a sign of God's favor. Max Weber ([1905]1992) theorized that at least

some strains of religious observance are in harmony with, and even further, capitalism.

47. I sketched some of this religious narrative in an earlier article, which I incorporate here (Deery 2004b).

48. Some of these confessional elements are borrowed from earlier television talk shows (e.g., Gamson 1998; Dovey 2000; Glynn 2000) whose therapeutic culture echoes earlier religious traditions. For more on confessional or therapeutic talk shows, see Shattuc (1990) and White (1992). For a history of confession as a ritual used in the production of truth, see Foucault ([1976] 1978).

49. Motley (2006) suggests that being born again through Christ could be seen as the ultimate makeover (66–7). In her examination of *Plastic Surgery: Before and After,* Crawley (2006) links the surgical makeover to a more secular form of rebirth, which is the story of immigrants coming to America to emancipate themselves from Old World history and personal ancestry.

50. Bauman's fluid society combines high levels of consumption within an expanding market and lack of stable or centralized institutions.

51. Jones (2008a) likens *The Swan's* mirror scene to a screen-birth during which "the endometrial richness of the curtains" and "their slow vulval parting" give rise to the subject's birthing of herself (517). This is certainly an intriguing interpretation, though it may not be a true parthenogenesis given the subject's loss of agency.

52. At least one group is prepared to assign all the glory to God. They claim that *Home Edition's* good works are all part of God's plan and His blessing to people of faith and prayer. See http://www.adventistreview.org/article.php?id=365 (accessed May 16, 2009).

53. For an account of the shift from moral character and service to personal appearance, see Brumberg (1998).

54. Some have identified a three-step evolution from cultivation of the soul (traditional religious society), to cultivation of character (nineteenth century, ethical), to emphasis on personality and presentation of self (early twentieth century, impression); for example, Haiken (1997).

Chapter 5

1. Oprah Winfrey has gone on to launch an entire channel (OWN, 2011–) devoted to the kind of imperative programming she featured on her long-running talk show.

2. Other style makeovers include: *How Do I Look?* (Style, 2004–), *Look-a-Like* (TV Guide, 2004), *Ambush Makeover* (Style, 2004–05), *Tim Gunn's Guide to Style* (Bravo, 2007), *You're Wearing That?* (We, 2010–), *Trinny and Susannah Undress* (ITV, 2006–07) and *Making Over America with Trinny and Susannah* (TLC, 2009).

3. I will not be able to do justice here to the complex issue of class on RTV, but it is a topic I pursue in another upcoming publication. See McRobbie (2004); Palmer (2004, 2007, 2008); Skeggs and Wood (2008).

4. The Build-a-Bear site is available at: http://www.buildabear.com/babw/us/pages/aboutus/ourcompany/factsheet.pdf (accessed June 2, 2008).

5. The term metrosexual was coined by British journalist Mark Simpson in 1994 (*The Independent,* November 15).

6. "Busy" is the root of the word business, only branching off from it in the seventeenth century.

7. A classic study here is Mauss' ([1950] 1990) account of gift economies.

8. Redden (2007) also touches on this neglect of social determinants in the likes of Beck and Giddens.

9. Sumptuary laws were in circulation in Europe from the medieval to the industrial era. Until the nineteenth century, these stipulations about clothing and behavior were read annually in church in England (Slater 1997, 68).

10. One 2006 survey estimated that there are 40,000 life or work coaches in the United States and this $2.4 billion industry is growing 18 percent per year (Gauntlett 2008, 235).

11. Viewers' comments can be viewed on bravotv.com.

12. See http://tlc.discovery.com/fansites/whatnottowear/episodes2/mirella/mirella.html (accessed June 28, 2008).

13. For commentary on this *How Do I Look?* episode and defense of the subject's defiance, see: http://new.music.yahoo.com/blogs/realityrocks/89826/how-do-i-look-plum-crazy/ (accessed June 28, 2008).

Chapter 6

1. Available at: http://www.disney.co.uk/DisneyDVDs/DVDs/cinderella-royal-edition.jsp (accessed May 30, 2011).

2. Available at: http://www.alfredangelo.com/disney/ (accessed May 30, 2011).

3. Available at: http://www.wetv.com/shows/platinum-weddings/about (accessed June 10, 2011).

4. Available at: http://www.auditionsfree.com/2011/bridezillas-casting-call/ (accessed May 30, 2011).

5. An image that resembles Grant Wood's iconic 1930 painting is available at: http://www.history.com/shows/american-pickers (accessed August 20, 2011).

6. Available at: http://www.history.com/shows/american-pickers/articles/about-the-series (accessed May 30, 2011).

7. See http://community.history.com/forums/160/t/American-Pickers.html (accessed August 20, 2011).

8. Though it is a matter of speculation, it may be that one of motives for the suicide of a *Real Housewives* husband (Russell Armstrong) in August 2011 was his financial failure as well as his impending divorce and so he may be the first serious causality.

9. For exhaustive information on couponing see http://jillcataldo.com/node/16258 (accessed May 12, 2011).

10. Quite detailed evidence of fraud is presented on http://jillcataldo.com/node/16258 (accessed May 12, 2011).

Chapter 7

1. Surgical makeover series are usually exported in their original American version rather than as a local adaptation. Disney/ABC has distributed local editions of *Extreme Makeover* in the United Kingdom, Holland, India, Belgium, Scandinavia, Hungary, and Colombia.

2. Franco (2008) notes that northern Europeans who do produce their own version of *Extreme Makeover* de-medicalize it and downplay the surgery in favor of telling the individual's personal narrative (475).

3. For a seminal discussion of the body in sociology, see Turner (1984). For an overview of body image and the role of the media, see Wykes and Gunter (2005).

4. Blum (2003) records that 85 percent of plastic surgeons are men (87).

5. Aristotle discusses male and female roles in human reproduction in his *Generation of Animals,* chapter 21.

6. In the 1980s, the body and its relation to individual identity moved front and center in sociology, though much of this ground had been pioneered by feminists since the 1960s.

7. The word for "inch" is similar to the word for "thumb" or "finger" in several languages. In French, *pouce* (inch/thumb); in Spanish, *pulgada* (inch), *pulgar* (thumb); in Swedish, *tum* (inch), *tumme* (thumb); in Dutch, *duim* (inch/thumb), all of this going back to the Sanskrit *Angulam* (inch), *Anguli* (finger).

8. Conventionally we think of a thing as without consciousness, which makes thinghood an extreme form of objectification.

9. Kavka (2008), who also discusses privacy in reality television, notes that one starting point is to define privacy as "the quality of being able to exercise the power of possession over the contents of selfhood: information, bodies and bodily spaces, identities" (69).

10. The phrase "prostitution whore" was a slur infamously slung at another housewife by Teresa Giudice of *The Real Housewives of New Jersey.* The phrase has since begun to circulate more widely in popular culture.

11. Science fiction writers have for some time predicted that surgically altered bodies would become fashion statements and status symbols: for example, William Gibson's *Neuromancer* (1984) and Marge Piercy's *He, She and It* (1991).

12. It wasn't until the mid- or late nineteenth century that various US states and European nations allowed women to keep their own assets after marriage and in many parts of the world today a woman continues to be treated as chattel, either legally or as a matter of custom and with the strong backing of religions.

13. In the UK version of *10 Years Younger* subjects stand in public but not always in a box.

14. See http://www.bravotv.com/Queer_Eye_for_the_Straight_Guy/About_Us/ website (accessed February 7, 2006).

15. It was unusual when on one British episode producers decided to OK two separate operations and take 12 weeks instead of six because, as the surgeon confirmed, this would be safer for the patient.

16. There are now numerous studies demonstrating the impact of media imagery on perceptions of body attractiveness. Typical results are the raising of the beauty standards that viewers feel obliged to reach and consequent mental and physical ill-effects. See, for instance, Bessenoff (2006), Botta (1999), Henderson-King, Henderson-King and Hoffman (2001), Lew et al. (2007), Moriarty and Harrison (2008), Strahan et al. (2008), Tiggemann (2003, 2005), and Tiggemann and Slater (2004).

17. Brumberg (1998) refers to ideal models as "hyperbolic bodies" (124).

18. For fear of sociobiological reductionism, some feminists dispute biological underpinnings as deterministic; for example, Wolf (1991).

19. One of the best known studies is Etcoff (2000) and there is a more recent publication by Rhode (2010). For an overview of several such studies see Sullivan (2001, 26–28).

20. Some have criticized Butler (1990) for going too far in claiming that (ordinarily and without surgical intervention) biology/sex is merely a discursive product, a deep from of performance; see, for example, Bordo (1993).

21. Rhode (2010) calculates that the US investment in appearance currently totals over $200 billion a year (2).

22. See also Lakoff and Scherr (1984).

23. Another example is Kathryn Pauly Morgan who candidly reports that she goes back and forth between the two extremes of liberation/oppression and wishes to avoid having to settle for a picture of either agency or victimhood (2009, 70–72).

Works Cited

Adams, James Truslow. 1931. *The Epic of America*. Boston, MA: Little, Brown.

Andersen, Benedict. [1983] 2006. *Imagined Communities: Reflections on the Origin and Spread of Nationalism*. London: Verso.

Andrejevic, Mark. 2004. *Reality TV: The Work of Being Watched*. Lanham, MD: Rowan and Littlefield.

——. 2011. "Real-izing Exploitation." In Kraidy and Sender 2011, 18–30.

Aristotle. 1979. *Generation of Animals*. Translated by Arthur Leslie Peck. Loeb Classical Library. Cambridge, MA: Harvard University Press. Accessed June 18, 2009. http://www.archive.org/details/generationofanim00arisuoft.

Banet-Weiser, Sarah and Laura Portwood-Stacer. 2006. " 'I Just Want to Be Me Again!': Beauty Pageants, Reality Television and Post-Feminism." *Feminist Theory* 7 (2): 255–272.

Baran, Stanley. 2008. *Introduction to Mass Communication*, 5th ed. New York: McGraw Hill.

Barnouw, Eric. 1978. *The Sponsor: Notes on a Modern Potentate*. Oxford: Oxford University Press.

Barthes, Roland. [1957] 1972. *Mythologies*. Translated by Annette Lavers. New York: Farrar, Straus and Giroux.

Bartky, Sandra. 1990. *Femininity and Domination: Studies in the Phenomenology of Oppression*. New York: Routledge.

Baudrillard, Jean. [1968] 1996. *The System of Objects*. Translated by James Benedict. London: Verso.

——. [1970] 1998. *The Consumer Society*. Translated by C. Turner. London: Sage.

——. [1976] 1993. *Symbolic Exchange and Death*. Translated by Iain Hamilton Grant. Introduction by Mike Gane. London: Sage.

——. [1981] 1994. *Simulacra and Simulation*. Translated by Shiela Faria Glaser. Ann Arbor, MI: University of Michigan Press.

——. 1983. *Simulations*. Translated by Paul Foss, Paul Patton, and Philip Beitchman. New York: Semiotext(e).

——. [1987] 1988. *The Ecstasy of Communication*. Translated by Bernard Schutze and Caroline Schutze. New York: Semiotext(e).

——. [1990] 1993. "Operational Whitewash." In *The Transparency of Evil*. Translated by J. St John Baddeley, 49–56. London: Verso.

——. 1996. "Disneyworld Company." Accessed October 10, 2009. http://www.ctheory.net/articles.aspx?id= 158.

——. 2001. "Dust Breeding." Translated by Francois Debrix. Accessed November 3, 2003. http//www.ctheory.net/text_file.asp?pick= 293.html.

Baugham, James L. 2007. *Same Time, Same Station: Creating American Television 1948–1961.* Baltimore, MD: Johns Hopkins University Press.

Bauman, Zygmunt. 2007. *Consuming Life.* Cambridge, UK: Polity.

Bazalgette, Peter. 2005. *Billion Dollar Game: How Three Men Risked It All and Changed the Face of Television.* London: Time Warner Books.

Beck, Ulrich. 1992. *Risk Society: Towards a New Modernity.* London: Sage.

Beck, Ulrich and Elisabeth Beck-Gernsheim. 2001. *Individualization: Institutional Individualism and its Social and Political Consequences.* London: Sage.

Becker, Ron. 2006. " 'Help is on the Way!': Supernanny, Nanny 911, and the Neoliberal Politics of the Family." In Heller 2006, 175–191.

Benioff, Marc and Karen Southwick. 2004. *Compassionate Capitalism: How Corporations Can Make Doing Good an Integral Part of Doing Well.* Franklin Lakes, NJ: Career Press.

Benjamin, Walter. [1936] 2006. "The Work of Art in the Age of Mechanical Reproduction." In *Media and Cultural Studies: Keyworks,* revised edition, edited by Meenakshi Gigi Durham and Douglas M. Kellner, 18–40. Malden, MA: Blackwell.

Berger, John. 1972. *Ways of Seeing.* London: Penguin.

Bernays, Edward. [1928] 2005. *Propaganda.* Brooklyn, NY: Ig Publishing.

Bessenoff, Gayle. 2006. "Can the Media Affect Us? Social Comparison, Self-Discrepancy, and the Thin Ideal." *Psychology of Women Quarterly* 30: 239–251.

Biressi, Anita and Heather Nunn. 2005. *Reality TV: Realism and Revelation.* London: Wallflower.

Blum, Virginia. 2003. *Flesh Wounds: The Culture of Cosmetic Surgery.* Berkeley, CA: University of California Press.

Boddy, William. 1990. *Fifties Television: The Industry and its Critics.* Champaign, IL: University of Illinois Press.

Bone, James. 2005. "Anguish over Reality TV Leads to Lawsuit After 'Ugly Sister' Suicide," *The Times Online,* posted 20 September 2005. Accessed June 18, 2008. http://www.timesonline.co.uk/tol/news/world/us_and_americas/article568583.ece.

Boorstin, Daniel J. [1961] 1992. *The Image: A Guide to Pseudo-Events in America.* New York: Vintage Books.

Booth, Paul. 2010. *Digital Fandom.* New York: Peter Lang.

Bordo, Susan. 1993. *Unbearable Weight: Feminism, Western Culture, and the Body.* Berkeley, CA: University of California Press.

Botta, Renee. 1999. "Television Images and Adolescent Girl's Body Image Disturbance." *Journal of Communication* 49 (2): 22–41.

Bourdieu, Pierre. [1979] 1984. *Distinction: A Social Critique of the Judgment of Taste.* Cambridge, MA: Harvard University Press.

Bratich, Jack Z. 2007. "Programming Reality: Control Societies, New Subjects and the Powers of Transformation." In Heller 2007, 6–22.

Brooker, Will. 2001. "Living on Dawson's Creek: Teen Viewers, Cultural Convergence, and Television Overflow." *International Journal of Cultural Studies* 4 (4): 456–472.

Brumberg, Joan Jacobs. 1998. *The Body Project: An Intimate History of American Girls.* New York: Vintage.

Butler, Judith. 1990. *Gender Trouble: Feminism and the Subversion of Identity.* New York: Routledge.

Carey, James W. [1975] 1992. "A Cultural Approach to Communication." In *Communication and Culture: Essays on Media and Society,* 13–36. New York: Routledge.

Castells, Manuel. 2000. *The Rise of the Network Society,* 2nd ed. Oxford: Blackwell.

Cava, Marco R. della. 2004. "Queer Eye Has Keen Eye for Sales," *USA Today,* February 25: D5. Accessed September 8, 2007. http://www.usatoday.com/life/television/news/2004-02-25-queere-eye-marketing_x.html.

Chaney, David. 1996. *Lifestyles.* New York: Routledge.

Chomsky, Noam. 2002. *Media Control: The Spectacular Achievements of Propaganda.* New York: Seven Stories Press.

Chomsky, Noam and Edward Herman. 1988. *Manufacturing Consent: The Political Economy of the Mass Media.* New York: Pantheon Books.

Clarkson, Jay. 2005. "Contesting Masculinities Makeover: Queer Eye, Consumer Masculinity and 'Straight Acting' Gays." *Journal of Communication Inquiry* 29 (3): 235–255.

Cohen, Lizabeth. 2003. *A Consumers' Republic: The Politics of Mass Consumption in Postwar America.* New York: Knopf.

Coombs, W. Timothy and Sherry J. Holladay. 2007. *It's Not Just PR: Public Relations in Society.* Oxford: Blackwell.

Corner, John. 1996. *The Art of Record: A Critical Introduction to Documentary.* Manchester: Manchester University Press.

Crawley, Melissa. 2006. "Making Over the New Adam." In Heller 2006, 51–64.

Creeber, Glen and Royston Martin. 2008. *Digital Culture: Understanding New Media.* Maidenhead, Berkshire: Open University Press.

Crockett, Richard, Thomas Pruzinsky, and John Persing. 2007. "The Influence of Plastic Surgery 'Reality TV' on Cosmetic Surgery Patient Expectations and Decisions Making." *Plastic and Reconstructive Surgery* 120 (1): 316–324.

Cutlip, Scott M. 1994. *The Unseen Power: Public Relations, a History.* Hillsdale, NJ: Lawrence Erlbaum.

—— 1995. *Public Relations History: From the Seventeenth to the Twentieth Century. The Antecedents.* Hillsdale, NJ: Lawrence Erlbaum.

Cutlip, Scott M., Allen Center, and Glen Broom. 2006. *Effective Public Relations,* 9th ed. Upper Saddle River, NJ: Pearson.

Davies, Philip and Bruce Newman. 2006. *Winning Elections with Political Marketing.* New York: Routledge.

Davis, Aeron. 2002. *Public Relations Democracy: Public Relations, Politics and the Mass Media in Britain.* Manchester: Manchester University Press.

———. 2003. "Public Relations and News Sources." In *News, Public Relations and Power,* edited by Simon Cottle, 27–42. London: Sage.

Davis, Kathy. 2003. *Dubious Equalities and Embodied Differences: Cultural Studies on Cosmetic Surgery.* New York: Rowman and Littlefield.

Debord, Guy. [1967] 1995. *The Society of the Spectacle.* Translated by Donald Nicholson-Smith. New York: Zone Books.

De Certeau, Michel. [1980] 1984. *The Practice of Everyday Life.* Translated by Steven Randall. Berkeley, CA: University of California Press.

Deery, June. 2003. "TV.Com: Participatory Viewing on the Web." *Journal of Popular Culture* 37 (2): 161–183.

———. 2004a. Reality TV As Advertainment." *Popular Communication* 2 (1): 1–19.

———. 2004b. "Trading Faces: The Makeover Show as Prime-Time 'Infomercial,' " *Feminist Media Studies* 4 (2): 211–214.

———. 2006. "Interior Design: Commodifying Self and Place in *Extreme Makeover, Extreme Makeover: Home Edition,* and *The Swan.*" In Heller 2006, 159–174.

Delinsky, Sherrie Selwyn. 2005. "Cosmetic Surgery: A Common and Accepted Form of Self-Improvement?" *Journal of Applied Social Psychology* 35 (10): 2012–2028.

Dickinson, Greg. 2009. "Selling Democracy: Consumer Culture and Citizenship in the Wake of September 11." In *The Advertising and Consumer Culture Reader,* edited by Joseph Turow and Matthew P. McAllister, 295–311. New York: Routledge.

Di Mattia, Joanna. 2007. "The Gentle Art of Manscaping: Lessons in Hetero-Masculinity from the Queer Eye Guys." In Heller 2007, 133–149.

Dinan, William and David Miller, eds. 2007. *Thinker, Faker, Spinner, Spy: Corporate PR and the Assault on Democracy.* London: Pluto Press.

Donaton, Scott. 2004. *Madison and Vine: Why the Entertainment and Advertising Industries Must Converge to Survive.* New York: McGraw-Hill.

Dorfman, Bill, with Paul Lombardi. 2006. *Billion Dollar Smile: A Complete Guide to Your Extreme Smile Makeover.* Nashville, TN: Rutledge Hill Press.

Douglas, Mary and Baron C. Isherwood. [1979] 1996. *The World of Goods.* New York: Routledge.

Douglas, Susan. 1989. *Inventing American Broadcasting.* Baltimore, MD: Johns Hopkins University Press.

———. 2000. "Narcissism as Liberation." In *The Gender and Consumer Culture Reader,* edited by Jennifer Scanlon, 267–282. New York: NYU Press.

———. 2010. *Enlightened Sexism: The Seductive Message That Feminism's Work is Done.* New York: Henry Holt.

Dovey, Jon. 2000. *Freakshow: First Person Media and Factual Television.* London: Pluto Press.

Dow, Bonnie. 1996. *Prime-Time Feminism: Television, Media Culture, and the Women's Movement Since 1970.* Philadelphia, PA: University of Pennsylvania Press.

Ellul, Jacques. [1962] 1965. *Propaganda: The Formation of Men's Attitudes.* Translated by Konrad Kellen and Jean Lerner. New York: Knopf.

Escoffery, David, ed. 2006. *How Real is Reality TV? Essays on Representation and Truth.* Jefferson, NC: McFarland.

Etcoff, Nancy. 2000. *Survival of the Prettiest: The Science of Beauty.* New York: Anchor Books.

Ewen, Stuart. 1988. *All Consuming Images: The Politics of Style in Contemporary Culture.* New York: Basic Books.

——. 1996. *PR! A Social History of Spin.* New York: Basic Books.

Falk, Pasi. 1994. *The Consuming Body.* London: Sage.

Faludi, Susan. 2007. *The Terror Dream: Fear and Fantasy in Post 9/11 America.* New York: Metropolitan Books.

Featherstone, Mike. 1991. *Consumer Culture and Postmodernism.* London: Sage.

Fiske, John. 1987. *Television Culture.* London: Methuen.

Flew, Terry. 2002. *New Media: An Introduction.* New York: Oxford University Press.

Florian, Ellen. 2004. "Queer Eye Makes Over the Economy!" *Fortune* 149 (3): 38.

Foucault, Michel. [1975] 1977. *Discipline and Punish: The Birth of the Prison.* Translated by Alan Sheridan. New York: Pantheon.

——. [1976] 1978. *The History of Sexuality. Vol. 1: An Introduction.* Translated by Robert Hurley. New York: Vintage Books.

Franco, Judith. 2008. "Extreme Makeover: The Politics of Gender, Class, and Cultural Identity." *Television and New Media* 9 (6): 471–486.

Franklin, Robert. 1994. *Packaging Politics: Political Communications in Britain's Media Democracy.* London: Arnold.

Fraser, Kathryn. 2007. " 'Now I am Ready to Tell How Bodies Are Changed Into Different Bodies …' Ovid, The Metamorphoses." In Heller 2007, 177–192.

Gabler, Neal. 1998. *Life: The Movie.* New York: Vintage Books.

Gailey, Elizabeth Atwood. 2007. "Self-Made Women: Cosmetic Surgery Shows and the Construction of Female Psychopathology." In Heller 2007, 107–118.

Gamson, Joshua. 1998. *Freaks Talk Back: Tabloid Talk Shows and Sexual Nonconformity.* Chicago: University of Chicago Press.

Gane, Nicholas and David Beer. 2008. *New Media: The Key Concepts.* New York: Berg.

Gauntlett, David. 2008. *Media, Gender and Identity.* New York: Routledge.

Gibson, William. 1984. *Neuromancer.* New York: Ace.

Giddens, Anthony. 1991. *Modernity and Self-Identity: Self and Society in the Late Modern Age.* Stanford, CA: Stanford University Press.

Gill, Rosalind. 2007. *Gender and the Media.* Cambridge, UK: Polity.

Gillan, Jennifer. 2006. "Extreme Makeover Homeland Security Edition." In Heller 2006, 193–209.

——. 2011. *Television and New Media: Must-Click TV.* New York: Routledge.

Gilman, Sander L. 1999. *Making the Body Beautiful: A Cultural History of Aesthetic Surgery.* Princeton, NJ: Princeton University Press.

Glynn, Kevin. 2000. *Tabloid Culture: Trash Taste, Popular Power, and the Transformation of American Television.* Durham, NC: Duke University Press.

Gobe, Marc. 2001. *Emotional Branding: The New Paradigm for Connecting Brands to People.* New York: Allworth Press.

Goldstein, Carolyn M. 1998. *Do It Yourself: Home Improvement in Twentieth-Century America*. New York: Princeton Architectural Press.

Gordon, Michael and Bernard Trainor. 2007. *Cobra II: The Inside Story of the Invasion and Occupation of Iraq*. New York: Vintage.

Gore, Albert. 2007. *The Assault on Reason*. New York: Penguin.

Gray, Jonathan. 2003. "New Audiences, New Textualities: Anti-Fans and Non-Fans." *International Journal of Cultural Studies* 6 (1): 64–81.

Greer, Germaine. 1999. *The Whole Woman*. London: Doubleday.

Grogan, Sarah. 1999. *Body Image: Understanding Body Dissatisfaction in Men, Women, and Children*. New York: Routledge.

Habermas, Jurgen. [1962] 1991. *The Structural Transformation of the Public Sphere: An Inquiry into a Category of Bourgeois Society*. Cambridge, MA: The MIT Press.

Haiken, Elizabeth. 1997. *Venus Envy: A History of Cosmetic Surgery*. Baltimore, MD: The Johns Hopkins University Press.

Hall, Stuart. 1980. "Encoding/Decoding." In *Culture, Media, Language,* edited by Stuart Hall, Dorothy Hobson, Andrew Lowe, and Paul Willis, 128–138. London: Hutchinson.

———. 1988. *The Hard Road to Renewal: Thatcherism and the Crisis of the Left*. London: Verso.

Hart, Stuart L. 2007. *Capitalism at the Crossroads: Aligning Business, Earth, and Humanity,* 2nd ed. Foreword by Al Gore. Upper Saddle River, NJ: Wharton School Publishing.

Hartley, John. 1992. *The Politics of Pictures: The Creation of the Public in the Age of Popular Media*. London: Routledge.

———. 2008. *Television Truths*. Malden, MA: Blackwell.

Harvey, David. 1973. *Social Justice and the City*. London: Arnold.

Hearn, Alison. 2008. "Insecure: Narratives and Economies of the Branded Self in Transformation Television." *Continuum: Journal of Media and Cultural Studies* 22 (4): 459–504.

Heath, Robert L., Elizabeth Toth, Damion Waymer, eds. 2009. *Rhetorical and Critical Approaches to Public Relations II*. New York: Routledge.

Heinricy, Shana. 2006. "The Cutting Room: Gendered American Dreams on Plastic Surgery TV." In *How Real is Reality TV? Essays on Representation and Truth,* edited by David Escoffery, 149–164. Jefferson, NC: McFarland.

Heller, Dana, ed. 2005. *The Selling of 9/11: How a National Tragedy Became a Commodity*. New York: Palgrave Macmillan.

———. 2006. *The Great American Makeover: Television, History, Nation*. New York: Palgrave Macmillan.

———. 2007. *Makeover Television: Realities Remodelled*. New York: L. B. Tauris.

Henderson-King, Donna, Eaaron Henderson-King, and Lisa Hoffman. 2001. "Media Images and Women's Self-evaluations: Social Context and Importance of Attractiveness as Moderators." *Personality and Social Psychology Bulletin* 27: 1407–1416.

Herman, Edward and Noam Chomsky. 1988. *Manufacturing Consent: The Political Economy of the Mass Media*. New York: Pantheon.

Heyes, Cressida J. 2007. "Cosmetic Surgery and the Televisual Makeover: A Foucauldian Feminist Reading." *Feminist Media Studies* 7 (1): 17–32.

Hill, Annette. 2005. *Reality TV: Audiences and Popular Factual Television.* London: Routledge.

———. 2007. *Restyling Factual TV: Audiences and News, Documentary and Reality Genres.* New York: Routledge.

Holmes, Su. 2004. " 'But This Time You Choose!': Approaching the 'Interactive' Audience in Reality TV." *International Journal of Cultural Studies* 3 (2): 213–231.

Holmes, Su and Deborah Jermyn, eds. 2004. *Understanding Reality Television.* New York: Routledge.

Horkheimer, Max and Theodor Adorno. [1944] 1988. "The Culture Industry: Enlightenment as Mass Deception." In *Dialectic of Enlightenment.* Translated by John Cumming, 120–167. New York: Continuum.

Ihlen, Oyvind, Betteke van Ruler, and Magnus Fredriksson. 2009. *Public Relations and Social Theory: Key Figures and Concepts.* New York: Routledge.

Irigaray, Luce. 1985. *This Sex Which is Not One.* Translated by Catherine Porter. Ithaca, NY: Cornell University Press.

Isikoff, Michael and David Corn. 2006. *Hubris: The Inside Story of Spin, Scandal, and the Selling of the Iraq War.* New York: Three Rivers Press.

Jackall, Robert, ed. 1995. *Propaganda.* New York: NYU Press.

Jackall, Robert and Janice M. Hirota. 2000. *Image Makers: Advertising, Public Relations, and the Ethos of Advocacy.* Chicago: University of Chicago Press.

Jackson, Brooks and Kathleen Hall Jameson. 2007. *unSpun: Finding Facts in a World of Disinformation.* New York: Random House.

Jacobson, Michael F. and Laurie Ann Mazur. 1995. *Marketing Madness: A Survival Guide for a Consumer Society.* Boulder, CO: Westview Press.

Jaffe, Joseph. 2005. *Life After the 30-Second Spot: Energize Your Brand With a Bold Mix of Alternatives to Traditional Advertising.* Hoboken, NJ: John Wiley & sons.

Jameson, Fredric. 1991. *Postmodernism, or, the Cultural Logic of Late Capitalism.* Durham, NC: Duke University Press.

———. 1992. *Signatures of the Visible.* New York: Routledge.

———. 1998. *Cultural Turn: Selected Writings on Postmodernism 1983–98.* London: Verso.

Jenkins, Henry. 2006. *Convergence Culture: Where Old and New Media Collide.* New York: NYU Press.

Jhally, Sut. 1990. *The Codes of Advertising: Fetishism and the Political Economy of Meaning in the Consumer Society.* New York: Routledge.

Jillson, Calvin. 2004. *Pursuing the American Dream: Opportunity and Exclusion Over Four Centuries.* Lawrence, KS: University Press of Kansas.

Jones, Gerard. 1992. *Honey, I'm Home: Selling the American Dream.* New York: New Grove.

Jones, Meredith. 2008a. "Media-bodies and Screen-births: Cosmetic Surgery Reality Television." *Continuum: Journal of Media and Cultural Studies* 22 (4): 515–524.

———. 2008b. *Skintight: An Anatomy of Cosmetic Surgery.* New York: Berg.

Jost, Francois. 2011. "When Reality TV is a Job." In Kraidy and Sender 2011, 31–43.

Jowett, Garth S. and Victoria O'Donnell. 2005. *Propaganda and Persuasion*. London: Sage.

Kackman, Michael, Marnie Binfield, Matthew Thomas Payne, Allison Perlman, and Bryan Sebok, eds. 2010. *Flow TV: Television in the Age of Media Convergence*. New York: Routledge.

Kavka, Misha. 2008. *Reality Television, Affect and Intimacy: Reality Matters*. New York: Palgrave Macmillan.

Kellner, Douglas. 2002. "September 11, the Media, and War Fever." *Television and New Media* 3 (2): 143–151.

Kelly, Clinton. 2008. *Freakin' Fabulous: How to Dress, Speak, Behave, Eat, Drink, Entertain, Decorate, and Generally Be Better Than Everyone Else*. New York: Simon and Schuster.

——. 2010. *Oh No She Didn't: The Top 100 Style Mistakes Women Make and How to Avoid Them*. New York: Gallery Books.

Kilborn, Richard. 2003. *Staging the Real: Factual TV Programming in the Age of Big Brother*. Manchester: Manchester University Press.

Kilbourne, Jean. 1999. *Deadly Persuasion: Why Women and Girls Must Fight the Addictive Power of Advertising*. New York: Free Press.

King, Martin Luther, Jr. 1968. " The American Dream." *Negro History Bulletin* 31 (5): 10–15.

Klein Naomi. 2002. *No Logo*. New York: Picador.

Kotler, Philip and Nancy Lee. 2004. *Corporate Social Responsibility: Doing the Most Good for Your Company and Your Cause*. Hoboken, NJ: John Wiley & sons.

Kraidy, Marwan and Katherine Sender, eds. 2011. *The Politics of Reality Television: Global Perspectives*. New York: Routledge.

Kraut, Robert, Michael Patterson, Vicki Lundmark, Sara Kiesler, Tridas Mukhopadhyay, and William Scherlis. 1998. "Internet Paradox: A Social Technology That Reduces Social Involvement and Psychological Well-Being?" *American Psychologist* 53 (9): 1017–1032.

Kraut, Robert, Sara Kiesler, Bouka Boneva, Jonathan Cummings, Vicki Helgeson, and Ann Crawford. 2002. "Internet Paradox Revisited." *Journal of Social Issues* 58 (1): 49–74.

Lafayette, Jon. 2006. "Mark Burnett, Adman." TVWeek.com, December 20. Accessed March 14, 2007. http://www.tvweek.com/news/2006/12/mark_burnett_adman.php.

Lakoff, Robin T. and Raquel L. Scherr. 1984. *Face Value: The Politics of Beauty*. Boston, MA: Routledge & Kegan Paul.

Lardner, James and David A. Smith, eds. 2007. *Inequality Matters: The Growing Economic Divide in America and its Poisonous Consequences*. New York: The New Press.

Lasch, Christopher. 1979. *The Culture of Narcissism*. New York: Norton.

Lears, Jackson. 1994. *Fables of Abundance: A Cultural History of Advertising in America*. New York: Basic Books.

Lee, Martyn J., ed. 2000 *The Consumer Society Reader*. Malden, MA: Blackwell.

Lee, Waipeng and Eddie Kuo. 2002. "Internet and Displacement Effect: Children's Media Use and Activities in Singapore." *Journal of Computer-Mediated Communication* 7 (2). http://onlinelibrary.wiley.com/doi/10.1111/j.1083–6101.2002. tb00143.x/full.

Lefebvre, Henri. [1968] 1984. *Everyday Life in the Modern World*. Translated by Sacha Rabinovitch. Introduction by Philip Wander. New Brunswisk, NJ: Transaction Publishers.

———. [1974] 1991. *The Production of Space*. Translated by D. Nicholson-Smith. Oxford: Blackwell.

Lefler, Hugh T. 1967. "Promotional Literature of the Southern Colonies." *Journal of Southern History* 33: 3–25.

Lehu, Jean-Marc. 2007. *Branded Entertainment: Product Placement and Brand Strategy in the Entertainment Business*. London: Kogan

Leiss, William, Stephen Kline, and Sut Jhally. 1997. *Social Communication in Advertising: Persons, Products and Images of Well-Being*, 2nd ed. London: Routledge.

Leonhardt, David and Ben Werschkul. 2005. "How Class Works," *New York Times*, Special Section (online). Accessed June 15, 2009. http://www.nytimes.com/packages/html/national/20050515_CLASS_GRAPHIC/index_03.html.

Lew, Ann-Marie, Traci Mann, Hector Myers, Shelley Taylor, and Julienne Bower. 2007. "Thin-ideal Media and Women's Body Dissatisfaction: Prevention Using Downward Social Comparisons on Non-Appearance Dimensions." *Sex Roles: A Journal of Research* 57: 543–556.

Lewis, Tania. 2008. *Smart Living: Lifestyle Media and Popular Expertise*. New York: Peter Lang.

———, ed. 2009. *TV Transformations: Revealing the Makeover Show*. New York: Routledge.

———. 2011. "Globalizing Lifestyles? Makeover Television in Singapore." In Kraidy and Sender 2011, 78–92.

Lilleker, Darren G. 2006. *Key Concepts in Political Communication*. London: Sage.

Lister, Martin, Jon Dovey, Seth Giddings, Iain Grant, and Kieran Kelly. 2009. *New Media: A Critical Introduction*, 2nd ed. London: Routledge.

London, Stacy and Clinton Kelly C. 2005. *Dress Your Best: The Complete Guide to Finding the Style That's Right For Your Body*. New York: Three Rivers Press.

Lunt, Peter. 2008. "Little Angels: The Mediation of Parenting." *Continuum: Journal of Media and Cultural Studies* 22 (4): 537–546.

Lury, Celia. 1996. *Consumer Culture*. Cambridge, UK: Polity.

MacRury, Iain. 2009. *Advertising*. New York: Routledge.

McAllister, Matthew. 1996. *The Commercialization of American Culture: New Advertising, Control and Democracy*. Thousand Oaks, CA: Sage.

McGee, Micki. 2005. *Self-Help, Inc.: Makeover Culture in American Life*. Oxford: Oxford University Press.

McMurria, John. 2009. "Global Realities: International Markets, Geopolitics, and the Transcultural Contexts of Reality TV." In Murray and Ouellette 2009, 179–202.

McNair, Brian. 2011. *An introduction to Political Communication.* New York: Routledge.

McRobbie, Angela. 2004. "Notes on 'What Not To Wear' and Post-Feminist Symbolic Violence." *The Sociological Review* 52 (2): 97–109.

Magder, Ted. 2009. "Television 2.0: The Business of American Television in Transition." In Murray and Ouellette 2009, 141–164.

Manovich, Lev. 2002. *The Language of New Media.* Cambridge, MA: MIT Press.

Marchand, Roland. 1998. *Creating the Corporate Soul: The Rise of Public Relations and Corporate Imagery in American Big Business.* Berkeley, CA: University of California Press.

Marcuse, Herbert. 1964. *One Dimensional Man.* Boston, MA: Beacon Press.

Markey, Charlotte and Patrick Markey. 2010. "A Correlational and Experimental Examination of Reality Television Viewing and Interest in Cosmetic Surgery." *Body Image* 7 (2): 165–171.

Marling, Karal Ann. 1996. *As Seen on TV: The Visual Culture of Everyday Life in the 1950s.* Cambridge, MA: Harvard University Press.

Massey, Doreen. 1994. *Space, Place, and Gender.* Cambridge, UK: Polity.

Mauss, Marcel. [1950] 1990. *The Gift: The Form and Reason for Exchange in Archaic Societies.* Translated by W. D. Halls. Foreword by Mary Douglas. New York: Norton.

Merchant, Carolyn. 1980. *The Death of Nature: Women, Ecology, and the Scientific Revolution.* New York: HarperCollins.

Merrin, William. 2005. *Baudrillard and the Media.* Cambridge: Polity.

Miller, David and William Dinan. 2008. *A Century of Spin: How Public Relations Became the Cutting Edge of Corporate Power.* London: Pluto Press.

Miller, Mark Crispin. 1990. "Advertising: End of Story." In *Seeing Through Movies,* edited by Mark Crispin Miller, 186–246. New York: Pantheon.

Miller, Toby. 2006. "Metrosexuality: See the Bright Light of Commodification Shine! Watch Yanqui Masculinity Made Over!" In Heller 2006, 105–122.

——. 2008. *Makeover Nation: The United States of Reinvention.* Columbus, OH: Ohio State University Press.

Morgan, Kathryn Pauly. 2009. "Women and the Knife: Cosmetic Surgery and the Colonization of Women's Bodies." In *Cosmetic Surgery: A Feminist Primer,* edited by Cressida Heyes and Meredith Jones, 49–77. Burlington, VT: Ashgate.

Moriarty, Cortney and Kristen Harrison. 2008. "Television Exposure and Disordered Eating Among Children: A Longitudinal Panel Study." *Journal of Communication* 58 (2): 361–381.

Motley, Clay. 2006. "Making Over Body and Soul: In His Steps and the Roots of Evangelical Popular Culture." In Heller 2006, 85–103.

Murray, Susan. 2005. *Hitch Your Antenna to the Stars: Early Television and Broadcast Stardom.* New York: Routledge.

Murray, Susan and Laurie Ouellette, eds. 2009. *Reality TV: Remaking Television Culture,* 2nd ed. New York: NYU Press.

Nabi, Robin L. 2009. "Cosmetic Surgery Makeover Programs and Intentions to Undergo Cosmetic Enhancements: A Consideration of Three Models of Media Effects." *Human Communication Research* 35 (1): 1–27.

Nadel, Alan. 2005. *Television in Black-and-White: Race and National Identity.* Lawrence, KS: University Press of Kansas.

Negrine, Ralph. 1996. *The Communication of Politics.* London: Sage.

Negroponte, Nicholas. 1995. *Being Digital.* New York: Alfred A. Knopf.

Nelson, Joyce. 1989. *Sultans of Sleaze: Public Relations and the Media.* Monroe, ME: Common Courage Press.

Nie, Norman H. and Lutz Erbring. 2000. "Internet and Society: A Preliminary Report." Stanford, CA: Stanford Institute for the Quantitative Study of Society.

Nie, Norman H. and D. Sunshine Hillygus. 2002. "The Impact of Internet Use on Sociability: Time-diary Findings." *IT and Society* 1 (1): 1–20.

Norton, Michael and Dan Ariely. 2011. " Building a Better America—One Wealth Quintile at a Time." *Perspectives on Psychological Science* 6 (9): 9–12.

Nye, David E. 2003. *America as Second Creation: Technology and Narratives of New Beginnings.* Cambridge, MA: MIT Press.

Nye, Joseph, Jr. 2004. *Soft Power: The Means to Success in World Politics.* New York: PublicAffairs.

Obama, Barack. 2006. *The Audacity of Hope: Thoughts on Reclaiming the American Dream.* New York: Crown.

Official Companion Book. 2005. *Extreme Makeover: Home Edition.* New York, Hyperion.

O'Shaughnessy, Nicholas J. 2004. *Politics and Propaganda: Weapons of Mass Seduction.* Ann Arbor, MI: University of Michigan Press.

Otnes, Cele and Elizabeth Pleck. 2003. *Cinderella Dreams: The Allure of the Lavish Wedding,* Berkeley, CA: University of California Press.

Ouellette, Laurie. 2002 *Viewers Like You? How Public TV Failed the People.* New York: Columbia University Press.

Ouellette, Laurie and James Hay. 2008. *Better Living through Reality TV: Television and Post-Welfare Citizenship.* Oxford: Blackwell.

Palmer, Gareth. 2003. *Discipline and Liberty: Television and Governance.* Manchester: Manchester University Press.

———. 2004. " 'The New You': Class and Transformation in Lifestyle Television." In *Understanding Reality Television,* edited by Su Holmes and Deborah Jermyn, 173–190. New York: Routledge.

———. 2007. "Extreme Makeover: Home Edition: An American Fairy Tale." In Heller, 165–176.

———. 2008 "Introduction—The Habit of Scrutiny." In *Exposing Lifestyle Television: The Big Reveal,* edited by Gareth Palmer, 1–13. Burlington, VT: Ashgate.

———, ed. 2008. *Exposing Lifestyle Television: The Big Reveal.* Burlington, VT: Ashgate.

———. 2011. "Governing Bodies." In Kraidy and Sender, 65–77.

Philips, Deborah. 2008. "What Not to Buy: Consumption and Anxiety in the Television Makeover." In *Exposing Lifestyle Television: The Big Reveal,* edited by Gareth Palmer, 117–128. Burlington, VT: Ashgate.

Piercy, Marge. 1991. *He, She and It*. New York: Knopf.

Pine, B. Joseph and James H. Gilmore, 1999. *The Experience Economy: Work is Theatre and Every Business a Stage*. Boston, MA: Harvard Business School Press.

———. 2007. *Authenticity: What Consumers Really Want*. Boston, MA: Harvard Business School Press.

Pozner, Jennifer. 2010. *Reality Bites Back: The Troubling Truth about Guilty Pleasure TV*. Berkeley, CA: Seal Press.

Punathambekar, Aswin. 2011. "Reality Television and the Making of Mobile Publics: The Case of Indian Idol." In Kraidy and Sender 2011, 140–153.

Putnam, Robert. 1995. " Bowling Alone: America's Declining Social Capital." *Journal of Democracy* 6 (1): 65–78.

Raphael, Chad. 2009. "The Political Economic Origins of Reali-TV." In Murray and Ouellette 2009, 123–140.

Redden, Guy. 2007. "Makeover Morality and Consumer Culture." In Heller 2007, 150–164.

Rhode, Deborah. 2010. *The Beauty Bias: The Injustice of Appearance in Life and Law*. Oxford: Oxford University Press.

Ricks, Thomas. 2006. *Fiasco: The American Military Adventure in Iraq*. New York: Penguin.

Roberts, Martin. 2007. "The Fashion Police: Governing the Self in What Not to Wear." In *Interrogating Postfeminism: Gender and the Politics of Popular Culture*, edited by Yvonne Tasker and Diane Negra, 227–248. Durham, NC: Duke University Press.

Robinson, John P., Kevin Barth, and Andrew Kohut. 1997. "Social Impact Research: Person Computers, Mass Media, and Use of Time." *Social Science Computer Review* 15 (1): 65–82.

Rose, Gillian. 1993. *Feminism and Geography*. Minneapolis, MN: University of Minnesota Press.

Rose, Nikolas. 1996. *Inventing Our Selves: Psychology, Power, and Personhood*. Cambridge: Cambridge University Press.

Rosenberg, Buck Clifford. 2008. "Property and Home-Makeover Television: Risk, Thrift and Taste." *Continuum: Journal of Media and Cultural Studies* 22 (4): 505–513.

Ross, Sharon. 2008. *Beyond the Box: Television and the Internet*. Malden, MA: Blackwell.

Ruoff, Jeffrey. 2002. *An American Family: A Televised Life*. Minneapolis, MN: University of Minnesota Press.

Samuel, Lawrence R. 2002. *Brought to You By: Postwar Television Advertising and the American Dream*. Austin, TX: University of Texas Press.

Scahill, Jeremy. 2007. *Blackwater: The Rise of the World's Most Powerful Mercenary Army*. New York: Nation Books.

Scanlon, Jennifer. 2005. " 'Your Flag Decal Won't Get You into Heaven Anymore': US Consumers, Wal-Mart, and the Commodification of Patriotism." In *The Selling *of 9/11: How a National Tragedy Became a Commodity,* edited by Dana Heller, 174–199. New York: Palgrave Macmillan.

Schor, Juliet. 1999. *The Overspent American: Why We Want What We Don't Need.* New York: Harper Perennial.

Schor, Juliet and Douglas Holt. 2000. *The Consumer Society Reader.* New York: The New Press.

Secunda, Eugene and Terence P. Moran. 2007. *Selling War to America: From the Spanish American War to the Global War on Terror.* Westport, CT: Praeger Publishers.

Seiter, Ellen. 1992. "Semiotics, Structuralism, and Television." In *Channels of Discourse, Reassembled,* 2nd ed., edited by Robert C. Allen, 31–66. Chapel Hill, NC: University of North Carolina Press.

Sender, Katherine. 2006. "Queens for a Day: Queer Eye for the Straight Guy and the Neoliberal Project." *Critical Studies in Media Communication* 23 (2): 131–151.

Sennett, Richard. [1974] 1992. *The Fall of Public Man.* New York: Norton.

Shattuc, Jane. 1990. *The Talking Cure: TV Talk Shows and Women.* London: Routledge.

Shilling, Chris. 2003. *The Body and Social Theory,* 2nd ed. London: Sage.

Shim, Young Soo. 2007. "The Impact of the Internet on Teenagers' Face-to-Face Communication." *Global Media Journal* 6 (10). See http://lass.calumet.purdue.edu/cca/gmj/sp07/graduate/gmj-sp07-grad-shim.htm (accessed September 14, 2010).

Shufeldt, Madeleine and Kenra Gale. 2007. "Under the (Glue) Gun: Containing and Constructing Reality in Home Makeover TV." *Popular Communication* 5 (4): 263–282.

Sivulka, Juliann. 1998. *Soap, Sex, and Cigarettes: A Cultural History of American Advertising.* Belmont, CA: Wadsworth.

Skeggs, Beverley and Helen Wood. 2008. "The Labor of Transformation and Circuits of Value around Reality Television." *Continuum: Journal of Media and Cultural Studies* 22 (4): 559–572.

Slater, Don. 1997. *Consumer Culture and Modernity.* Cambridge: Polity.

Smith, Marc A. and Peter Kollock, eds. 1999. *Communities in Cyberspace.* London: Routledge.

Smythe, Dallas Walker. 1981. *Dependency Road: Communications, Capitalism, Consciousness, and Canada.* Norwood, NJ: Ablex.

Soja, Edward W. 1989. *Post-modern Geographies: The Reassertion of Space in Critical Social Theory.* London: Verso.

Sperry, Steffanie, J., Kevin Thompson, David B. Sarwer, Thomas F. Cash. 2009. "Cosmetic Surgery Reality TV Viewership: Relations with Cosmetic Surgery Attitudes, Body Image, and Disordered Eating." *Annals of Plastic Surgery* 62 (1): 7–11.

Spigel, Lynn and Jan Olsson, eds. 2004. *Television after TV: Essays on a Medium in Transition.* Durham, NC: Duke University Press.

Stanger, Patti, with Lisa Johnson Mandell. 2009. *Become Your Own Matchmaker.* New York: Atria.

Stauber, John and Sheldon Rampton. 1995. *Toxic Sludge is Good for You: Lies, Damn Lies and the Public Relations Industry*. Monroe, ME: Common Courage Press.

Steger, Wayne P., Sean O. Kelly, and J. Mark Wrighton, eds. 2006. *Campaigns and Political Marketing*. London: Routledge.

Stiegler, Bernard. 2010. "Memory." In *Critical Terms for Media Studies*, edited by W. J. T. Mitchell and Mark Hansen, 64–87. Chicago: University of Chicago Press.

Stone, Joseph. 1992. *Prime Time and Misdemeanors: Investigating the 1950's Quiz Scandal: A D.A.'s Account*. New Brunswick: Rutgers University Press.

Strahan, Erin, Adele Lafrance, Anne Wilson, Nicole Ethier, N., Steven Spencer, and Mark Zanna. 2008. "Victoria's Dirty Secret: How Sociocultural Norms Influence Adolescent Girls and Women." *Personality and Social Psychology Bulletin* 34: 288–301.

Streeter, Thomas. 1996. *Selling the Air: A Critique of the Policy of Commercial Broadcasting in the United States*. Chicago: University of Chicago Press.

Sullivan, Deborah. 2001. *Cosmetic Surgery: The Cutting Edge of Commercial Medicine in America*. New Brunswick, NJ: Rutgers University Press.

Tait, Sue. 2007. "Television and the Domestication of Cosmetic Surgery." *Feminist Media Studies* 7 (20): 119–135.

Tasker, Yvonne and Diane Negra, eds. 2007. *Interrogating Postfeminism: Gender and the Politics of Popular Culture*. Durham, NC: Duke University Press.

Thussu, Daya Kishan. 2007. *News as Entertainment: The Rise of Global Infotainment*. London: Sage.

Tiggemann, Marika. 2003. "Media Exposure, Body Dissatisfaction and Disordered Eating: Television and Magazines Are Not the Same!" *European Eating Disorders Review* 11: 418–430.

——. 2005. "Television and Adolescent Body Image: The Role of Program Content and Viewing." *Journal of Social and Clinical Psychology* 24: 361–381.

Tiggemann, Marika and Amy Slater. 2004. "Thin Ideals in Music Television: A Source of Social Comparison and Body Dissatisfaction." *International Journal of Eating Disorders* 35: 48–58.

Tincknell, Estella and Parvati Raghuram. 2002. "Big Brother: Reconfiguring the 'Active' Audience of Cultural Studies?" *European Journal of Cultural Studies* 5 (2): 199–215.

Turner, Bryan S. 1984. *The Body and Society*. Oxford: Blackwell.

Vogel, David. 2006. *The Market for Virtue: The Potential and Limits of Corporate Social Responsibility*. Washington, DC: Brookings Institution Press.

Volcic, Zala. 2009. "Television in the Balkans: The Rise of Commercial Nationalism." In *Television Studies after TV: Understanding Television in the Post-Broadcast Era*, edited by Graeme Turner and Jinna Tay, 115–124. New York: Routledge.

Volcic, Zala and Mark Andrejevic. 2011. "Commercial Nationalism on Balkan Reality TV." In Kraidy and Sender 2011, 113–126.

Wasko, Janet. 2001. *Understanding Disney: The Manufacture of Fantasy*. Cambridge, UK: Polity.

Wearing, Sadie. 2007. "Subjects of Rejuvenation: Aging in Postfeminist Culture." In *Interrogating Postfeminism: Gender and the Politics of Popular Culture*, edited by Yvonne Tasker and Diane Negra, 277–310. Durham, NC: Duke University Press.

Weber, Brenda. 2009. *Makeover TV: Selfhood, Citizenship, and Celebrity*. Durham, NC: Duke University Press.

Weber, Max. [1905] 1992. *The Protestant Ethic and the Spirit of Capitalism*. London: Routledge.

Wernick, Andrew. 1991. *Promotional Culture: Advertising, Ideology and Symbolic Expression*. London: Sage.

White, Mimi. 1992. *Teleadvising: Therapeutic Discourse in American Television*. Berkeley, CA: University of California Press.

Whyte, William H. 1957. *The Organization Man*. New York: Doubleday.

Williams, Raymond. 1980. *Problems in Materialism and Culture: Selected Essays*. London: Verso.

Wolf, Naomi. 1991. *The Beauty Myth: How Images of Beauty Are Used Against Women*. New York: William Morrow.

Wykes, Maggie and Barrie Gunter. 2005. *The Media and Body Image: If Looks Could Kill*. London: Sage.

Index